Olympic Games as Performance and Public Event

Olympic Games as Performance and Public Event

The Case of the XVII Winter Olympic Games in Norway

Edited by

Arne Martin Klausen

Berghahn Books
New York • Oxford

First published in 1999 by

Berghahn Books
Editorial offices:
55 John Street, 3rd Floor, New York, NY 10038, USA
3 NewTec Place, Magdalen Road, Oxford OX4 1RE, UK

Front cover photo by Jarle Kjetil Rolseth

Library of Congress Cataloging-in-Publication Data

Olympic games as performance and public event: the case of the
  XVII Winter Olympic Games in Norway / edited by Arne
  Martin Klausen.
     p.   cm.
  Includes bibliographical references and index.
  ISBN 1-57181-706-9 (hbk)
  ISBN 1-57181-203-2 (pbk)
     1. Winter Olympic Games (17th : 1994 : Lillehammer, Norway)
  2. Olympics–Social aspects–Norway. 3. Nationalism and
  sports–Norway. I. Klausen, Arne Martin, 1927- .
  GV842 19940595 1998   98-49638
  796.98–dc21   CIP

British Library Cataloguing in Publication Data
A catalogue record for this book is available from the British Library

Printed in the United States on acid-free paper

Contents

Contents

List of Figures and Tables

Figures

Tables

The Editor wishes to thank the copyright holders for their kind permission to reproduce the illustrations.

ABBREVIATIONS LIST

ABC	American Broadcasting Company
AUB	Autonomous University of Barcelona
BBC	British Broadcasting Corporation
CBS	Columbia Broadcasting System
CEO	Centre d'Estudis Olimpics
COOB	Barcelona Organising Committee
EC	European Community
EU	European Union
FIS	International Ski Federation
HOA	Hamar Olympic Enterprises
IF	International Sports Federations
IOC	International Olympic Committee
LAOOC	Los Angeles Olympic Committee
LOOC	Lillehammer Olympic Organising Committee
NOC	National Olympic Committees
NOK	Norwegian Olympic Committee
NRK	Norwegian State Broadcasting Corporation
NSF	National Ski Federation
NTB	Norwegian Press Agency
OL	Olympic Games
OLGA	OL-Gruppa (The Olympic Research Group)
OOOC	Oslo Olympic Organising Committee
ORTO	Olympic Radio and Television Organisation
PBS	Public Broadcasting Service
SLOOC	Seoul Olympic Organising Committee
TVE	Spanish Television
WHO	World Health Organization

PREFACE AND ACKNOWLEDGEMENTS

This book consists of a collection of essays written by five social anthropologists working in Norway, as well as an overview chapter by the American social anthropologist, Professor John MacAloon. The essays are mainly based on research related to the 1994 XVII Olympic Winter Games in Lillehammer, although for Chapter 9 fieldwork was also conducted during the XVI Olympic Winter Games in Albertville 1992.

While the empirical material explored in the book is drawn from two particular Winter Games, our more general focus is on the relationship between Olympic elite sports and subjects indicated by catchwords such as tradition, modernity, national identity and cultural performance.

As the initiator and leader of the research project, I would like to express my warmest thanks to the members of the research team for stimulating, creative and friendly collaboration over four years. A special thanks goes to Ellen Aslaksen, research assistant for the project group for more than three years and co-author of our book in Norwegian on the torch relay.

The research process was financed mainly by the Norwegian Research Council as part of its 'Research Programme for Culture and Tradition'. The University of Oslo, the Eastern Norway Research Institute, and the Regional College at Lillehammer have also contributed financially. Four members of the research team work at the Department and Museum of Anthropology, University of Oslo and one works at the Regional College in Lillehammer. We take this opportunity to express our thanks to these institutions for their economic support and technical assistance. During the fieldwork The Nansen School (Norwegian Humanistic Academy) in Lillehammer provided office room and library facilities as well as accommodation for the team members.

Many staff members of the Lillehammer Olympic Organising Committee (LOOC) patiently and kindly lent of their scarce time as informants and as conversation partners in more informal gatherings. We are grateful to our informants at all levels of the Olympic hierarchy and particularly to the staff in the Cultural Section for the confidence they showed in us and for putting up with our presence as observers.

Finally, we are particularly grateful to our colleague Professor John J. MacAloon from the University of Chicago – nestor in anthropological studies on the Olympic Games – for his inspiring support of our project and his contribution to this book.

Arne Martin Klausen
Hvaler, Norway, 1999

Chapter 1

INTRODUCTION

Arne Martin Klausen

The Background to the Research Project

In the book *Anthropology at Home* the editor Anthony Jackson writes: 'doing anthropology at home is of benefit when the researcher has prior experience of fieldwork abroad before turning homewards, since this aids the "distanciation" process.'

All of the members of the research team satisfied these prerequisites before embarking on the exciting but difficult task of studying aspects of Norwegian society and culture as they unfolded in the planning and execution of the Seventeenth Olympic Winter Games in Lillehammer, Norway in 1994.

Norwegian anthropologists have shown interest not only in things exotic, but also in the complex and the modern and have therefore, also gained some experience in doing 'anthropology at home'. In 1984 ten social anthropologists working in Norway published a collection of essays entitled *Den norske væremåten* (The Norwegian Way of Life) (Klausen 1984).[1] The book is mainly of an impressionistic genre and only partly based on fieldwork. It almost achieved a bestseller status, thereby confirming the stereotype of Norwegians as very self-centred. As the editor of this book, I was invited to deliver an introductory lecture at a conference on Norwegian culture in an Olympic context, arranged by the Lillehammer Olympic Organising Committee (LOOC) in autumn 1989. I was given a title for the address which translates roughly into English as 'Norwegian Culture at a Ski-Jump Take-Off Point' (Norsk kultur på hoppkanten). Using this metaphor from ski jumping, the LOOC wanted to indicate that the Olympic Winter Games would provide Norwegian culture with the opportunity to soar to new heights.

The conference brought together almost 300 people involved in Norwegian culture: folk musicians, singers, authors, artists and media people as well as representatives from the artist's associations, which are fairly influential in Norway. After the introductory address almost all of them stood up and crowded round the rostrum, using the opportunity to inform the LOOC about how important a part they could play in a successful staging of the Winter Olympics. This was in great contrast to the stereotype I had of artists and intellectuals in Norway as being rather snobbish towards sports.

I decided there and then that someone ought to look into this response, which struck me as slightly exotic, and follow the anticipated artistic contributions, and perhaps even make it the subject of a research programme.

At the same time, the administration of the Norwegian Research Council's Programme for Research on Culture and Tradition invited me to formulate a project under the title 'The 1994 Olympics and Culture' (OL-94 og kulturdimensjonen). Four senior anthropologists and one research assistant working at the University of Oslo and one anthropologist and media researcher from the Regional College at Lillehammer were later involved in this project. (The group was known under the acronym OLGA derived from the Norwegian *OL-gruppa*.) We monitored the planning and execution of the Winter Olympics over a period of four years, two of us on a full-time basis and four on a part-time basis. Our focus was on culture in the two main senses of the word: i.e. firstly, culture as art and other aesthetic expressions, and secondly culture as group identity and way of life.[2]

A Few Facts about the Lillehammer Games

The XVII Olympic Winter Games at Lillehammer, which took place from 12 to 27 February 1994, was the most expensive staging and the most complex and spectacular event in Norwegian history. The number of participants and organisers, and the magnitude of the spectators at the arenas exceeded all previous formal public events. The only comparable occurrences in Norwegian history might be the spontaneous celebration of peace in May 1945 and the return from exile of the late King Haakon the same year.

Never before had Norway, its landscape and culture, been exposed to the rest of the world on the same scale as through the television coverage of the Games. In the United States, 204 million Americans watched one or more programmes transmitted by CBS. The figures for the Albertville Games two years previously were 184 million. During the sixteen days of the Games, more than 90 per cent of American households watched part of the Lillehammer programme. Some media experts claim that the transmissions from Lillehammer had the highest ratings in the history of American television (Svabø 1994).

We know that the 'soap-opera' conflict between the two figure skaters Nancy Kerrigan and Tonya Harding certainly contributed to such a high rating in the United States (see Chapter 8). Even so we also have reports from the rest of the world indicating exceptionally high ratings.

The twelve years that passed from Norway's first application for the Games in 1982 until the Games in 1994, saw a marked change in the scope of the Games. The initiators, local bankers, business people and a couple of Olympic medalists envisaged an event somewhat similar to an enlarged national championship. The Games might also, it was hoped, have some beneficial economic spin-offs for the local community, a district marked by unemployment and economic stagnation.

The plans for the non-sporting aspects of the Games such as exhibitions, performances, festivals etc., were rather marginal and unspecified. Gradually, however, the planning entered a phase of exponential – and, in a way, Olympic – growth with regard to both economy and complexity. During the first year after the awarding of the Games in 1988, the budget increased from 1.7 billion Norwegian Kroner to 7 billion. More important was the fact that two governments, one right wing and one socialist, had approved this development and wanted to exploit the Games for more general national ends. The organising committee, the LOOC, was gradually taken over by non-local leaders, mainly recruited from the oil industry and other commercial enterprises. The main scope of the Games was now formulated metaphorically as 'a showcase of modern Norwegian society'. The cultural dimension became very important, both in the sense of culture as artistic activities and in the sense of culture as identity and way of life.

There are numerous examples throughout the history of the modern Olympic Games that sports contests have been multifunctional and served a variety of political and national interests. In Norway, e.g., one Labour and one Conservative government and the parliament, with only two opposing votes, were persuaded to compete for the right to host the Games in order to benefit the economic development of the country, and particularly the economically stagnating region around Lillehammer. Furthermore, Norwegian sporting achievements, combined with artistic performances of Olympic standard, as demanded in the Olympic Charter, would contribute towards putting Norway on the international map. We would show ourselves as a modern industrialised country, but still firmly anchored in what we perceive to be traditional and positive Norwegian values. These traditionally oriented values and attitudes have not been irreconcilable with the development of a modern Norwegian industrial society in which welfare ideology has been strong. Thus – paradoxically – Norway is small scale and traditional but, at the same time, with high scores on parameters indicating a modern social structure, for instance the existence of an efficient bureaucracy and advanced modern technology. This dichotomy of traditional and modern with reference to Norwegian culture will be critically analysed in this volume.

Methodological and Theoretical Approach

Since all of the contributors are social anthropologists, we tend to use a basically inductive method; problems, hypotheses and theories all originate from observations we have made mainly through fieldwork. Fully aware of the difficulties in conducting conventional fieldwork in an Olympic context, we still wanted to get as close to it as possible. Two members of the research team attended the Winter Games in Albertville in 1992 in order to get some fieldwork experience in advance of the problems that would confront us in Lillehammer. Chapter 9 in this volume is a result of data gathered from the Albertville Games. Even though a strictly comparative approach on Winter Games was beyond our ambitions, the experiences from Albertville provided a contrasting background for our work in Lillehammer and contributed to our methodological planning of our research project.

In Lillehammer we participated in all the important Olympic events from 1991 until 1995, one year after the Games. We observed inauguration ceremonies in all the arenas, cultural performances in Norway and abroad, including presentations of Norwegian art and industry in Atlanta, Tokyo and Barcelona. During the Games the research group spent three weeks in a rented flat in the very centre of Lillehammer, covering all the venues, most of the competitions, cultural programmes and the well-planned 'spontaneous' folk life.

After some reluctance we were accepted by LOOC and given access to the inner circles of the organisation, such as board meetings and other staff meetings. During the Games we were provided with accreditation as observers, but without access to the VIP areas.

Our work was not applied research or consequence analysis in a restricted sense, but basic research with a more interpretative approach. The contributors' previous research experience and individual theoretical orientation guided the selection of the research focus, which is mirrored in more detail in the various essays. In spite of our differences we do, however, have some basic theoretical points of departure in common.

Anchored in general anthropological theory of ritual we share the view that the Olympic Games may be interpreted as a gigantic 'secular ritual' (Moore and Meyerhoff 1977). As such, the Games express and legitimise fundamental values of modernity. The Olympic motto 'Citius, Altius, Fortius' is a condensed expression of the values inherent in the creative and innovative endeavours, characteristic of everything that is modern in manufacture, science, art and self-realisation. The achievements of the human body through competitive sports serve as a general symbolic repertoire of such values, comprehensible across cultural barriers, but at the same time potent with culturally specific elaboration.

We have also been inspired by John MacAloon's analysis of the various performance types in his book *Rite, Drama, Festival, Spectacle* (MacAloon 1984). He claims that Olympic Games are the prototype of spectacle, and the performance genre most adequately expressing the essence of modernity and thus – paradoxically – they function as a modern secular ritual.

Related to the concept of secular ritual is Don Handelman's concept of 'public event' (1990). According to Handelman, public events serve to *present* (mirror) existing social order directly, *re-present* it more indirectly, and/or *model* socio-cultural reality in a way that may imply change. This conceptual framework fits in very well with the functional role of the Games and with their multisemic interpretational potential. Most of the essays illustrate, more or less explicitly, how aspects of Norwegian society and culture, through the Games, were related to these three functional modes.

Contributions to this Volume

In Chapter 2, John MacAloon presents a general overview of anthropological research on the Olympic institution and the Games as a performative genre.

Chapter 3, written by the Editor, focuses in greater detail on the conflicts that emerged in the Olympic process in Norway. One assertion is that some aspects of the Norwegian ethos are rooted in the idea of a pre-modern egalitarian social structure, on which modern socialist ideology was superimposed. In the encounter with modern olympism and its commercialised sponsoring system, the research group envisaged the possibility of conflicts, but the intensity of the ensuing confrontations surpassed our imagination. This chapter also describes how the President of IOC, Juan Antonio Samaranch, and the LOOC leadership solved the problems with a kind of Olympic diplomacy which John Hoberman characterised as 'playing the chameleon' (Hoberman 1986).

Odd Are Berkaak deals in Chapter 4 with how the Olympic ideology is marked by exponentiality and how this is articulated in the rhetoric with hyperbole as the dominant trope. His essay shows how the LOOC adopted this mode and how it was mirrored in important visual symbols and the narrative style of Olympic texts. His analysis also demonstrates how the Olympic ideology and its symbolic repertoire fits in with the logic and ideology of the market. His contention is that for the first time in Norwegian cultural history and nation building, it became legitimate to evaluate cultural forms and performances in terms of their market potentialities which represented, in fact, a new cultural ideology emerging within the Olympic process.

While Chapter 3 deals with internal conflicts in Norway, Chapter 5 (also by the Editor) describes an external one, that between Norway and Greece on the Olympic and ritual status of the Norwegian 'Olympic' flame. This was lit for the first time in 1952 as part of the Olympic ceremonies in Oslo, and since then has been associated with the Winter Games. For the Lillehammer Games a similar, but much more elaborate, Norwegian torch relay was planned. The idea was that the two flames, the Greek from Olympia and the Norwegian from Morgedal, 'the cradle of skiing', should unite in a spectacular ceremony in Oslo before proceeding to Lillehammer. Exploiting the potentials of the flames for the marketing of Norway and Morgedal resulted in strong reactions and protests from Greece.

In Chapter 6, Roel Puijk analyses the planning process and the accomplishment of the opening ceremony both from the point of view of the audience present in the arena and as a media event. With reference to Handelman's functional modes, referred to above, he finds an interesting difference between the national and the international context. The image of Norway as interpreted abroad was in the presentational mode, whereas in the national context the ceremony was interpreted both as re-presentation and even modelling. We know that hosting the Olympic Games usually implies comprehensive changes to landscapes and urban layout due to new dominant buildings and arenas. In Chapter 7, Odd Are Berkaak is concerned with the relationship between inhabitants and their landscape or habitat. He presents a detailed description and theoretical analysis of the transformation of an old farm estate on the 'western' or 'wrong side' of the valley, into the alpine venue of Kvitfjell.

In Chapter 8, Ingrid Rudie focuses on the athlete as key symbol in order to analyse two problems. The first is the relationship between sports and changing societal discourses regarding gender. This chapter demonstrates the complex and contradictory messages regarding gendered scripts in international sports, in which principles of gender hierarchy coexist alongside those of gender equality. The second problem is concerned with the degree to which meaning can be shared across cultures. On one level, the Games promote universality and global homogenisation, on another level particular sporting disciplines have developed within the context of specific local traditions, so that a sport often carries a rich load of tacit social memory. The symbols attached to this memory are not easily translatable, and may foster a sense of cultural fragmentation. Three cases are used as background for the analysis: first, the development of women's cross-country skiing in Norway; second, women's fight for access to the men's alpine arena in Kvitfjell; third, the performance of women's figure skating with focus on the three most exposed athletes, Tonya Harding, Nancy Kerrigan and Oksana Baiul.

Eduardo Archetti pursues the gender perspective in Chapter 9. His focus is on masculinity, however, and analyses how athletes deploy their maleness in contexts conditioned by values conveyed by Olympic ideals, media and the adoring spectators. Competing forms of masculinity are produced and negotiated in different social arenas with different actors. Archetti's main actors, the Norwegian cross-country skier Vegard Ulvang and the Italian alpine champion Alberto Tomba, are compared as participators at the Albertville Games.

Notes

1. Although the book is not available in English, it has been translated into French with the title *Le savoir-être norvegien. Regards anthropologiques sur la culture norvégienne,* 1991, L'Harmattan: Paris.

2. As part of the research project we also arranged five workshops for scholars interested in sport and culture. Five reports containing papers presented at these workshops have been published with Roel Puijk as the editor. The reports, *OL-94 og forskningen I-V* are distributed by The Eastern Norway Research Institute, Lillehammer, Norway.

References

Handelman, D. (1990) *Models and mirrors: towards an anthropology of public events*, Cambridge University Press: Cambridge.

Hoberman, J. (1986) *The Olympic Crisis. Sports, Politics and the Moral Order*, Aristides D. Caratzas Publishers: New York.

Jackson, A. (ed.) (1987) *Anthropology at Home, ASA Monographs 25*, Tavistock: London/New York.

Klausen, A.M. (ed.) (1984) *Den norske væremåten*, Cappelen: Oslo. (French translation 1991: *Le savoir-être norvégien. Regards anthropologiques sur la culture norvégienne*, L'Harmattan: Paris.)

MacAloon, J.J. (1984) 'Olympic Games and the Theory of Spectacle in Modern Societies' in John J. MacAloon (ed.) *Rite, Drama, Festival, Spectacle. Rehearsals Toward a Theory of Cultural Performance*, Institute for the Study of Human Issues Press: Philadelphia.

Moore, S.F. and B. Meyerhoff (eds) (1977) *Secular Ritual*, Van Gorcum: Amsterdam.

Svabø, T. (1994) *'Lillyhammer' OL '94 sett fra utlandet*, Cappelen: Oslo.

Chapter 2

ANTHROPOLOGY AT THE OLYMPIC GAMES:
An Overview

John J. MacAloon

The artifact of an important initiative in the anthropology of the Olympic Games, this volume explores the motivating and mediating effects of international Olympic forces on the constitution and performative communication of Norwegian identities in the context of the Lillehammer Winter Games. By extension, the book will inspire analysts of other large-scale intercultural and multicultural performances and challenge all concerned with the future of anthropology in the 'globalising' and 'post-modern' moment. As a veteran of this kind of ethnology, I feel privileged to have been asked by Arne Martin Klausen and his colleagues (of the OLGA-group) to help situate their Lillehammer projects in the context of Olympic anthropological research.

In Lillehammer, anthropological investigation of an Olympic Games was for the first time undertaken by a sizeable team of established collaborators, drawn from a single major university department and a host-city research institute in the Olympic country. This team was supported by foreign colleagues, stabilised by a common research agenda, and organised with enough lead time for required fieldwork *practica* inside the local organising committee, the International Olympic Committee, and at a prior Olympic Games. In this overview, I will outline the international scholarly context of the OLGA group's work, highlight some of the difficulties our Norwegian colleagues overcame, and indicate the significance of their results for future anthropologies of cultural identity and global spectacle.

John J. MacAloon

Theory and the Olympic Games

Professional anthropology of mass festivals like the Olympic Games may seem a bit *outré*, but the pedigree for this work goes back to ancient times. In classical Greece, the *theoria* were delegations of official observers sent by the city-states to the great panhellenic gatherings – the Olympic Games above all – with the duty to report back on the doings of exotic or rivalrous others and on the overall condition of what Thucydides called *ton anthropinon*, the 'human thing'. The *anthropologoi* recounted by these theorists were among the first ethnologies, forming the practical, political and diplomatic counterpart to the narratives composed by historians. (Thus, with the publication of their Olympic research, our Norwegian colleagues join the small band of the only true theorists in anthropology!)

In the eighth century B.C., the three great assertions of panhellenic identity were institutionalised: Homeric poetry, the Delphic oracle and the Olympic Games. This happened at the self-same moment as the city-state model arose from the ruins of the palace cultures and the subsequent 'Dark Age' to provide powerful, segmented local identities for the Greek-speaking peoples. Therefore, far from opposing processes, the titration of Eleans, Corcyrans, Athenians, Corinthians, Spartans, and the rest, and the creation of the common identity of 'Hellenes' mutually entailed one another. Among the Greeks, cultural and political diversification was but the other side of the same coin as cultural interconnection and standardisation.

Historically speaking, nearly everything about the nineteenth-century European 'restoration' of the Olympic Games has been contested as more an invention of tradition than any straightforward revivalism. Structurally speaking, however, the homology is quite exact: at the very moment the nation-state emerged as the model of segmentary identity, setting out upon its course toward global domination, the Olympic Games were 'reborn' as one institution asserting and at least ideologically and discursively performing a transnationally common human identity. Moreover, as the functional equivalent of the standardising ancient epic poetries, world cosmopolitan popular and material cultures emerged and eventually won out, demographically speaking, over such rivals as 'world literature' or 'world religions'. As for the structural transformation of the Delphic oracle, modern science, or at least modern 'scientism' was destined for universal rule in the domain of authoritative knowledge and prediction, while journalism and publicity were to attain their own global powers in the domain of popular cultural knowledge.

In the name of science itself and only implicitly for any political assembly, the new discipline of modern anthropology began sending out its ethnographers to live with and observe distant peoples and events. Replicating the Janus-faced segmentation/unification process of the macro-social forces which produced them, the observational practices of these modern *theoria* were organised by the twin dogmas of cultural relativism and the psychic unity of humankind. As we know, however, the term 'theory' in our intellectual world was fated to retain its prestige but to lose its ancient meaning. Instead of physical presence and eyewitness observation, recording and reporting, 'theorisation' became the very opposite thing: the home-bound rendering into general and abstract formulae of some other persons' empirical observations of distant public events, relayed in texts of one or another sort, today including those delivered by simulacra of sight such as the television and the computer screen.

Considering the widest world of public speech, the modern Olympic Games have hardly ever lacked for this kind of theorising. Journalists of news, sports, politics and culture, literary figures, archaeologists, classical philologists, popular historians, physical educationists, military scientists, social and educational reformers, nationalist philosophers, and class and commercial codifiers of fashion, entertainment, and life-style practices were among those busy constructing theoretical fields for themselves well before the modern Olympic movement articulated its own official, transnational version of 'Olympism'. When scientific anthropology finally entered the Olympic game in the 1970s and 1980s, it was the last of the established social sciences to do so.

Though frequently disorganised, nationally segregated and marginal within their own disciplines, sociologists, psychologists, political economists, political scientists, social historians and critical theorists were already active in Olympics-related research. As exemplified in James Riordan's pioneering studies of Soviet sports systems, formal ethnography had as yet performed only an ancillary service to other methods of enquiry. However, no sooner did professional anthropologists begin to test their own distinctive ethnographic skills against Olympic objects than they found themselves propelled into rivalries and alliances with these newly professionalised 'sport sciences' on the one side, and with the upstart disciplines of communications and cultural studies, on the other. Practitioners in the latter field have proved especially prone to 'theorising' an Olympic object they have never seen first-hand, much less struggled with under the established methodological strictures of participant observation. Our Norwegian colleagues are only the latest to have had to do the ethnographic work while defending its value against the quicker fixes of purely deductive critical theorising.

Ethnography under New Conditions

Several reasons can be adduced for anthropology's slow entry into Olympic terrain. Obviously, little there responds to the traditional anthropological research model, in either its scientific or its romantic version, of long-term participant observation by a single scientist in a small-scale, autonomous and localised community in some exotic corner of the world. As I have suggested elsewhere, to begin to approach phenomena like the Olympics, anthropology had to alter that radical relativism which literally could not conceptualise the direct and explicit interaction of hundreds of cultural units in a way which did not automatically reduce itself to the imperialistic formulae of Marxist or liberal modernisationist theory. Moreover, as a bottom-up social science, anthropology had rarely applied its considerable talent to the direct ethnographic study of elites, especially cosmopolitan elites necessarily associated with large, international, mass-mediated, prestigious and expensive public works and projects like the Olympic Games.

Finally, there is always the professional's disdain for the popular version of his or her own science. As I have emphasised in my own historical anthropology, the Olympic movement has traditionally seen itself as an enterprise of intercultural and cross-cultural education and the Olympic Games as the practice of cultural encounter and mutual redefinition, simultaneously on a global and a micro-festive scale. Anthropologists – already being challenged and even set aside by federal culture ministries, national museums and indigenous cultural rights organisations – have hardly been in any mood to respect the claims to popular ethnography and intercultural practice made by the 'mere (capitalist) spectacle' of the Olympic Games. This effect has been especially pronounced in countries such as the United States where, in contrast to much of Western Europe and North-eastern Asia, intellectuals are like other citizens in having no regular source of information about the Olympic Games alternative to what they see and hear on commercial television.

Olympic anthropology had its modest beginnings in a 1960s and 1970s intellectual context of semiotic and structural anthropologies, of cultural performance theories born from renewed interest in the old topoi of myth, symbol and ritual, and of consequentially culturalist approaches to national and nationalist phenomena. The geopolitical context of that time was structured by the conjuncture of de-colonising nationalisms at the peripheries and Cold War neo-colonialisms at the centre of a 'world system' distinguished above all by the final global triumph of the nation-state form. Not surprisingly, the Olympic Games themselves – with their core calculus of representational identities: Individuality, Nationality, Humanity – experienced a quantum leap in acquired social, cultural and economic capitals during this same period.

Conducted in a post-Cold War world of increasingly significant transnational entities and forces, the maturing Olympic anthropology represented in this volume both reflects and takes advantage of a new theoretical state of affairs in the 'post-modern' human sciences. For example, these studies are concerned with such familiar issues as the production of national identity on international occasions, traditional versus modern forms of each, and the recruitment and fate of individual actors in these mass-mediated public dramas. However, these matters are conceptualised herein more as public 'discourses' – sometimes successfully stage-managed, often self-consciously popular and always contested – than as given social structural realities, much less as the purely 'etic' theoretical constructions of self-absorbed social scientists. Given this ethos, and in the context of a much-proclaimed death of the conventional anthropological field, the essays in this book will meet an anthropological audience more theoretically disposed to take an interest than the one available to Olympic researchers in previous decades.

At the same time, colleagues in the Lillehammer study are pushing the envelope of contemporary theoretical practice in the 'new' anthropology. I refer especially to the consistent, progressive and truly anthropological commitment in these chapters to attend as equally as possible to all the various social segments engaged in the making and interpretation of the Olympic events of Lillehammer. This commitment shows itself above all in the treatment of elites as human beings and not as ciphers of structure, and of ordinary citizens as actors with their own intentions, projects and powers. The consequence of this commitment, it seems to me, is to turn the 'negotiation of meaning and power' from a post-structuralist mantra into a research finding, to be evaluated like any other scientific result according to its greater or lesser success against other disciplinary approaches in representing, interpreting and explaining the events in question.

One suspects that the OLGA team's success owes much to the special conditions for this intellectual work in Norway, where, as Arne

Martin Klausen points out in his introduction, Olympic-scale events have been rare, university professors have a habitus of relatively familiar relations with government and media officials, and there has been surprisingly little tradition of analytical scholarship on 'Norwegian national identity'. This special combination of circumstances has not obtained in the previous contexts of anthropological research on the mutual inflections of the Olympics and its host cultures.

But progress in the face of the persistent methodological difficulties of Olympic anthropology should not be underestimated in grasping the attainments of the Norwegian research team. While the theoretical milieu has changed in a way more favourable for Olympic anthropology, and the arrival of the Games in Lillehammer provided a particularly supportive environment for its practice, relatively little has changed in the 'Olympian' character of the methodological challenges.

Methodologies of Scale

Above all, even for Winter Games, there are the challenges of scale and complexity. Whether or not hyperbole is the master trope for grasping Olympic matters, as Odd Are Berkaak asserts in Chapter 4, it is the case that nearly every person, and certainly every researcher, attending an Olympic Games for the first time is a little awe-struck by how much more vast is the terrain of goings-on than had been imagined in advance. This is because the cinematic, journalistic and academic sources of prior knowledge and expectation are constituted by one or another sort of reductionist, controlling and authoritative gaze. Moreover, in addition to the more boundary-crossing characteristics of these meta-discursive genres, researchers, whether they like to admit it or not, arrive at the object preconditioned by one or another national Olympic curriculum, often remarkably different from the discourses of even closely neighbouring countries, but each equally partial and confining.

For example, as Klausen points out in Chapter 3, few Norwegians, because of their own historical sports discourse, had much awareness of international Olympic organisations prior to Lillehammer. Most were notably innocent – by comparison with publics, say, in Britain, France, or Germany – of contemporary journalistic attacks on the integrity of the present IOC and IF leaderships. As a consequence, the already stretched Lillehammer anthropologists had to respond almost instantaneously, adding to their research agenda a new and powerful Norwegian public drama which they had been unable to anticipate.

First-time fieldworkers can also be ignorant of quite normative Olympic performance forms, and sometimes this is an advantage with ethnographic pay-off. When I arrived in Montreal to do fieldwork at the 1976 Olympic Games, I had put considerable time into a history of the Olympic revival, including time spent at IOC headquarters in Lausanne. I had also spent years as a participant in related elite sports contexts, had studied the cultural politics of events preliminary to the 1968 and 1972 games, and had learned a bit of the way around sports science organisations. Still, because of the exclusionary routines of U.S. television and the failure of my own anthropological imagination, I had no clue about the rich and intriguing popular festival which literally surrounds and encompasses the sports venues in every Olympic City.

Forced 'outside' by limited ticket funds (access credentials and research funding for a young Olympic anthropologist were hardly imaginable then), I discovered and commenced to document intercultural interactions among ordinary people which made Olympic ideology seem more credible than it ever had been to me. I was also forced by this ethnographic experience to begin to develop more complex performance system models than the anthropological ones available to me at that time. I began to allow differences among experiences of Olympic festival, ritual, game and television spectacle to make a theoretical difference; that is to say in the older vocabulary of theory, I saw that they did and tried to find new stories in which to report these data back.

In Chapter 9 of this volume, Eduardo Archetti pushes the study of Olympic festival-goers forward in an important new way, focusing on the behaviours and discourses of skiing supporters and documenting their quite different cultural constructions and celebrations of the athletic masculinities literally and differentially embodied in sports heroes. Archetti also provides readers with a wonderfully true account of that impossible Olympic fieldwork requirement, even for a single circumscribed project, of being several places at once each day of a Games. I well remember Archetti's exasperated (but also, it seemed to me, excited) query on opening day of the Albertville Games: 'How can you do anthropological fieldwork when there's no one place and everyone and everything is continuously in movement?' The answer is that the ethnographer must be in constant motion too. Archetti's account in his chapter of the continuous and quite exhausting oscillation from participant observation and face-to-face interviewing to the fill-in-the-blanks of bar gossip, late-night television, and morning newspapers will strike a chord of recognition in every Olympic fieldworker. James Clifford has called for supplementing the 'village in-dweller' root metaphor of ethnography with a second, that of the 'intercultural traveller'. For the Olympic anthropologist, the shift is very nearly a total one.

Scale, complexity and mobility of the object require a second major methodological shift, namely to team research. Although team fieldwork has been positively discouraged in traditional social anthropology and still is unusual today, it offers the only possibility for building any true ethnology of massive, mobile and periodic events like the Games. After recognising the absurdities of going it alone in Montreal, I began to design models for anthropological Olympic teams, and in 1984, the Wenner-Gren Foundation provided the funds to assemble such a team for Los Angeles.

The Los Angeles Model

I chose for this model a multinational and tri-generational cadre of anthropologists and sociological ethnographers who shared a general theoretical orientation toward symbolic anthropology and who had worked on state-level as well as local-level cultural performances. While team members were well known to one another from prior conferences, lectures and memberships in Victor Turner's circle, and some were close friends, we were unlike the Lillehammer team in having no prior history of working together in the field or even in the academic routines of shared departmental life. Moreover, we had no opportunity or funding for trial research projects or even preliminary meetings. Each person more or less developed his or her field project, got off the aeroplane, and went at it.

I alone had worked at previous Olympic Games and knew generally what to expect, and only Laurence Chalip and Pamela Chalip, besides myself, knew their way around the 'alphabet soup' of international and national Olympic organisations. The rest of the team knew a lot of anthropology of performance and quite a bit about their own national sport traditions, but also next to nothing about the institutions of the Olympic movement. This proved debilitating, as the rush of the Games is hardly the best setting for learning the territories of power and interaction in this complex field.

Moreover, the team itself became the object of media attention, with a film crew from the American public television trailing our members around, and a score of other press outlets daily seeking interviews. This degree of press interest in anthropologists studying their own societies in an international context was revelatory, and it influenced the initiatives later taken by one of the group, James Peacock, when he became president of the American Anthropological Association. It also set me to developing a method of exploring, as cultural data, the edits between controlled inputs into journalists and their outputs of produced texts, a method which offers a key corrective to cultural studies approaches which deal only with finished texts and performances. For example, certain taboos in American media coverage of religion became apparent through our Los Angeles work with the PBS Macneil-Lehrer Program, and I was able to use these insights to comparative advantage at subsequent Games in Seoul, Barcelona, and Atlanta. However, other members of our Los Angeles team were dubious of the media's attention, believing that it dangerously blurred the lines between scientific and journalistic commentaries, and we all agreed to curtail that attention when it became seriously disruptive of our common life.

As mentioned earlier, the Olympic scene is bifurcated into those with and without access credentials to the various backstages, and this is another matter which all subsequent Olympic research teams have had to face. In Los Angeles, Roberto DaMatta was credentialed as a television broadcast commentator for Brazilian TV Globo, working the cultural affairs 'beat' and providing the first backstage field study of Olympic media installations and routines. (Intercultural communication through Olympic mass media was a research area destined for significant development, as evidenced by Roel Puijk's exceptional chapter in this volume.) Through the intervention of the Puerto Rican government, whose Olympic policies I had studied, I had a distinguished guest credential in Los Angeles which permitted me to do the first fieldwork in the 'deep backstage' areas reserved for international elites.

Other colleagues on the Los Angeles team were confined to the public sphere, and though there was research pay-off in this diversity of field sites – 'highland' and 'lowland', 'riverine' and 'jungle', as we called them in self-conscious parody – tensions were introduced as well. For example, the Olympic specialists and those spending each day with internal actors of various sorts – athletes, officials, media, LAOOC personnel, diplomats – were more cautious in their interpretations, whereas the non-specialists and those spending their time in and as audiences were encouraged toward globalising interpretations and judgements.

These quite normal interpretative struggles become sharply defined in the context of late-Reaganite 'America', segmented and segregated

Los Angeles, extreme LAOOC commercialisation of the Games, and the hopelessly chauvinistic ABC television coverage of them. Intellectuals often pride themselves as being beyond the nationalist consciousness of fellow citizens, but our team discovered in Los Angeles that nations live inside the bodies of anthropologists too. Under the pressures of Olympic circumstances and representations, intellectuals can be nationalised in their moral sentiments. One of our number even took to refusing to appear in public without his country's flag worn as a scarf around his neck. It was a lesson to be relearned by our multinational research teams in Seoul and Barcelona, though avoided, so it seems, by the more ethnically homogenous Lillehammer group.

Probably the smaller scale and the friendlier, more 'wintry', and in Berkaak's terms less hyperbolic atmosphere of a Winter as against a Summer Games contributed to this effect as well, as it surely did to the more integral character of the research reported in this volume and the publications by the OLGA group. The Los Angeles team published their results independently. Papers important to later Olympic scholarship included: Don Handelman and Leah Shomgar-Handelman's pioneering study of the Israeli Olympic team as a mediating political and financial resource between the Israeli government and the Israeli-American and Jewish-American communities in Los Angeles; and the Chalips' analysis of the rigid selection and symbolic typing of athletic heroes in American mass media coverage of these Games. DaMatta's contrastive study of Olympic sport and World Cup *futbol* in Brazilian cultural structure and ideology helped to inspire Ingrid Rudie's treatment of gender hierarchy and equality in Chapter 8 of the present volume. The Los Angeles Olympic ethnography also helped inspire the important theoretical contributions of Bruce Kapferer's *Legends of People, Myths of State*, on comparative nationalisms, and Don Handelman's *Models and Mirrors*, an approach to public events referenced by several of the Lillehammer researchers. My own commitment to a ramified performance system model, which the Lillehammer colleagues are kind enough to cite, was deepened by the differential experiences and discourses of the researchers themselves in Los Angeles.

The Seoul Model

The summons which drew Arne Martin Klausen into Olympic anthropology, described here in Chapter 1, duplicated the experiences which brought Kang Shin-pyo to leadership of an extensive programme of social science research and scholarly events which accompanied the Seoul Olympics. As a distinguished anthropologist of Korean culture, and living – like the Norwegian colleagues – in a society whose government authorities habitually consult with such scholars, Kang was among those called upon for initial ideas by the organising committee for the 1986 Asian and the 1988 Olympic Games. Prior to this, the Olympic festival had not been on his radar as an anthropological object, but Kang realised immediately the monumental project of Korean cultural reconstitution and world presentation that would ensue. He got in touch with me, and together with our respective colleagues we refined a research model in which leading social scientific experts in the cultures of the host country and city collaborated intensively over a period of years with anthropologists and historians of the Olympic and international sport systems.

This research strategy was designed to mirror on the level of scholarship the phenomena themselves on the level of their Olympic practice, in which international, transnational, 'globalised' institutions and performances encounter, transform and are transformed by the practices, representations and institutions of the national and local host cultures. This process itself has emerged as the most general object of Olympic anthropology and what we continue to believe to be a special opportunity for our discipline to preserve its historical research traditions and accomplishments while at the same time opening itself up to the new interests in and conditions of intercultural exchange in the contemporary 'world system'. Odd Are Berkaak's exploration of the dialectic between local and global place-naming practices in Chapter 7 wonderfully conveys and develops this spirit.

In Seoul, we also sought to remedy particular deficiencies in the Los Angeles effort. Pilot projects were judged essential to establishing collaboration and beginning the transfer of knowledges of Korean social and cultural formations and of the international Olympic system. I had long been interested in the Olympic flame ceremonies and relay, and Kang well understood the importance in Korean terms of surveying the political and cultural reflections of the foreign forms throughout the peninsula and not just in Seoul. Together we studied the 1986 Asian Games flame-lighting ceremonies at Kyongju and travelled for hundreds of kilometres with the flame relay on its three routes through the country. In several towns, local academics had prepared briefings for us on the debates, planning decisions and political struggles in their areas. This became a model for us when we repeated the study with the 1988 Olympic relay, paying especially close attention to the changes wrought by the intervening national political transormation. We were able to show how – away from the capital city, the foreign elites, and international media attention – local political and social forces used against the centre the very resources the centre provided for national identity performances. The OLGA group was to make similar observations in its laborious Lillehammer torch relay study.

Of course, ethnographic experience and theoretical understanding does not necessarily translate into authority with Olympic organisers. On the basis of the Korean two-flames innovation, as well as of long experience with the Hellenic Olympic Committee, I was able to assure LOOC torch relay director Olemic Thomessen – at a meeting arranged and attended by Odd Are Berkaak – that the Lillehammer plan for two flames would lead to serious conflict with the Greeks. But the message went unheeded, and Arne Martin Klausen documents the ensuing drama in Chapter 5 of this volume.

In 1986, the Seoul organising committee had refused to help Kang and I with our research. But in the typical Korean way, our perseverance was being measured by the authorities as a test of our 'sincerity', and SLOOC president Park Seh-jik became a personal friend to all our work in 1988, supporting our official presence on the Olympic flame relay, and providing credentials, shared residence in the Olympic Family Town, and access to his office during the Games. Moreover, Park's and SLOOC's Olympic anniversary conference in 1989 would permit our teams to report and publish our research results in common.

In order to maintain continuity with the Los Angeles anthropology project while avoiding its Olympic-period difficulties, Kang adopted a double strategy. Roberto DaMatta, together with legal expert and Los Angeles Olympic heritage authority Stan Wheeler, joined us for the Asian Games opening ceremonies in Seoul. For a large-scale 1987 conference and cultural study tour of Korea, funded chiefly by a major Korean newspaper foundation, Kang assembled: Chalip, DaMatta, Kapferer and myself from the Los Angeles team; additional anthropologists interested in transnational phenomena, including Yamaguchi Masao, Ulf Hannerz, Edith Turner, Juan Ossio, Chun Kyong-soo, Yoneyama Toshinao, Joe Gusfield, Arjun Appadurai, Kim Choong-soon; and Olympics experts from other disciplines, including Bruce Kidd, James Riordan, Nadejda Lekarska, Dietrich Quanz, Oleg Milschstein, Gyongi Foldesine Szabo, Wojciech Liponski, Phyllis Berck, and Peter Macintosh.

In Los Angeles we had managed only informal relations with a mass communications research team led by Eric Rothenbuhler and including Daniel Dayan and Elihu Katz, but through Kang's Seoul conferences, much closer relations were developed with Olympic television researchers Miquel de Moragas, Nancy Rivenburgh, Lee Sang-hwe, James Larson, and Park Heung-soo. The post-Olympic conferences further thickened the network of researchers and commentators, through inclusion of additional sports specialists like Arnd Krüger and Robert Barney, and anthropologists like Marnie Dilling, Harumi Befu, and Marshall Sahlins. We were beginning to build a critical mass of experienced Olympic fieldworkers, and both the anthropological research community and the IOC also had begun to take notice.

At the same time, a decision was made to select for the core field study team during the Seoul Olympic Games themselves only Olympic specialists, regardless of discipline, who were experienced in the practical milieu of the Olympic festival and who shared a developed knowledge of Olympic organisations and histories. (The political historians Kidd, Liponski and Riordan, for example, had been NOC officials and the first two were past Olympic competitors.) Together with all the preliminary work, Kang's enormous energy and network of Korean contacts, and the quite different conditions of Olympic Seoul (easy transportation, common living within an Olympic venue and SLOOC credentialling as official observers), this shared institutional knowledge base and self-organised activity made common life easier and more productive.

Certainly, we came away as a team feeling that we had a much more complete and integrated understanding of the international and intercultural politics of these Olympics, from such global thematics as the end of the Cold War and of military rule in Korea, Korea-Third World interactions, and the creation of a Korean diaspora culture, to such Olympic cultural politics as strengthened Eurocentrism in the movement and the Ben Johnson case. But the solution was not perfect, not only because the same nationalist conflicts occasionally rose up within this team as in the Los Angeles one, but also because the cultural anthropological and political economic paradigms for interpreting the data being collected did not always comfortably coexist. Without SLOOC (or rather, its successor Sports Promotion Foundation) undertaking to publish the multivolume anniversary conference report, we might again have had difficulty with a common final publication of our research. The OLGA team's avoidance of such problems is admirable to their predecessors in Olympic team anthropology.

The Barcelona Model

Of course, it was in Seoul that Lillehammer was selected to host the 1994 Winter Olympic Games, setting in motion the recruitment of Klausen and his colleagues into colleague-ship and leadership in Olympic anthropological studies. Though preoccupied with other matters, our Seoul team took note of the strong impact of the Norwegian Prime Minister and other female members of the government on Korean television audiences as well as on the IOC. Both gender and 'green' issues were prominent in the run-up to, and the celebration of Lillehammer's victory, and there was much winking commentary in Seoul about the Norwegians beating out the Swedes. Members of our team were more directly concerned, however, with the failure of the Sofia bid committee to understand the seriousness of the Turkish minority issues in international and IOC opinion. The continued erosion of 'East bloc' Olympic voting also attracted our attentions, as it echoed the autonomous behaviours of Eastern European countries vis-à-vis the Soviet Union, the Seoul Games and South Korea.

Meanwhile, our new colleague Miquel de Moragas was already laying out his plans for Barcelona. In the event, Moragas and his colleagues preserved the previously developed model of sustained research collaboration between Olympics scholars and local experts in Catalan and Spanish cultures, while pioneering a new institutional basis for such team research projects. Attracting the support of the authorities of the Autonomous University of Barcelona, Moragas established a free-standing Centre d'Estudis Olimpics (CEO), housed in the AUB Faculty of Communication, with a staffed Olympic library and documentation centre, and with a mission to serve as a common meeting ground for domestic, European and international Olympics researchers through the entire Barcelona Olympiad of 1988-1992. (University courses, conferences, and degree programes were subsequently developed as well.) As in Seoul, preliminary conferences and study tours permitted a dozen prior Olympic research collaborators to report their research and acclimate themselves in Barcelona, and to contribute to Catalan and Spanish research projects on Barcelona 1992.

Moragas was to obtain far less interest from the Barcelona organising committee (COOB) than Kang had managed with SLOOC in Seoul or Klausen would obtain with LOOC in Lillehammer. At the same time, however, Moragas won support for the CEO from the Catalan Autonomous Government, the Spanish National Olympic

Committee, and finally and most unprecedentedly from the IOC itself. President Samaranch officiated at the Centre's dedication, and the IOC and the Lausanne Olympic Museum have commissioned studies from it. The on-site games research team – mass communications specialists Moragas, Rivenburgh and Montserrat Llines, anthropologists Kang, Guadalupe Rodriguez, myself; and the political economist John Hargreaves – for the first time enjoyed IOC-issued credentials.

After the Barcelona Olympics, the Centre has persisted through Moragas's remarkable leadership, the Autonomous University's steadfastness, and the Samaranch administration's continued support. Indeed, new programmes have been inaugurated through this important collaboration, including the International Chair of Olympic Studies, its attendant IOC symposia at which OLGA research results have been presented, and normalisation and co-ordination of university based Olympic Studies Centres throughout Europe and North America.

In Barcelona, Rodriguez contributed an important new form of Olympic anthropological study, monitoring the impact of the Games on a metropolitan, immigrant working-class neighbourhood in Barcelona, in which she had already completed two years of distinguished (and somewhat more conventional) fieldwork. Kang followed the experience of the Korean delegation in Catalonia, and I worked on Greek-Spanish-IOC relations in the Greek segments of the flame celebrations. We all worked together on the cultural representations of the opening ceremonies, primarily as an anthropological support to the real focus and achievement of the Barcelona team's research: Moragas, Rivenburgh, and Llines's twenty-five-nation comparative content analysis of the national television coverage's of these ceremonies.

This unique and inestimably important work, conducted with the assistance of resident researchers in the twenty-five study countries on all of the continents, put the lie once and for all to the familiar postulations of media homogenisation and homogeneity by conventional and universalising critical theories, left and right. By combining sophisticated media-institutional analysis, sustained ethnography of media production, and end-product content analysis, Moragas, Rivenburgh, Llines and company demonstrated empirically that the law of cultural production in the global system today applies to media representations too: that far from the elimination of cultural differences, standardisation of media forms and institutional routines are, in the Olympic context at least, the source of the production of difference in content.

The OLGA Group

When, as we waited for the Albertville opening ceremonies, Eduardo Archetti wondered how this kind of fieldwork could ever be possible, I was tempted to respond that he would not be alone in the stadium that night, that Fernand Landry, Alan Tomlinson, Bernard Jeu, and I, and others who had worked for years on Olympic cultural phenomena would be present too. Moreover, whether anthropologists or not, these would all be theorists in the old Greek sense of the term, as was the Norwegian team. But the real assurance was that Archetti himself was there, as Puijk would be in Olympia, and Klausen in Lausanne and Athens, and Berkaak in Georgia; as Olympic veterans from several fields and countries would be for the preliminary conferences in Lillehammer; and as Rudie and Aslaksen and the whole OLGA team would be in LOOC meeting rooms, along the Lillehammer flame relay, and bustling in and out of their Nansen School headquarters during the Games. What the team saw when it got to this gigantic, ramified, ever-moving 'there', and how members held the local and the global in theoretically binocular visions, are recorded in these pages. To improve upon them, the next anthropological Olympic team is going to have to pioneer means to see the Games from the outside while sustaining the Lillehammer team's remarkable accomplishment of an inside-out view.

References

Chalip, L. and P. Chalip (1989) 'Olympic Athletes as American Heroes' in R. Jackson and T. McPhail (eds) *The Olympic Movement and Mass Media*, Hurford Enterprises Press: Calgary, Alberta, pp. 11/3-11/27.

Clifford, J. (1992) 'Travelling Cultures' in L. Grossberg (ed.) *Cultural Studies*, Routledge: London, pp. 96-112.

Dayan, D. and E. Katz (1992) *Media Events: The Live Broadcasting of History*, Harvard University Press: Cambridge, Mass.

Dilling, M. (1990) 'The Familiar and the Foreign: Music as a Medium of Exchange in the Seoul Opening Ceremonies' in Koh Byong-ik (ed.) *Toward One World Beyond All Barriers: The Seoul Olympic Anniversary Conference*, Seoul Olympic Sports Promotion Foundation/Poon Nam Publishing: Seoul. Vol. 1, pp. 160-175.

Handelman, D. (1990) *Models and Mirrors: Towards an Anthropology of Public Events*, Cambridge University Press: Cambridge.

Kang, Shin-pyo, J. MacAloon and R. DaMatta (eds) (1988) *The Olympics and Cultural Exchange*, Hanyang University Press: Seoul.

Kapferer, B. (1989) *Legends of People. Myths of State*, Smithsonian Press: Washington.

Kidd, B. (1989) 'The Culture Wars of the Montreal Olympics' in M. de Moragas and M. Ladron (eds) *Olympic Games, Media, and Cultural Exchanges*, Autonomous University Press: Barcelona, pp. 19-26.

Landry, F., M. Landry, M. Yerles (eds) (1991) *Sport: The Third Millenium*, Laval University Press: Quebec City.

Klausen, A.M. (1996) *Lillehammer-OL og olympismen*, Ad Notam: Oslo.

Klausen, A.M., O.A. Berkaak, E.K. Aslaksen, I. Rudie, R. Puijk and E. Archetti (1995) *Fakkelstaffetten – en olympisk ouverture*, Ad Notam: Oslo.

Koh, Byong-ik (ed.) (1990) *Toward One World Beyond All Barriers: The Seoul Olympic Anniversary Conference*. 3 Volumes. Seoul Olympic Sports Promotion Foundation/Poon Nam Publishing: Seoul.

MacAloon J. (1984) 'Introduction: Cultural Performance, Culture Theory' and 'Olympic Games and the Theory of Spectacle in Modern Society' in J. MacAloon (ed.) *Rite, Drama, Festival, Spectacle. Rehearsals Toward a Theory of Cultural Performance*, Institute for the Study of Human Issues Press: Philadelphia, pp. 1-15, 241-280.

MacAloon J. (1989) 'Festival, ritual, and television' in R. Jackson and T. McPhail (eds.) *The Olympic Movement and Mass Media*, Hurford Enterprises Press: Calgary, Alberta, pp. 6/21-6/41.

MacAloon J. (1992) 'Comparative Analysis of Olympic Ceremonies, with Special Reference to Los Angeles' in M. de Moragas and M. Ladron (eds) *Olympic Games, Media, and Cultural Exchanges*, Autonomous University Press: Barcelona, pp. 35-54.

MacAloon J. (1995a) 'Interval Training' in S. Foster (ed.) *Choreographing History*, University of Indiana Press: Bloomington, Ind., pp. 32-53.

MacAloon J. (1995b) 'Humanism as Political Necessity? Reflections on the Pathos of Anthropological Science in Pluricultural Contexts' in J. Fernandez and M. Singer (eds) *The Conditions of Reciprocal Understanding*, Center for International Studies: Chicago, pp. 206-235.

MacAloon J. and Kang Shin-pyo (1990) '*Uri Nara*: Korean Nationalism, the Seoul Olympics, and Contemporary Anthropology' in Koh Byong-ik (ed.) *Toward One World Beyond All Barriers: The Seoul Olympic Anniversary Conference*, Seoul Olympic Sports Promotion Foundation/Poon Nam Publishing: Seoul, Vol. 1, pp. 117-159.

Moragas, Miquel de, and M. Ladron (eds) (1992) *Olympic Games, Media, and Cultural Exchanges*, Autonomous University Press: Barcelona.

Moragas, Miquel de, and M. Botella (eds) (1995) *The Keys to Success: The Social, Sporting, Economic, and Communications Impact of Barcelona '92*, Autonomous University Press: Barcelona.

Moragas, Miquel de, N.K. Rivenburgh and J. Larson (eds) (1995) *Television and the Olympics*, John Libbey: London.

Riordan, J. (1977) *Sport in Soviet Society*, Cambridge University Press: Cambridge.

Rothenbuhler, E. (1989) 'The Olympics in the American Living Room' in R. Jackson and T. McPhail (eds) *The Olympic Movement and Mass Media*, Hurford Enterprises Press: Calgary, Alberta, pp. 6/41-6/50.

Chapter 3

NORWEGIAN CULTURE AND OLYMPISM:
Confrontations and Adaptations

Arne Martin Klausen

Introduction

In this chapter I will discuss the socio-cultural and political tensions which arose during the preparations for and during the Olympic Winter Games in Lillehammer in 1994. Our preliminary hypothesis was that important features of the Norwegian ethos, especially in its rhetorical aspects, would necessarily come into conflict with certain features of Olympism as this diffuse ideology is administered by the IOC.

Olympism has never occupied any dominant position in the Norwegian sporting community. Organised sports emerged from national and military preparations for complete independence in the second half of the nineteenth century. From early on there was a certain rivalry between the German-inspired gymnastics movement, called a 'circus' by its opponents, and the disciplinary gymnastics of the Swede P.H. Ling. Herein lies the germ of the continuous division of Norwegian sports into two camps. The one lays emphasis on health and self-discipline; the other stresses competition and the cultivation of elites. As time passed, these two movements merged to form what sports historians have called 'the Norwegian system' (Olstad and Tønnesson 1987). In the Norwegian history of sports, the dominant trend has been sports for the masses and the health aspect, in keeping with other aspects of what many people perceive to be the Norwegian ethos.

Norway was not represented at the first modern Olympic Games in Athens in 1896, but four years later Norway sent a rifle team to the Paris Games which was directly sponsored by the Storting (parliament). A small gymnastics team, whose application for financial support was turned down, found itself a private sponsor. One of the athletes won a bronze medal in pole vaulting, jumping 3.2 metres. In the extraordinary Games in Athens in 1906 Norway was represented by a team of thirty-two sportsmen. The gymnastics team won the gold medal, and the home-coming festivities were spectacular. This was the year after Norway's secession from Sweden, and the king of this new nation came out to welcome the triumphant athletes home. The speeches and other ceremonies were dominated by a spirit of nationalism, but other aspects of this home-coming were reminiscent of Coubertin's style and rhetoric. The festivities also bore a striking resemblance to Fridtjof Nansen's triumphant return to Oslo in 1896, subsequent to his research expedition across the Arctic Ocean.

Norway's first contact with Coubertin and the IOC was through General Henrik A. Angell. He had skied across Montenegro, trained Greek soldiers during the war with Turkey, and had founded the first ski school in France. He was truly a man after Coubertin's heart. He is, however, not even mentioned in the most extensive history of Norwegian sports.

Up until the 1980s the Olympics had not dominated Norwegian sports. Even the Norwegian member of the IOC from 1928 to 1948, the ship owner Thomas Fearnley, sided with the Norwegian sports leadership when they organised the Norwegian relations to the IOC in a way that conflicted with the Olympic charter. This arrangement lasted until 1965, when a separate Norwegian Olympic Committee was established, following subtle intervention from the IOC and now in keeping with the charter. The sports historians Finn Olstad and Stein Tønnesson describe the IOC as follows:

> Socially the Olympic movement had its origins in the upper classes of Western societies – French, German, Italian and Danish princes and counts, English lords, American and Swedish industrial magnates and Norwegian ship owners... The Norwegian ship owners were for a long time the lowest class in the CIO. [IOC][1] (Ibid. p. 183.)

One would have expected that the IOC's plans to arrange the Olympic Winter Games in addition to the summer Games would have received an enormous amount of support in Norway. However, this was not the case; indeed they even met with resistance among sports administrators. Norwegian skiing was associated with a romantic communion with nature, and was strongly influenced by the sharp criticisms of competitive sports of Norway's national hero, the Arctic explorer Fridtjof Nansen. Despite the fact that Norway participated in the Olympics in Chamonix and St Moritz with some success, the Winter Olympics did not prove to be an effective means of increasing the status of the IOC or Olympism among the Norwegian sports leadership.

In Norway, sports were an important arena for the class struggle. The organisational division into bourgeois and socialistic sports was not eliminated until after the Second World War. The Winter Games in Oslo in 1952 became a symbol of 'national unity'; it was hoped that the Games would demonstrate that the nation had recovered from the war and the Occupation.

Nevertheless, the 1952 Winter Olympics in Oslo were almost a purely sporting event, with few secondary functions, modest ceremonies, and only a few artistic elements. It is symptomatic that the only non-sporting arrangement undertaken by the Olympic committee was an international conference about sports and health, carried out in a clearly social-democratic spirit.

In the so-called 'Oslo resolution' which was sent to the World Health Organization (WHO), and not to the IOC, we can read:

> Branches of sport which presuppose collective participation and co-operation should be encouraged, if necessary at the expense of those branches which presuppose individual 'sports stars'... To a far greater degree than now, sport must be regarded by all parties as a health issue, as opposed to a question of financial investments or national prestige. (Translated from *VI Olympiske vinterleker 1952*)

In the plans for the Lillehammer Olympics there were no formulations to any such effect. Indeed, here it was precisely economics, national profile and other meta-messages which were employed as a legitimisation of the huge expenses modern sports events incur. Before we look at the 1994 Olympics more closely, however, it is necessary to present some aspects of the Norwegian ethos.

Modernism, Olympism, and Norwegian culture

An analysis and comparison of the distinguishing features of both Norwegian society and Olympism can be based on a simplified version of the dichotomy traditional/modern. As ideal types they can be characterised by eight sets of parameters, as follows:

Traditionalism	*Modernism*
Social norms are stable	Everything may be disputed
Change is slow	Change is very rapid
Unambiguousness	Ambiguity
Social sectors multiplex	Social sectors specialised
Collectivity	Individualism
Perspicuity	Complexity
Low mobility	High mobility
Economy based on reciprocity	Economy based on market

To the extent that the so-called Olympism constitutes an ideology and is to be placed along the continuum of traditional/modern, my assertion is that it has to be placed close to the modern end of the continuum, with Norwegian culture closer to the other end. From its very beginning the Olympic movement has been one of the vanguards of modernism. Pierre Coubertin belonged to a group of artists and academics characterised as pioneers of modernism. (MacAloon 1981) Coubertin's great optimism and faith in future development and his enthusiasm for the innovatory possibilities of modern technology were unshakeable. The IOC has, in its more recent history (at least according to most sports historians) not only been very adaptive to the mainstream aspect of modernism, but has also been an integrated and active part of modern liberal capitalism. Rhetorically, the Olympic movement has always claimed to be apolitical, and Coubertin himself used the metaphor 'playing the chameleon' in a positive way, proud of the movement's ability to remain outside politics (Hoberman 1986). In fact, the movement has always been conservative, but still adaptive to various mainstream developments – like capitalism itself – including, after Lillehammer, 'environmentalism'.

The Olympic Games may thus be interpreted as the most distinct, secular ritual of modernity. No international event realises the concept of 'the global village' more distinctly than do the Games, and the Olympic slogan 'higher, stronger, faster' is the most pronounced rhetorical expression of the ideals of modernity. The Games, as a public event (Handelman 1990) are also polysemous and thus functional to modern pluralism and relativism: the Games may serve a broad spectrum of interests.

Several non-Norwegian social scientists who have studied contemporary Norwegian society support the assertion that the distinguishing characteristics of the Norwegian manner are closer to the traditional end of the continuum than to the modern. The German author Hans Magnus Enzenberger (1984) called his book on Norway

Norsk u-takt (Norway Out-of-Step) implying that it is not on a par with mainstream European modernism.

John Barnes, the well-known British anthropologist, was the first to reveal, after his fieldwork in Norway around 1950, the similarities between the socio-political structure of a Norwegian local community and traditional, small-scale societies in so-called exotic parts of the world (Barnes 1954; see also Eckstein 1966).

The Norwegian Paradox

Some years ago the BBC made a television programme comparing the various royal families in Europe. They sent a team to Norway to find out why the most popular and successful monarchy in Europe was to be found in a social democracy and a society proud of its egalitarian and non-hierarchical structure.

This paradox was visualised by means of shots from the Ski Museum at Holmenkollen, where a famous royal tableau has been reconstructed in one of the showcases. The story dates back to the oil crisis of the early 1970s when the Norwegian government prohibited the use of private cars on Sundays. The late King Olav V, loyal citizen that he was, travelled up to Holmenkollen for his regular Sunday ski excursion on the public tram, and the moment was captured in a photograph as he paid for his ticket from his own pocket. This unusual picture was distributed world-wide, and the reconstructed situation in the museum now functions as a semi-sacred symbol of Norway's alleged egalitarianism.

In 1984 ten Norwegian social anthropologists wrote a collection of essays on the subject of 'The Norwegian Way of Life' (Klausen 1984). This slim volume is certainly not the 'Bible' of Norwegian culture, but many non-Norwegians have claimed to understand more about aspects of Norwegian culture, which had previously been a mystery to them, after having read it. Its generalisations coincide well with research done by others. A few extracts from the book should illustrate those aspects of the Norwegian ethos relevant to the analysis of conflicts which emerged both before and during the Games at Lillehammer.

Tord Larsen's essay 'Peasants in the Town' sets the tone for a topic which is also discussed in several other articles. His most important contention is that Norwegian culture demands order, seriousness and responsibility, and that Ola Nordmann – the archetypal Norwegian – is no *homo ludens*; play for the sake of play itself is a morally dubious activity in Norway.

Furthermore, Larsen rewrites the so-called Jante Law – a law formulated by the Norwegian author Axel Sandemose, and which according to him is the first commandment in Scandinavian local communities. The Jante Law states that 'You must not think that you are better than anybody else'. In Larsen's rewritten Norwegian version it goes: 'You may well think that you are better than everybody else, as long as you make it quite clear that it is on behalf of something, preferably an organisation or some kind of community'.

He maintains further that the 'Norwegian configuration' is characterised by the fact that attitudes, meanings, values and even behaviour and etiquette are, and should be, connected in long standardised chains. This means that if you know one or two things about a person, you should quite easily be able to deduce the rest of the chain. This is another way of talking about the pressure to conform. Tord Larsen and many other scholars maintain that the town and urbanism are a foreign element of culture in Norway. Such features call to mind traits which we associate with stable, small-scale, local rural communities.

In the same volume, Hans Chr. Sørhaug tries to find 'the Norwegian totem' in the sense of a key symbol and structural model for society at large. He rejects the idea that the king is Norway's uniting totem symbol. Nature is possibly a strong candidate, but, according to Sørhaug, the real totem is the 'local community' (*bygda* in the vernacular). It is in the characteristic features of the local community that Norwegians find the sacred elements of their worship, and it is the local structures that they try (sometimes desperately) to get to function as a mould and model for the modern state as well.

The South African anthropologist Julian Kramer found the Norwegian state to be not fully integrated, and that Norway reminded him of the tribal structure of his homeland. When he participated in the national celebrations on 17 May for the first time, his interpretation of the extensive use of various national costumes (even in Oslo) was one of regionalism, rather than national unity.

The insights presented in Klausen's book and its generalisations may certainly be, and indeed have been, criticised. Still, it is possible to summarise what both foreign and native scholars consider to be the four main characteristics of 'Norwegianness':

1. Norway is a small-scale society by Euro-American standards, which means that its social structures are more multiplex than in other modern societies. This in turn implies, among other things, a higher degree of informal social control, and not only at the local level.

2. The ideal of equality is also important. Historically, this is explained by the fact that, in contrast to Denmark and Sweden, Norway never adopted the continental system of feudalism. The Norwegian peasant has seldom been a tenant farmer. Norwegian socialism and welfare ideology were, so to speak, built on a pre-existing egalitarian social structure.

3. TheNorwegian strong sense of fairness and equal rights serves to strengthen egalitarianism. Not only must people be equal, but they must also have equal rights and access to all sorts of things. The Freedom of Information Act (*Offentlighetsloven*) gives the press and ordinary citizens extensive rights of insight into public affairs, a fact that caused conflicts during the planning of the Winter Games.

4. Finally, there is the regionalism and importance of local sub-cultures to be further elaborated upon in Chapter 5 of the present volume.

It is important to emphasise that the strong traditional elements in Norwegian culture and the somewhat weaker modern elements are in some way superimposed on the structure of party politics. The conventional right/left-wing dimension in party politics does not always coincide with Norway's dichotomy. The result of the 1994 referendum on the European Union is a case in point. To many foreign observers it was a surprising result, based as it was on equally surprising political alliances. The political opposition to the Olympic Games in Lillehammer bore a strong resemblance to a similar structure, probably with a stronger infusion of value-conservative intellectuals.

These traditionally oriented values and attitudes have, however, not been irreconcilable with the development of a modern Norwegian industrial society. The present trend in Norwegian socio-cultural development is certainly oriented towards the modern end of our continuum. The Winter Games, in spite of all the folkloric and traditional symbols activated during the ceremonies, served as a catalyst in this process of modernisation.

The Fight For and Against the Olympics

The pro-Olympic circles stressed right from the beginning and throughout the entire planning period that the 1994 Winter Games would present Norway to the world as a modern industrialised country, but with a solid anchor in traditional Norwegian values. Some quotations from the official programme illustrate how the LOOC leadership chose to present these values:

> The Lillehammer Games are intended to demonstrate Norway's tradi-
> tions as a winter sport nation, and will draw on Norwegian culture and
> national character so as to reflect our basic attitude towards the individ-
> ual and society beyond the realm of sport. *(Lillehammer '94 Guide)*

It was also said that the Games will 'provide a showcase for Norwegian sport, architecture, environment, culture and industry'. The Games were to be built on five 'genuine values', namely a spirit of 'community, participation, enjoyment, spontaneity and fair play'. These values are specified in thirteen sub-points, which coincide well with the generali-sations researchers have made about the Norwegian ethos.

In the local political discussion about whether to bid for the right to host the Olympics or not, an alliance was formed between the social-democratic party and the conservatives, both of whom wanted to bid. The opposition consisted mostly of left-wing socialists and lib-erals, with the Christian and agrarian parties as hesitant and critical bystanders. Those who were in favour of bidding for the Olympics belonged to the same circles which later also fought for Norwegian membership in the EU, and can thus be seen as the champions of modernism. Since, however, the Winter Olympics are basically syn-onymous with winter sports – something most Norwegians have a strong relationship with – opposition to the Olympics was not as easy to mobilise as opposition to the EU. The call for a referendum about the Olympics was turned down several times by a majority in the municipal council. Opinion polls showed that it would have been highly unlikely to find a majority against hosting the Olympics at any point in time.

One of the most vociferous groups opposing the Olympics con-sisted of environmental and conservation groups. They maintained that the construction of arenas and the necessary infrastructure would entail a vast upheaval in the ecosystem. A few experts claimed that the traditional and idyllic small town of Lillehammer would be ruined by the changes a mega-event like the Olympics would necessarily entail. The arguments against hosting the Olympics launched by value-conservative intellectuals, however, were of a more general nature, centring on a general reluctance to invest so many resources in a sports event.

The arguments of the conservationists were neutralised by Sama-ranch himself. After a meeting with demonstrators he effectively ordered the LOOC to move the ice rink 'Viking Hall' in Hamar further away from a wildlife reserve. This marked the beginning of a co-oper-ation between the IOC and a handful of young Norwegian environmental activists. The global commitment of the prime minister through the so-called Brundtland commission was activated in the Olympic rhetoric. The LOOC introduced what it called an environmental profile into its planning, and as one of the quality requirements. Subsequent to the Lillehammer Olympics, the IOC has claimed to have introduced environmental consideration as the third dimension of Olympism, alongside sports and culture. Whether the Olympic Games and Olympism can be said to represent positive factors in a wider sense of human and natural ecology is a matter of opinion. Because of the close ties with modern capitalism and market economy that the Olympic movement nurtures, its environmental conscience is first and foremost rhetorical and cosmetic, the critics claim.

The other opponents of the Olympics in Lillehammer had to concede in the end that the Games did not constitute a catastrophe for the town, either architectonically or socially. At the same time, the optimists' belief in the positive economic effects of the Olympics for the district has not borne fruit, and finding a use for the expensive arenas and infrastructure is proving to be quite a problem for the local communities.

Tension and Criticism During the Preparations for the Olympics

During the entire planning period there was a continuous debate about the kind of themes discussed in both the national and local media. Locally, there was an almost immediate polarisation between the two local newspapers: the social-democratic newspaper was consistently critical, while the conservative one was highly positive. The strong alliance that existed in the political arena about the advantages of hosting the Olympics was thus not reflected by a corresponding conviction in the local media. The social-democratic press in Norway entered into a national co-operation agreement on coverage of the Olympics. In particular two highly critical journalists based in the Olympic region exerted a strong influence on the national coverage of the Olympics in the social-democratic press. There was no corresponding co-operation in the conservative and liberal press. Here, the views expressed were much less uniform. The entire press corps did, however, agree on one point of criticism of the LOOC: they felt that the organisation interpreted the Freedom of Information Act far too restrictively, refusing the public access to all sorts of information – a breach of a central element in the Norwegian ethos.

At an early stage in the process, the critical journalists in Lille-hammer mediated ideas from the book *The Lords of the Rings* which was soon translated into Norwegian (Simson and Jennings 1993), and Andrew Jennings was invited to Lillehammer's press club to hold a lecture. As mentioned earlier, Olympism and the IOC had not previously played a central part in Norwegian social debate. Only a handful of sports managers had close contact with the IOC and the unique organisation and style that permeates the interna-tional Olympic community. Nor had the scandals and power strug-gles within this idiosyncratic international organisation received much attention in Norwegian public debates. The descriptions in the book of the power struggles in elite professional sports, the com-mercialisation and undemocratic forms of recruitment to the IOC came as a shock to the Norwegian public.

The Norwegian Confederation of Sports had initiated a so-called moral values campaign the year before the Olympics, the aim of which was to place problematic aspects of modern sport on the agenda of the various organisations involved. In the first advertise-ment for the campaign we read: 'Today Norwegian sporting circles are facing their most important match. It is not about winning nine gold medals in Lillehammer, but about a future as a popular move-ment'. This campaign can be interpreted as a parallel to the health conference of 1952. Then as now, campaigns and resolutions were powerless against mainstream tendencies in modern sports. The campaign drowned in the initial enthusiasm over the Olympics. Moreover, ever since the Games the media have first and foremost been preoccupied with the economic scandals which have enveloped the organising body of our national sport, Norges Skifor-bund (The Norwegian Ski Association).

Many people have claimed that self-complacency and moralism are typical Norwegian characteristics. Once criticism of the IOC was on the agenda and LOOC's plans to accommodate the IOC's requirements for service and comfort became known, a debate arose in which most voices demanded greater Norwegian efforts to reform the IOC in the direction of a democratic organisation.

Alongside this, a power struggle within Norwegian sports manage-ment was being played out. It had been decided that the traditional division into Olympic and other sports, with two presidents, should be abolished, and that all sports should be administered by a common body with a single president. In the discussion about the new structure there were two main themes which are relevant to our context. One was the ability of local sport organisers to influence the national organisations at the top of the pyramid i.e., a centre-periphery dimension. The other was whether the Norwegian IOC members were to have ex officio seats in the new organisation. Scepticism towards the IOC was also great in sporting circles. Norway has a long tradition of sports being connected to the state through economic support. The requirements of the Olympic Charter that the national Olympic Committees are to be completely independent, have also been a cause for conflict in Norwegian sports organisations. At times there has also been conflict as to which president is to represent Norwegian sports in Olympic contexts. On a couple of occasions the IOC has attempted to influence this power struggle, but has generally shown great diplomacy and has not openly intervened. In the organisational reforms which are now taking place, the goal is to create an administration which also satisfies the Olympic requirements.

During the 1994 election campaign in Norway for the new presidency, the Olympic president competed against a female candidate who had solid support in the popular, mass sports milieus. The Olympic president won the election, and became the first joint president of mass sports and Olympic sports.

The strong criticism of the IOC, which had been publicised by two British jounalists in *The Lords of the Rings*, thus found ideal conditions in Norway and flourished. Few sports managers contradicted its findings and, indeed, many even shared its fundamentally critical attitude. The people who were most critical of the book were the central actors in the LOOC, whose own experience of meetings with Samaranch and other IOC leaders did not merit such harsh criticism. These people were, however, also probably more familiar with the style that marks not only the IOC, but also other power centres.

A weighty argument for awarding Lillehammer the Games was that its application emphasised the concept of 'compact Games', meaning that the different arenas were located within short distances. The initiative for this, the formulation of two applications, and an unusually active and successful lobbying among the IOC members was carried out by a small group of people from the town of Lillehammer. One of the main arguments in its request for state guarantees was that hosting the Games would provide an economically stagnant area of Norway with new opportunities for growth. From the very beginning then, there was a correspondence between the characteristic Norwegian regionalism and the IOC's two principles: first, that it is towns rather than countries which are awarded the Olympic Games, and second, the desire for compact Games. As it turned out, however, there was a movement away from these two principles as the event itself loomed closer. Highly unrealistic calculations and weaknesses in the locally recruited leadership necessitated major changes. The Games became a national affair under the auspices of a new leadership recruited from large-scale industry, not least the oil industry. (These changes are described in detail by the political scientist Jon Helge Lesjø, 1992) This process was an example of accommodation, and to a large degree its drama was acted out behind closed doors, and it was thus not publicised as a conflict to the same degree as the conflicts we will discuss below, which received widespread media coverage.

Some Cases of Conflict

Hosting a modern Olympic Games entails great challenges to administration and leadership. Conflicts of personality and interests are normal. Tensions arose at a very early stage between the original 'natives' and the multitude of 'immigrants', who held leading positions in the LOOC. Such conflicts are not unusual in cases of 'boomtowns' and other sudden changes. The form this conflict took in Lillehammer, however, is probably related to the strong Norwegian ideology of equality. What provoked the local population most of all were claims that LOOC employees used their institution as a justification for special treatment at restaurants and similar establishments. There was a lot of debate about this in the press, and it became known as 'the snob debate'. This debate became so serious that it had to be taken up within the LOOC by the LOOC president.

Once volunteers had been recruited, the seeds of a conflict among this group were also sown. One of the volunteers, an organisational psychologist at the regional college, stated that the structure of the LOOC was military and authoritarian, and appointed himself spokesman of a movement for a more egalitarian and democratic form of leadership. Both of these conflicts were quickly toned down, but the fact that they surfaced at all is typical of the Norwegian way of being.

A central feature of Norwegian society is the power and influence of voluntary organisations. Trade unions and professional associations enjoy a strong position and have the right of co-determination. Unusually, Norwegian cultural policy is also greatly influenced by artists' associations (see Klausen 1984). In two cases this force made its presence felt when the LOOC initiated measures in two areas without having contacted the relevant professional associations. The first case was the development of the design programme for LOOC, and the second was an art exhibition which was shown across the entire country as part of the Olympic cultural programme, and sealed with the Olympic hallmark.

During the bidding and early stages the design work was carried out by private advertising agencies and the chairman of the IOC's cultural committee, Pedro Ramirez Vasquez. He also provided a lot of support for Lillehammer in the application phase. His son, Javier Ramirez Campuzano, who accompanied his father to Lillehammer on a visit, offered to draw an Olympic mascot, an offer which the director of the LOOC accepted. He drew a Walt Disney-inspired 'Peter Pan' type of figure, which was supposed to represent the old Norwegian childking Haakon. This figure was used in the marketing of Lillehammer at the Calgary Games.

When this became known in Norway, there was a storm of protest from the arts community, and the issue of the 'non-Norwegianness' of the figure was even raised in the Storting by a member of the Socialist-Left party. He reacted to the fact that the LOOC had not consulted professional Norwegian artists, but had left the work to the son of the head of culture in the IOC.

As a result of this massive protest from artists, the LOOC started to discuss the development of an extensive and professional design programme. Under the direction of a Norwegian designer, but with a great deal of help from foreign experts, the mascot was Norwegianised, in co-operation with Campuzano. (A complete report in English on the development of the design programme can be found in Klausen 1993).

The main objective for the designers was to give the 1994 Winter Olympics a visual profile based on traditional Norwegian designs and colours. The objective was also to withstand resorting to what professional artists perceived as vulgar symbols of 'Norwegianness', such as 'Vikings, moose and shepherdesses'. The Norwegian identity was to be mediated in a modern way. The final solution was achieved by returning to structures within the Norwegian landscape; snow flakes and ice crystals were abstracted to form a pattern that was repeated throughout all the visual material. A cave carving from the Bronze Age, which is believed to be the oldest representation of a skier, formed the prototype for the pictograms. The abstract and the structural, the figurative and the ancient were thus, in an innovative way, combined to represent the meaning of traditional and modern at the same time.

On two previous occasions in Norwegian history, in the 1850s and at the turn of the century, artists have played an active role in nation-building and the development of what can be said to be the typically Norwegian. It is interesting to note that on the threshold of the twenty-first century, modern Norwegian artists are not as preoccupied with 'Norwegianness' as before. The professionals who now define and develop Norway's image are the modern industrial designers who create our products. It is often non-Norwegians who decide this form, in an era when ethnic and national designs can be used to profile products in marketing. Whereas the contribution of artists to the process of nation-building was formerly inward-oriented, aiming to make the population aware of its identity, it can be said that the modern applications of national and ethnic symbols are now outward-oriented, and as such, are a form of marketing. The final design programme was generally perceived to be a huge success, even by its original critics.

The so-called graphic arts conflict was another case where LOOC was criticised by the artists' organisational establishment.

It all started with a private art dealer who wanted to market Norwegian prints with the Olympic rings as part of the trademark. His contact in the LOOC was the marketing department, which organised all forms of sales under the licence of Olympic products such as souvenirs and clothing. This was a purely commercial trade in art, but the art dealer managed to employ the head of the professional association of graphic artists as the director of the touring exhibition. During the course of 1993 and 1994 they planned to sell approximately 40,000 prints by twenty-six professional Norwegian graphic artists throughout Norway. Again, there was a storm of protest from a number of well-known artists, led by a professor at the art academy.

This protest embraced three dimensions of conflict. First of all, it was a reaction against the LOOC as a state-funded institution lending out the rings to a purely commercial art sales venture, which was in competition with galleries run by artists. They believed that this venture would saturate the market for graphic art for years ahead. Local gallery owners took part in the protest. Secondly, the choice of artists whose work was to be sold had not followed the rules laid down by the artists' organisations. Thirdly, there was clearly a great amount of scepticism towards the Olympics in general among the artists who opposed the Olympic graphic art project, which was voiced in the many articles which appeared in the press. The project did not receive unconditional support from the LOOC's own cultural department either. When a portfolio of graphics was received from the art dealer in connection with the official Olympic art exhibition 'Vinterland', the museum people and art historians demanded its removal, thus displaying their solidarity with the opponents of the Olympic graphics project. These same people also demanded that their leader resign from her position.

The official Olympic art exhibition 'Vinterland', which was shown in Tokyo and the Olympic cities of Atlanta, Barcelona and Munich before arriving in Lillehammer, was also a main element of the commercial marketing of Norwegian industry and tourism. It was sponsored by the oil company Statoil. The Export Council of Norway also accompanied the exhibition to all the cities. 'Vinterland' can thus be interpreted as a modern version of the Trobriand Islanders' Kula trade, where the ceremonial trade of prestige items precedes the commercial market trade. 'Vinterland' was explicitly intended as a door-opener for Norwegian trade and industry. We might have expected that some artists, in light of this, would have registered their anti-commercial attitudes in connection with this venture, but this was not the case. This is probably because the works of art selected for the exhibition were chosen by Her Majesty Queen Sonja, who has studied the history of art, and was the first honorary president of LOOC's cultural committee. When selecting the works she consulted advisors from the most prestigious Norwegian art galleries. The project was thus integrated into the official Norwegian arts system. It was easier to accept the state using art for commercial purposes than private enterprises doing the same.

Peace work and humanitarian commitment are important aspects of Norway's self-image. The Arctic researcher and skiing hero Fridtjof Nansen laid many of the foundations for this image with his international refugee work after the first world war. As a result of his work the bestowal of the Nobel Peace Prize was conferred to a committee appointed by the Norwegian Storting. In more recent times 'The Oslo Accord' in the Middle East has become a similar symbol. Norway's international humanitarian commitment is said to be known throughout the world. There are, of course, people who believe that this is pure rhetoric and represents a far too chauvinistic self-image.

When the planning of the Winter Games started, many voiced a warning against Norway's tendencies towards self-criticism, moralism and folklorism. In an early discussion about a possible Olympic slogan, one of the participants argued for peace promotion to be explicitly expressed in the slogans. The suggestion was rejected at this stage by the majority as being too banal, moralistic and puritanical, and bearing too much resemblance to Norwegian stereotypes.

This negative attitude towards peace as an important element in the Norwegian Olympic rhetoric changed when the idea of Olympic

Aid to Sarajevo was launched, via Norwegian television from Barcelona. Later, this issue became an important part of the non-sportive elements of the Games. Samaranch made a symbolic one-day trip to Sarajevo during the Games at Lillehammer, and in the final ceremony included an improvised salute to the former Olympic city. During the national torch relay, the peace message of Olympism was often associated with Sarajevo and the ethnic conflicts in the Balkan states.

After the 1994 Olympics the king of speed skating, Johan Olav Koss, followed the Norwegian tradition and worked to ensure that the IOC would include a permanent humanitarian element in the Games, however, this endeavour was without success.

The Climax of Conflict

Another Norwegian sporting hero, the cross-country skier Vegard Ulvang, also became a major actor in the general Norwegian criticism of the IOC. He had been selected to take the Olympic oath during the opening ceremony. In the period leading up to February 1994, a recurrent theme in Norwegian newspapers was how it was possible to relate to the upper echelons of the IOC and at the same time, in an educated, but definite way, mark Norwegian values and ways of being. In January, Vegard Ulvang had already made a public statement in which he strongly criticised the IOC, first and foremost for the fact that the active sportsmen did not have sufficient influence over the administration of the resources of the organisation. He also criticised the undemocratic way in which the IOC recruited its members.

Far more dramatic was the opinion poll which the largest newspaper in the country undertook and published at the same time as the first IOC members were arriving in Lillehammer. This opinion poll showed that the Norwegian public had a predominantly negative opinion of Samaranch and the IOC. The Norwegian LOOC president, who over several years had built up a close relationship with the leadership of the IOC, also made some critical comments in another newspaper. The interview with the president remained with the editors for a while, but was printed at about the same time as the opinion poll.

No one in Norway had imagined that the conflict would become as dramatic as it did in the week before the opening ceremony. The extent and seriousness of the conflict was not made public until a good while after the Olympics.

The meeting of the IOC with Norway was thus characterised by an unexpectedly critical attitude, clearly to its great surprise and irritation. It was, in fact, so dramatic that several IOC members threatened to leave Lillehammer, and others felt that Ulvang should be relieved of his duties. The president of Norwegian Olympic Committee (NOK), Arne Myrvold, countered this by threatening to withdraw the entire Norwegian team if Ulvang was removed. In this highly volatile situation Norwegian sports managers, with the LOOC president Gerhard Heiberg in the forefront, and assisted by the Prime Minister and the Norwegian State Broadcasting System (NRK), were faced with a formidable diplomatic challenge to try to appease the IOC tempers. An important part of this was the Prime Minister's 'message' to the Norwegian people on an evening news broadcast. She said:

> I think it is important to underline that we are arranging an event with a Norwegian character. Nevertheless, we are doing so in an international arena, we have accepted the role of host, and there are people other than social democrats and Norwegians in the world... We Norwegians are more used to egalitarian ways of thinking than perhaps any other nation, and it is a fine aspect of our culture and our community.

In his book about the Olympics (Heiberg 1995) the LOOC president relates how he even had to mobilise the King and Queen in his efforts to quell the conflict.

The day after the results of the opinion poll were published Ulvang once again appeared on television to criticise Samaranch for his background in the Franco regime and the lack of democracy in the IOC. Heiberg and Samaranch now chose to exhibit diplomacy and arrange a meeting between Ulvang and Samaranch, at which Ulvang assured Samaranch that his criticism was not meant personally, but was aimed at the system. Samaranch was then invited to dine with Ulvang in the Olympic village, an invitation that he accepted.

The conflict was resolved and the festivities could begin, with Vegard Ulvang as the oath-taker.

To Samaranch's closest colleagues all of this appeared to display an unheard of lack of common courtesy and gratitude. The director general of the IOC, François Carrard, made the following statement to the press:

> IOC does not care what Norwegians think. The opinions of four million people in a small province in Europe about the IOC do not concern us. There are many hundreds of millions of people in the world who support the IOC and welcome us.

Conclusions

The planning of opening ceremony got off to a difficult start. Several artists had presented their ideas, and here too there were warnings against creating a performance based on banal Norwegian symbols; instead the aim was to show a modern Norway using contemporary ways and means.

It was therefore a surprise that the final version of the ceremony was based to such a great extent on national traditions and ideas, and was in many ways an orgy of folkloric elements (see Chapter 6 this volume). Once it had been carried out, however, it was deemed to be a huge success. The many Norwegian medalwinners, the weather and the enthusiasm of the spectators dispelled earlier problems and conflicts. During the closing ceremony, to the great enthusiasm of the Norwegians, Samaranch said that this has been 'The best Winter Games ever' – a description that malicious cynics claim he always uses about the most recent Games.

It has been claimed that the success of the Winter Games strengthened Norwegian confidence and the belief that even a small Norwegian provincial town is able to arrange a mega-event like the Olympics. In the autumn of 1994, after the second referendum in twenty years about whether to join the EU, i.e. when there had again been a surprising majority against membership, speculation started about the cause of this. Serious political commentators contended that the successful hosting of the Olympics had strengthened the anti-EU cause.

According to the present author's view no dramatic change has taken place in the structural pattern of 'Norwegianness' due to the Games alone. In order to identify the more subtle changes it is necessary to comment on this from two different perspectives: first from the perspective of symbolic expressions and rhetoric, and secondly from the perspective of *realpolitik*.

During the last ten to twenty years, among Norwegian elites, or what may be called the modern sector, there has been a tendency to disparage some of the traditional values, or caricature them with negative metaphors. For example, the Norwegian people's positive concern with being Norwegian – doing it our way – is inverted to the Norwegian expression *nisselue-mentalitet*, an expression which originates in the belief that goblins (*nisser*) pull their caps so far down that their eyes and ears are concealed, thus making them oblivious to their surroundings. This has been one of the favourite derisory expressions of those who have wanted to speed up the modernisation process through internationalisation and integration into the European common market. Our egalitarian ideology is often presented negatively as the 'Jante Law', implying envy of the success of others and a lack of generosity. Our concern with fairness, equal rights and insight into public affairs is presented as an obstacle to efficiency and progress. A often-heard satirical expression, also during the planning period for the Lillehammer Games, was that 'Norway is a country consisting of four million consultants'.

When the final version of the objectives of the Lillehammer Games was worked out, surprisingly, it mirrored many of the stereotypes mentioned above – and not that reluctantly either, but quite outspokenly and sometimes even with a pathos more common to Olympic rhetoric than to Norwegian. In the chapter on international objectives in LOOC's guide it says that the aim is to 'enhance respect for our values and the role we play in the international community and promote interest in Norwegian business and industry'. Business and industry are secondary to 'Norwegianness' in this rhetoric. In the next paragraph of the Olympic Guide this is repeated when the text stresses the importance of building the Games on Norwegian qualities and genuine values, and, as quoted previously, to 'create a positive attitude to Norwegian culture and our way of life'.

The 'genuine values' are specified in the subsequent paragraphs and are all in keeping with the most positive self-image that Norway has, the 'spirit of community', 'participation', 'enjoyment' specified as 'making room for everyone', 'spontaneity' specified as 'a down-to-earth event' and finally Olympic 'fair play', which in a Norwegian context may have connotations to the quest for justice in a more general sense than simply sporting competitions alone.

The concept of 'the green Games', a modern derivative of traditional Norwegian nature-orientation, played an important role in the rhetoric after the protests from the Norwegian grass-roots organisations, and the IOC's adaptation to environmental concerns.

It is our impression that the LOOC establishment also gradually withdrew from the tendency to view things Norwegian in an inverted perspective, and that it became fully legitimate to be proud of our alleged 'Norwegianness'. (The LOOC president Gerhard Heiberg's argument for joining the EU: 'It is the best way to preserve our own special, national character'.)

The torch relay was supposed to mobilise interest and enthusiasm in the whole country for the hosting of the Games. Certainly, the Games had this kind of integrative function. Nevertheless, as shown in

Chapter 5, the local communities used the torch symbol for their own purposes. Moreover, Norwegian regionalism was demonstrated with an enormous, post-modern inventiveness, imagination and creativity, but still by using traditional myths and folklore as raw material.

If we add that the media coverage abroad very often focused on the traditional and exotic aspects of the Norwegian way of life, I think we can conclude that the rhetoric and symbolic message of the Winter Games enhanced the image of Norway as *Annerledeslandet* (the country where everything is different) – the title of a poem by the famous Norwegian poet Rolf Jacobsen. From its poetic origins this expression has also been inverted to something negative, and used as a slogan by those in favour of Norwegian membership of the EU.

Finally, let us comment on what we called *realpolitik*. In spite of Norway's reluctance to join the modern political developments in Europe, it is not unaffected by the strong pull of modern technology and market economy. As mentioned above, the Olympic movement is part and parcel of this regime. Like all other modern countries Norway competed for the right to arrange the Games and thus signalled that it is – basically – not so very different from the mainstream of Western civilisation.

Norway's state-owned oil company, Statoil, as one of the main sponsors, adopted the Olympic slogan in their advertisements. The most fascinating artistic expressions in the Olympic information centre were the models of the world's most spectacular buildings; one could recognise the Eiffel Tower, the Cheops pyramid, the Empire State Building and the Hamar Olympiahall. Towering above all the others, however, and firmly placed in the middle, was the oil rig Troll, one of the tallest constructions in the world at 430 metres. This oil rig was symbolically linked to the old Norse tree of life – the ash tree Yggdrasil. The text accompanying this artistic installation which, in fact, was not the work of an artist, but of a commercial advertising agency, was taken from 'Voluspá', the poetic, old Norse myth of creation.

In a paradoxical way the Winter Games at Lillehammer became an occasion for revitalising traditional Norwegian identity, and particularly its artistic expression while, at the same time, it became an arena for presenting Norway's modernity. And as always, Norwegians did it their way!

The criticisms regarding the IOC, elitist sports and the commercialisation of the Olympics has now almost died out, along with the Olympic flame.

Note

1. Empirically this generalisation has been criticised by John MacAloon who claims that the statement may be interpreted more as a Norwegian projection on to the IOC than an accurate historical statement about the organisation (personal communication).

References

Barnes, J. (1954) 'Class and Committees in a Norwegian Island Parish', *Human Relations,* vol. 7, no. 1.

Det offisielle OL programmet (1994), LOOC: Lillehammer.

Eckstein, H. (1966) *Division and Cohesion in Democracy: A Study of Norway,* Princeton University Press: Princeton.

Enzenberger, H.M. (1984) *Norsk u-takt,* Universitetsforlaget: Oslo.

Handelman, D. (1990) *Models and mirrors: towards an anthropology of public events,* Cambridge University Press: Cambridge.

Heiberg, G. (1995) *Et eventyr blir til – veien til Lillehammer,* Cappelen: Oslo.

Hoberman, J. (1986) *The Olympic Crisis. Sports, Politics and the Moral Order,* Aristides D. Caratzas Publishers: New York.

Klausen, A.M. (ed.) (1984) *Den norske væremåten,* Cappelen: Oslo. (French translation 1991: *Le savoir-être norvegien. Regards anthropologiques sur la culture norvégienne,* L'Harmattan: Paris.)

Klausen, A.M. (1993) 'Construction of the Norwegian Image – Reflections on the Olympic Design Programme' in R. Puijk (ed.) *OL 94 og forskningen III.* Rapport fra forskerkonferanse, Østlandsforskning Rapport 5-93: Lillehammer.

Lesjø, J.H. (1992) 'OL på Løvebakken' in R. Puijk (ed.) *OL 94 og forskningen II,* Østlandsforskning Rapport 12-92: Lillehammer.

Lillehammer '94 Guide (English Edition) (1993), Universitetsforlaget: Oslo.

MacAloon, J.J. (1981) *This Great Symbol. Pierre de Coubertin and the Origins of the Modern Olympic Games,* The University of Chicago Press: Chicago and London.

MacAloon, J.J. (1984) 'Olympic Games and the Theory of Spectacle in Modern Societies' in J.J. MacAloon (ed.) *Rite, Drama, Festival, Spectacle. Rehearsals Toward a Theory of Cultural Performance,* Institute for the Study of Human Issues: Philadelphia.

Moore, S.F. and B.G. Meyerhoff (eds) (1977) *Secular Ritual,* Van Gorcum: Amsterdam.

Olstad, F. and S. Tønneson (1987) *Norsk idretts historie,* vols I and II, Aschehoug: Oslo.

VI Olympiske vinterleker (1952) Official Report of the Organising Committee: Oslo.

Simson, V. and A. Jennings (1992) *The Lords of the Rings,* Simon and Schuster: London.

Chapter 4

'IN THE HEART OF THE VOLCANO':
The Olympic Games as Mega Drama

Odd Are Berkaak

During the summer of 1991 spokesmen for the XVII Olympic Winter Games at Lillehammer in 1994 started to use the concept 'mega event' when referring to the arrangement. They emphasised the great number of people involved and the economical and physical volume of the forthcoming event. The word 'mega' denoted the unprecedented scale of the event, emphasising the fact that there was really no adequate format or pre-existing yardstick which could be used, not only in Norway but throughout the world. The Games meant something out-of-this-world, not only as a sports performance or media event, but also as an economic venture and a construction project. The message that the organising committee (the LOOC) was repeatedly insisting on in the public debate was that they were going to do something that would surpass any previous event the world had seen. Phrases such as 'set new standards', and 'raise the stakes', became standard. The musical conductor of the opening and closing ceremonies at Lillehammer, for example, explained that the only reason that he took on the task was its sheer volume. He said it would be bigger than anything he would ever work with, that there were really no economical or physical limitations to his artistic ideas. The kick he got out of it was the format itself – without precedence or parallel and, importantly, without limits.

It has been suggested by students of the Olympic movement that this quest for the bigger than life is endemic to the genre, the kind of grandiose spectacles to which the Olympic Games belong. It has been described as 'a de novo enterprise born with few precedents'

(MacAloon 1984:242), and 'an institution without parallel in nature and scope in the 20th century' (MacAloon 1988:280).

All these uses of the category 'mega' point to a distinctly hyperbolic discursive feature of the Olympic movement which also reveals itself when viewed historically. This feature is not simply that the Games are something big and impressive but that they are steadily getting bigger and becoming more and more impressive, both in quantitative and in experiential terms. The so-called Olympic idea is telling in this context: 'Citius, Altius, Fortius' – 'Faster, Higher, Stronger'. The comparative is essential.

> In 1896 the first modern Olympic Games were arranged in Athens. 311 athletes from 13 countries participated... Today the number of participants is more than ten thousand, the audience numbers hundreds of thousands, and the number of TV-viewers is beyond imagination.[1]

Again, the same feature is emphasised in the literature: 'In scarcely 90 years the Games have grown from a fin-de-siècle curiosity into an international culture performance of global proportions' (MacAloon 1988:279). This exponential character creates something of a millennial expectation for the Olympics. When, in 1988, the announcement was made from Seoul by the president of the International Olympic Committee, Juan Antonio Samaranch, that Lillehammer had been selected to host the XVII Olympic Winter Games with his now famous phrase, 'and the decision is Lillyhammer!'[*sic*], it caused instant euphoria in the Norwegian media. Large sections of the population, and certainly all those who had been involved in its planning, felt as though they had crossed the limits of the possible. It was, in other words a mega experience. The television pictures of the classical violinist who smashed his instrument to pieces in exaltation has become immortal in the national Olympic imagology. Samaranch's formulation became an instant cliché and was later used in the standard advertising texts from LOOC, as in the following excerpt:

> '...and the decision is Lillehammer.'
> 15 September 1988 IOC president Juan Antonio Samaranch stated the words of redemption. For years a group of enthusiasts had been working with the 'impossible'. Suddenly it was possible.

According to this logic it follows that if one is 'enthusiastic' enough one can achieve the 'impossible'. The utopia of the mega event seems to bring about a euphoric experience of breaking through the barriers of the physical and socio-cultural environment as we know it into a space of unrestricted possibilities. These almost millenarian expectations were also confirmed in retrospect in the post-festum process of public exegesis. The minister of education stated at a seminar in Lillehammer in February 1995 that the Games had set the nation on the road to 'common development towards higher goals and expansion of the limits of the possible.'[2]

The Olympic ideology of exponentiallity was made explicit by the president of the LOOC, Gerhard Heiberg, at a moment in the planning process when it was suggested by the press that the volume of the arrangement could perhaps be reduced somewhat without detracting from the quality of the event:

> We can not reduce much, we have to think of the tremendous expectations that the IOC have of us which are that our Games are going to be the best ever. The products we have promised the leadership in Lausanne we have so far delivered and we also have to follow up on this delivery.

The point that the organising committee was putting across at Lillehammer was that they were going to do something that would surpass the format of any previous Games. One of the great triumphant moments for the directors in LOOC was that the president of the International Olympic Committee, Juan Antonio Samaranch, himself confirmed the success of their ambitions in his final statement at the closing ceremony: 'It has been the best Games ever!' Two years later, at a ceremony in Oslo, when the Norwegian hosts were given a prize for their effort, he repeated the same statement which was widely publicised in national media. It had by then become a standard phrase reminding the nation of the megalomaniac ambition that the best is not good enough, to be a success things have to be better than the best.

The importance of the Olympic Games as an ongoing global spectacle, then, is the hyperbolic expectation to exceed all limits, break all boundaries and burst all formats, to reconfirm bi-annually that the human condition is to transcend its own condition. The Olympic movement thus seems to represent an ideological cult of the impossible which rests on the ideological predicament that from any point in any development, any condition or any level of achievement, it is always possible to move one step further. The significance of the Games does not lie in the ideological or symbolic declarations as we find them, for instance, in the Olympic Charter and the official symbolic repertoire, but in the continuous experience by the audiences of the unprecedented.

Hyperbole as Symbolic Form

This hyperbolic orientation is evident both as a rhetoric figure and as an overall discursive pattern as well as a mode of experience and imagination. In the remainder of this chapter I will explore the concept and its implications in the study of the Olympic Games. The concept of hyperbole was introduced into cultural analysis by Aristotle as a rhetorical trope with the basic meaning of 'exaggeration'. It is formed from the Greek 'hyper'- above and 'ballein'- to throw, literally. 'to throw over'. A parallel in the Norwegian language is the expression: 'To shoot over the goal'. Aristotle sees it as a particular kind of metaphor and uses as an example a black eye: 'One could say of a man who received a black eye that "one could think that it was a basket of mulberries". The lesion around the eye is red and blood-shot, but this expression would exaggerate it strongly'.

In the Olympic rhetoric, however, the notion of metaphor is somewhat awkward because it implies an equation and a form of continuity, however fictitious. The rhetorical figures used in the Olympic context extend in their grandiose references beyond metaphor and denote that for which there is no equation. The Olympic achievements are beyond compare. Hyperbole, defined as a rhetorical trope evokes illusions and expectations of the unprecedented, 'something exceeding the realistic or the probable' (Eide 1990:64). Such achievements are driven by the desire for the unprecedented, the infinite and the limitless, in short: *mega*.

On the most elementary level we can thus define hyperbole as an exaggeration, but it is also clear that it is a special kind of exaggeration with some particular epistemological premises and discursive implications. Perhaps we can develop a more precise concept of the code that is in operation if we look for a moment at how hyperbole is defined in geometry. A hyperbole is a graphic figure which moves towards a straight line (asymptote) when the x-value (denominator in the function) moves towards infinity. In my old maths book it is defined as something that 'grows limitlessly' and that is 'moving toward infinity'.

The use of such tropes, when they are institutionalised and become idiomatic, generates a cumulative or exponential discursive pattern. To maintain its referent, i.e., the hyperbolic expectation, the sign object has to be expanded each time it is repeated. To put it simply, one has to use more and more extravagant rhetoric to maintain the extravagance. For the Olympic Games this was made evident by LOOC president Heiberg in his address referred to above, where he insists on creating the 'best Games ever'. Any decrease in spectacular scale and intensity is utterly contra-final to his vision of the Games and of Olympism.

Let us now turn to the concrete expressions of this mentality as they were developed during the better part of a decade before the Games. The motto of the Lillehammer Games was developed by a marketing company: 'They said it could not be done, so we did it.' As a combination of seemingly contradictory and incongruous statements, this is a classic example of oxymoron, which Brooks notes as the typical figure of melodrama besides hyperbole and antithesis (Brooks 1985:40). The motto presents us with a schismatic narrative universe – Us against Them. 'They' represent the negative voice insisting that the unspecified 'it' cannot be done and, implicitly, that there are limits to ambitions and achievements. The positive voice – Our voice – has already broken the implied barriers and states quite flatly that 'it' has been done. What was impossible has now become possible.

The same ideological conceptions are also expressed in designs and figurative forms. The leader of the design programme, Petter Moshus, sums up the intentions of the programme in the following statement:

> The image of Norway we wanted to project was to be contemporary and innovative rather than nostalgic and cliché ridden. Norwegian nature and history were to serve as a source of inspiration – not as a model to be copied. And the design was also to incorporate the Olympic ideal of conquering new frontiers.[3]

Both 'nature' and 'history' are here regarded as points of departure, sources of 'inspiration' which are to be transcended, not boundaries or given limitations as in a 'model'. The hyperbolic gaze and style of thought were thus present as a driving force at the very heart of the symbolic production at Lillehammer. From the beginning the design section assumed what they themselves termed 'a pace-setting role' for the other sections of the organising committee playing a central role in formulating the vision and goals to be adopted by the Games as a whole.

The most important Olympic symbol of them all, and the only one that is actually prescribed in the Olympic Charter, is the Olympic flame, kindled by the sun itself at Olympia and carried to each Olympic site to ignite the flame of each individual Games. The flame is thus a ritual compound legitimising and defining places and events as Olympic. This structural position of the flame naturally makes the torch on which the flame is borne, into a central expressive element. For the Lillehammer Games the torch was moulded directly on the hyperbole.

Figure 4.1 The Olympic torch of the 1994 Lillehammer Games
(Copyright: Jarle Kjetil Rolseth, Lillehammer)

One of the first official symbols created in connection with the Lillehammer Games was a logo in which the central motive is a graphic representation of the Northern Lights. This is a slightly modified gestalting of the hyperbole. It is formed as a series of parallel white lines (light rays) spreading out and upward in a wave-like motion over a cobalt blue background (the sky). A concrete objectivation of the ideological vision that the Lillehammer Games would reach out across the universe. It literally grows limitlessly towards infinity like the myth of the tree that grows into the heavens, echoing the geometrical definition of the hyperbole.

This is also in line with the hyperbolic symbols and gestures of melodrama as described by Peter Brooks:

> The action played out on the stage is ever implicitly an emblem of the cosmic ethical drama, which by reflection illuminates life here below, makes it exciting, raises its stakes. Hence melodrama's mode must be centrally, radically hyperbolic, the mode of the bigger-than-life, reaching in grandiose reference to a noumenal realm.(1985:54)

Figure 4.2 The first logo of the Lillehammer Games (left) and the final version with the text 'Limit-less profiling of Norway' (translated literally) *(Copyright: Norges Olympiske Komite)*

The last part of this sentence could be a description of the logo. Celestial symbolism is utilised as a primordial expression of the experience of the infinite and limitless. Another image expressing the same notion of unboundedness was a postcard issued in a series with the official design of the Lillehammer Games showing the ski-jump hill, which forms an aspiring movement towards the 'great blue yonder' of the winter sky directly pointing to the full moon right on top of the hill. The definition of hyperbole in my old maths book again describes the image perfectly: 'moving towards infinity'.

Another ideological echoing of this hyperbolic notion was conjured up in a Norwegian newspaper report from the opening of the Tokyo Games in 1964, by the prominent culture journalist Henning Sinding-Larsen:

> We found ourselves in a solemn silence, before the temple bell from Nara was brought to us on electronic wings. We heard music of the spheres and relived ancient Man's belief that the stars were tuning keys for celestial harpstrings. (Sinding-Larsen 1976)

Figure 4.3 Shoot the moon. Lysgaardsbakken Olympic ski-jumping hill *(Copyright: Johan Brun, Lier)*

His vision of the celestial harpstrings is a direct textual parallel to the
graphic design of the Lillehammer logo, the quest for the unbounded
'spheres' through the image of the exponential, parallel lines extend-
ing into the sky. The function of the open sky in this symbolic scenario comes very close to the verbal category *mega,* the vision of the
undifferentiated space beyond the restrictions and inhibitions of life
as we know it here below.

The first versions of this logo were invented in the initial stages of
the bidding process as early as 1983. As seen in Figure 4.2 the original had the Northern Lights placed under the name of the city, and
the reference to the nation was included both in the subtitle and in
the colours of the logo itself which were red and blue. The name of
the country as well as the colours were dropped in 1988, after Lillehammer had been awarded the Games. In March 1990, after LOOC
had been organised, the central motive of the Northern Lights was
turned upside down, and, finally, in February 1991, the national
colours were dropped and simultaneously the whole motive was
'compressed' to give a more aspiring impression. There are several
significant moments in this design process, but the turn around of the
central motive element is the most telling. The original is characterised by a centred and markedly descending orientation in the per-

spective, while the final version is more top-heavy, indicating a movement upwards from 'life here below'. The compression of the emblem supports the same general re-orientation.

When a place or an area is defined as Olympic it has to be marked off from the surrounding landscape in an unambiguous way. Some signs have to be visible in the surroundings demarcating the Olympic from the non-Olympic. At Lillehammer this was done by erecting three great obelisks on the main highways into the area, one along the E6 south of Hamar, one west of Gjøvik on the R4 and one north of Ringebu on the E6. The shape of these obelisks also has a hyperbolic form.

Similarly, the most prestigious sponsor organisation Olympiatop-pen (The Olympic Summit) cre-ated a logo that even more clearly demonstrates the hyperbolic senti-ment. Its motive is a stylised moun-tain peak formed as a hyperbole pointing towards the Olympic rings reminiscent of the post card of the Kanthaugen ski-jumping hill.

When the successful Norwe-gian competitors from the 1992 Winter Games in Albertville returned home in triumph, two so-called 'count-down monuments' were erected, one in front of the central railway station in Oslo and the other on Lilletorget square in Lillehammer. After the Games, the one from Oslo was installed at Holmenkollen, the national skiing arena, while the one in Lilletorget remains permanently in place. These monuments were made

Figure 4.4 Entering the Olympic area *(Copyright: Jarle Kjetil Rolseth, Lillehammer)*

Figure 4.5 The logo of the 'Olympic summit' *(Copyright: Norges Olympiske Komite)*

from a beam of laminated wood formed as an up-turned hyperbole. On the top of the structure is a digital watch showing the number of days, hours and minutes to the opening of the Games. Something resembling a lantern mast cuts the movement of the hyperbole carrying displays with the logos of the main sponsors. These evoke the association of a ship under sail, which, in the European tradition, is a key symbol for exploration and movement into the unknown.

One of the medieval legends that was used in the presentation of Lillehammer was that of the Birkebeiner ('birch legs'). The Birkebeiner were a group of warriors active between 1174 and 1218 in the civil war, most famous for supporting King Sverre. After Sverre's death they shifted their loyalty to his infant son, Haakon Haakonson. In 1206 two of the Birkebeiners took the two-year-old prince the fifty-five kilometres across the mountains from Lillehammer to Østerdalen on skis to safety from his enemies. Each year since 1932 a commemorative cross-country event has been arranged with thousands of participants following more or less the same trail. In the coat of arms of the town of Lillehammer there is a Birkebeiner on skis, making Lillehammer the only town in the world to have a skier in its seal. In the television productions presenting the Games internationally this episode was dramatised to emphasise the fact that the town of Lillehammer has age-old heroic skiing traditions. As part of

Figure 4.6 The count-down monument *(Copyright: Jarle Kjetil Rolseth, Lillehammer)*

Figure 4.7 The Birkebeiner monument in the town square in Lillehammer *(Copyright: Jarle Kjetil Rolseth, Lillehammer)*

the Olympic cultural programme a statue of the Birkebeiner heroes was erected in the town square. The base of this statue was also formed as a hyperbole.

Hyperbole as Narrative

This imagery and style of design showed a prolific mutability during the Olympic process from the early 1980s and into the mid 1990.
    In the official Cultural Plan from the LOOC it says:

> The Olympic idea and the joy of breaking new barriers, is also going to be disseminated through the cultural events by appreciating great achievements. The audience and the performers will find pleasure in participation in things they have never experienced before.[4]

Likewise, in the *Rammeprogram for kultur og seremonier* (General Programme for Culture and Ceremonies) it says in the introduction to Chapter Two, entitled 'Premisser, mål og strategier' (Premises, Goals and Strategies) that 'Concentration, intensity, maximal physical effort and record-breaking results – that is how we imagine the world of sports. These are the basic characteristics of the culture of sports.'

Here, the structure of the hyperbolic narrative is formulated more or less explicitly as three syntagmatic moments. First, a phase of restraint and discontent is implied. Secondly, through intensification of mental and physical powers, the restricting barriers are broken down and, thirdly, a condition of freedom and possibilities is opened up.

Of course, the Olympic rhetoric does not operate on its own ideological preconditions removed from contemporary social processes and historical conditions. Several intertextual parallels carrying the same implicit – and sometimes not so implicit – narrative offer themselves up for inspection at this point. Let me take two such instances as examples. The first is an advertisement for Nike running shoes which was shown on television in Norway during the same period. The first scene shows a man running in an urban jungle environment resembling an airport runway or a motorway junction. He is slowly approaching a big, dark structure that blocks his way. We understand that he is facing 'The Wall'. He is breathing heavily and he is obviously under a lot of mental and physical strain. Then, miraculously, he suddenly runs through the wall and takes off like an aeroplane into the 'Great Wide Open', his footprints vanishing among the stars. From the world of sports and leisure consumerism this image is a visualisation of the same construction of the relationship between man and environment.

The other intertextual reference is to another genre of popular culture which even surpasses sports in commercial importance. The scenario of sexual intercourse and the modern description of the orgasm shows the same basic structure of the build-up of intensification and the sensation of breaking through a barrier to reach a level of total, uninhibited satisfaction. A standard description goes, for instance, like this: 'Harder and harder, faster and faster. Then I cried out for the first time in my adult life. It was the big bang, a real shake, a volcanic eruption, and the lava splashed and squirted through the air.' (*Cupido* 1994)

In February 1995, one year after the Games, in an important summing up address given by the minister of education[5] the opening ceremony was described in the following terms:

> It was bitterly cold, but at that moment our backs started tingling with warmth[6] – and the pride and courage in our breast[7] were rising and rising to a point where we in the end were overwhelmed by the fireworks,

standing amidst a sea of fire. Our hearts were pounding, the audience was steaming and we were spell-bound, in the heart of the volcano. (Hernes 1995)

The rhetoric figures and metaphors here, such as 'pounding', 'steaming', and 'spell-bound' come very close to the standard descriptive arsenal of the literature of ejaculation. The formulation 'rising and rising to a point were we in the end were overwhelmed' is also a parallel. The minister, in the same speech, also refers to a report which appeared in one of the national newspapers the day after the opening ceremony, in which the reporter talks about 'seething emotions bursting forth'. The grand finale of the opening ceremony, during which a globe in the form of an egg (the 'Tellus Egg') emerged from the ground and eventually opened to release hundreds of plastic peace doves, floating like semen into the dark winter sky, was described with the following ripe metaphors: 'The Tellus egg which emerged towards the end of the two-hour ceremony was a visual orgasm. Lava of pent-up love. Thank you so much!' The syntagmatic parallels between the genres of copulation narratives, sports advertising and Olympic achievements are striking indeed.

This narrative structure is a vehicle for the idiomatic mutability of the hyperbolic imagination across discursive boundaries into other social and cultural fields and genres, both popular and elite. Several agents and interests wanting to associate themselves with the Olympic process to promote their interests felt a strong affinity to the narrative of intensification and overcoming of limits. As we already have seen, the link to the 'cultural sector' and different art worlds became evident at an early stage of planning and was repeated throughout the 'Olympic process': 'To overcome personal limitations, to exploit physical and psychological resources, to exhibit strength, beauty, fantasy and playfulness to the audience, are characteristics that sports and art have in common.' This led to a discursive fusion of traditionally separate social and cultural fields such as sports, arts, business and politics, which shows that breaking through barriers was not only an ideology of the Olympic process but also a functional implication.

In this context it is important to understand why the hyperbolic rhetoric is notoriously formal and consistently avoids any item of substantial identification with the goals and values the process is meant to achieve. It is in the nature of hyperbolic discourse that it is exponential, which means that it necessarily has to transcend all established conditions, be they moral, functional or physical. From this it follows that the introduction of absolute values are logically alien to such processes. A substantial goal or a definite value in this connection is a barrier in itself and must be avoided. It is the overturning of barriers, and the euphoric sensation of having broken through to an unbounded space of unrestricted possibilities which is the 'goal'. The basic motivation seems not to be the achievement of goals, but to reach out *for,* and then surpass them. This follows logically from the epistemology of the hyperbole itself, as I have tried to show; any end-point or new 'order' or higher 'condition' would mean new boundaries and thus contradict the utopian expectation. This means that the process is not only anti-essentialist but anti-*essentials,* and thus, perhaps, nihilistic. Goals and values are inhibitions that tell us that we have reached a condition of fulfilment and contentment that reduces the further motivation to 'overcome personal limitations'.

This interpretation is confirmed by such central texts as the minister's official exegesis of the Games. The 'new order' or 'higher condition' that the Games were supposed to bring to the nation are here rhetorically implied but he carefully avoids defining it substantially:

> In short: the Olympic Games give us the possibility to redefine ourselves as a nation, to formulate common goals and to reach standards that raise the stakes, so that, when the arrangement is over, we not only have the opportunity to look back with joy and pride, but also forward because our average performance and capacity have raised us to a higher level… In other words, the Olympic Games should inspire Norway to transcend itself. (Hernes 1989)

This statement is symptomatic of the teleological paradox involved: the standard that one attains implies raising the standards. The new and higher standards will enable us to redefine our ambitions continuously in a never-ending quest for new standards. A standard is not understood as a final form or condition but as a new limit which in its turn, is going to be transcended. The process is not defined by a final goal or objective which will give it a general direction, but is depicted rhetorically as a grandiose quest beyond all metaphorical equations and, in the end, the world as we know it. No qualitative change or new condition of Norwegianness is indicated, only that the stakes are going to be higher. The nation is going to be 'mega-good', in an unrestricted environment for the unfolding of collective energies. In his official post-festum exegesis the minister referred back to his 1989 speech and confirmed his own forecast: 'We were successful in the attempt to set a new standard for our self-image.'

The whole Olympic project, as it was defined and interpreted by the minister of education was then for Norway to pull itself up like Münchaussen, by its bootlaces out of the quagmire of habits and traditional mentalities. The central ideological thrust of the Olympic process was that the Games would give Norwegians an opportunity to redefine and transform themselves, both as individuals and as a nation, and become something greater and better.

Hyperbole as Practice

In all cultural analysis it is important to understand the relationships between symbolic forms and other fields and processes that make up the social world. The ideological and symbolic do not operate in a historical or epistemological vacuum. In the case of the international Olympics these inter-relationships are very complex and rapidly changing. From the days of Coubertin, the festival, the ceremonial and ritual as well as the competition aspects of the Games were always intended to serve extrinsic ideological purposes. During the first decades of the Olympic movement, this purpose was humanistic, concerned with the issue of peace and political freedom. Later, and especially under the regime of Samaranch, economic motivations have come more and more into focus. Behind and beyond the joy and hedonism of the festival itself, lies a fundamentally pragmatic intention, as becomes explicit in the addresses of the minister. He wants the playfulness and the festival mood to serve an explicit purpose. It is characteristic of the Olympic discourse that these seemingly opposite orientations, the hedonism of the festival and the pragmatics of the political arena and the market place, always tend to coexist like light and shadow. The symbolic and artistic elements, the 'signifying materials of a culture', have clearly become instrumental in a way that is described by Andrew Wernick as typical of all promotional culture (1991:188).

A case that demonstrated this point in an exemplary manner was the media presentation of the American speed-skater Dan Jansen. He set a new world record for the 500 metres at a test race in the Vikingskipet, the new ice rink erected for the Lillehammer Games, in December 1993 just two months before the Games started. This record was a sensation in the world of winter sports because he was the first to break the thirtysix seconds barrier. In a television interview he interpreted his achievement as follows:

What does it mean for skating that you have broken a record?
I think it is very important for speed-skating… to take it to another level. It is a goal that I had, and a dream of mine. To be the first to do it is very exiting for me. Like I said yesterday I think the others are coming soon so I have to continue to go faster [laughter]. But for now I am very, very satisfied and happy to break that thirty six.

How fast is it possible for a human being to go 500 metres, do you think?
I think it is impossible to say. For me I don't like to set limits, because then you get there and there is nowhere to go, so… I always think I can go faster. And I think in the future things will change. Maybe the skates will change so the turns will become easier. But for now I just skate as fast as I can every time I go.[8]

Again there is the quest for the 'other level'; the description of the project of speed-skating comes very close to the description of the development of the nation as rendered by the minister of education. The two accounts are intertextually linked through hyperbolic structure. Jansen gives us a vivid picture of the modern athlete's symbolic 'burden'; life as a grand race in which competitors alternate for the front position but without anybody ever reaching the finish line. To win does not mean to achieve a goal in the traditional sense of having arrived at a final destination. All satisfaction and triumph is temporary and provisional in his world. He knows that the pack will catch up with him and overtake him if he does not 'continue to go faster'. We even sense a certain repugnancy towards the very idea of limits and final goals in general. Surprisingly enough he says that he becomes disoriented in relation to defined goals and that he has nowhere to go if he 'sets limits' for himself.

As this event was presented in the Norwegian media it was framed as a moral narrative relating to human values and personal integrity. As an international hero Jansen symbolises what it means to be an adequate person in the contemporary world and it was the symbolic and ideological significance that was in focus.

Immediately after the interview with Jansen, however, there followed an interview with a representative for Hamar Olympiske Anlegg (Hamar Olympic Enterprises, HOA), the organisation that built the hall and is responsible for its operation. Before the test race there had been speculations in the sports press as to whether the ice would be fast and attain a good reputation. If the arena was to meet expectations and make a profit for the owners some world records would have to be broken, even before the Games started. Johan Olav Koss's and Dan Jansen's races on 4 and 6 December 1993 proved that it would be among the fastest rinks in the world and relief was great in the HOA organisation. The investments were secured,as confirmed by Dan Jansen in the same interview:

> *The fact that the first 500 metres below the thirtysix second limit was made in the Olympic hall in Hamar is probably also a feather in your hat?*
> Absolutely! It is a boundary-breaker, and it will be remembered for many, many years, even if they will probably go faster in the years to come.

Here we see how the symbolic interpretative frames are intertwined with the pragmatic frames in ways that makes it impossible to disentangle them empirically. What is read as a general moral statement in one context is understood as an advertisement in the other. Jansen explicates his own experience in humanistic and existential terms while the HOA representative interprets that same experience as a marketing event. From events such as this it seems that the ground metaphor, the idiomatic situation, which expresses the central notions and categories of the hyperbolic discourse, is that of marketing, of attracting the attention of 'the world' to a place or a person cast as products, and to give them a 'positive profile' that will attract the Other as customer. In the discourse on barrier-breaking and 'visibility' it was openly and insistently referred to such pragmatic phenomena as 'market potential' and improved 'commercial performance' for Norwegian industry and tourism. The athletic achievements and the festive aspects of the Olympic events were meant to catch and hold the attention of the world and direct the 'eye of the world' to Norway, not just as a nation, but as a tourist destination and a production site, or, more generally, as a commodity.

This instrumentalisation of the symbolic and the cultural was accompanied by a more and more explicit reflexivity in relation to cultural forms, which became evident in a number of contexts and perhaps most explicit in documents published by the LOOC, as illustrated, for example, in this declaration of 'genuine values' from the group of official sponsors:

> The Olympic Winter Games at Lillehammer is going to be a sports festival and a popular festival based on genuine values.
> This is the vision that forms the frame for the Games at Lillehammer. But what do we mean by genuine values?
> Closeness: The arenas surrounded by 100,000 spectators, the venues in a close neighbourhood, people along the tracks, the dog on the slope[9] – and Norwegian business in focus on the home turf.

Participation: From the youngest to the oldest, for everybody regard-less of skills, nationality, or religion. The whole of Norway together in the Olympics – the business community too.

Happiness: The Lillehammer-cheer through the airwaves to 250 million people. The experience of participation in the largest sports festival of all times, either as a spectator, or by being part of the 'team' of co-operating companies.

Naturalness: Norwegians are born with skis on their feet. Norway is the cradle of skiing, our nature and climate was made for the Winter Olympics. Norwegian companies are the natural partners in making the 1994 Olympics possible.

Fair Play: An enthusiastic audience cheering all participants – not only the home favourites. Fair play and equal conditions for all – the commercial participants too.[10]

The question 'What do we mean by genuine values?' is a contradiction in terms because what we usually mean by genuine values is that they are doxic, self-evident an unconscious, and not a matter of opinion at all. Authentic or absolute norms are not made the object of conscious choice and do not enter into strategic thought, but are structural in the sense that they are the conditions on which choices and strategies are formed. They are habitual in Bourdieu's sense of being 'structuring structures'.

The Self as Hyperbole

The same rhetoric of 'visibility', 'attention' and barrier-breaking was also carried over to the Olympic reconstruction of the nation. There was seemingly a case of 'scheme transfer' between the pragmatic rhetoric of the market and the reformulation of our collective self as Norwegians.

A category that came into use very early on in the planning process was the noun 'profile' with its verb forms 'profile', 'profiling', accompanied by such derivative forms as 'profilisation', 'profile element', 'profile programme' and 'profile strategy'. These words, which were new in the Norwegian context at the time, confronted and gradually substituted more established concepts such as 'identity', 'heritage', 'national character', and 'tradition' which are all main rhetorical tropes of the narratives of the nation. The new categories signalled an acute reflexive awareness of the self and the nation as something gazed upon by 'the world'. The massive media presence was referred to as the 'eye of the world', and it was established in the planning of the media centre that the most important spectator had three legs, meaning the camera tripod. The central metaphor for the Games at a very early stage became quite simply 'an exhibition window'.

As it turned out, this rhetorical change indicated an ideological shift from an intrinsic to a markedly more extrinsic and other-oriented view of the self and the nation, which eventually set in motion a massive reflexive process of self-reconstruction on many levels and in highly diverse fields in Norwegian society. The national ideology of conceptualising culture in essentialist terms which had been hegemonical for the better part of two centuries was, perhaps for the first time, effectively challenged.

Parallel to the Olympic process driven by the LOOC, the Ministry of Foreign Affairs in collaboration with Nortra, the government tourist promotion agency, initiated the so-called Prosjekt Norgesprofil (Norwegian Profile Project) which stated that:

> Research on the international perception of different nations shows that Norway and the Norwegian people have a diffuse, vague image in the eyes of the world. These studies, which include research on the Norwegian self-image, reveal a definite discrepancy between the way the world sees us and the way we see ourselves.

The Profile Project, of course, was going to remedy this situation and bring the intrinsic and the extrinsic gaze on the nation in harmony. The Olympics is seen as the main context for this transformation precisely because it provides a context for reflexivity: 'With the 1994 Winter Olympics on the way to Lillehammer, Norwegians have become increasingly aware of the importance of our profile.' A method is also designated: 'This will ... take place through increasing our level of ambition at home, while raising our reputation and strengthening our image abroad.' The formulation echoes the Olympic motto directly: 'Faster, Higher, Stronger'. But again we see the use of rhetorical hyperbole conjuring up the image of exponential growth and increase without specifying its nature or scope.

This style of thought is typically hyperbolic because the image or the profile that is being constructed has as its main function the erasure of symbolic and functional barriers (difference) between Norway and the outside world, and is driven by an image of the world as one continuous space. The new promotional ideology does not focus attention on the character or the nature of the national culture, but on 'all the activities that make us visible to the world'. The aim is not to preserve or extend a heritage but to make something that is inaccessible accessible and desirable for the Other. Like hyperbole itself, Norway, when the 'strong positive profile' is established, will 'move towards infinity' and 'exceed all limitations'.

In addition, the LOOC itself was very active and quite explicit in formulating this new relationist cultural programme:

An Olympic event is an opportunity to be focused on – with an assured benefit... We have a lot to show the world and a lot we can point to and proudly say it is typically Norwegian.[11] This we can do standing upright and erect, without losing ourselves in our own reflection in the window pane. The glass is transparent. It allows us to see from the inside and the outside. It provides us with an opportunity to see ourselves with the eyes of strangers.

We can discover our blind spots, our way of life and culture. We will be able to see the good qualities, the comical aspects, and the more doubtful sides.

The sooner we start on this introspective task the sooner we will be able to choose which aspects we want to emulate, which we want to change, and which we want to retain as they are.'[12]

The LOOC newsletter *OL-Status* appeared during its four years of operation as a virtual textbook in post-modern self-reflection, or, in their own terminology, 'introspection'. Here, what were traditionally taken for granted, the nation and national identity, are referred to in a distanced and clinical language. Both entities are analytically dissociated and broken down into their constituent parts and made the object of a disinterested evaluation in which extrinsic criteria are applied – 'the gaze of the strangers'. The nature of Norwegian culture and mentality is no longer seen as endemic and self-evident but as a repertoire of potential instruments for communicating with others, i.e., profile elements. The national self-identity was, during the Olympic process, seen as somewhat pathological and a new collective self emerged rhetorically as a node in an open, continuous global network of similar selves and places. The world is represented as a limitless, homogeneous space without the central perspective of the nation or the subject-centred orientation of the localised sense of place. No longer could anyone hide behind the mirror of tradition but all positions now became visible from afar through 'the exhibition window'. Again, the hyperbolic utopia emerges as a basic template in the ideological expansion of the national self out of its historically bounded territory and into undifferentiated global space on the outside.

This new reflexive paradigm of self- and nationhood challenged the traditional cultural ideology of *norskdom* (Norwegianness) that had been predominant in the country from the 1830s onwards. In that typically national narrative framework the self was imagined in ecological terms by situating the person in a 'natural' habitat, the national landscape. By birthright or destiny it was imbued with an inherited identity which by definition it is essentially fixed and continuous, historically bounded and localised. This notion of identity rests on the idea of sameness and homogeneity through time, across space and between social strata within the national border which, accordingly, is conceived as ontologically discontinuous with the outside world. If the relationships between these dimensions are somehow broken or disturbed, a pathological condition arises in which the person loses his or her identity and is estranged from their natural/national environment.

A profile, on the other hand, as it emerged in the cultural ideology of the Olympics, is, as we have seen, something more outward and made the object of management and planning. While an integrated identity is a set of doxically anchored distinguishing features from which the person cannot and will not escape, a profile is more like a logo or a mask, consciously established and intended to attract the desire and trust of the Other. An identity in the national cultural paradigm is more or less ethnocentric, in the sense that it is constructed by an intrinsic discourse and an internal gaze and directed at an audience identical to the self. A national identity thus makes sense within the interpretative community but not as readily outside it. A profile, on the other hand, is allocentric, i.e., oriented towards the gaze and the perceptions of the stranger, or rather, the imagined stranger and thus strives to create an open space between the new set of global interlocutors.

In the above statements the public 'we' is encouraged to 'register those features of ourselves of which we are usually blind because they are an obvious part of our everyday life, our way of life and our culture'. This self-inspection is not an end in itself, or undertaken to bring a greater awareness of the values in our own culture, but to make us able to 'choose' what we want to 'emulate', what we want to 'change' and what we want to 'preserve' in order to construct an image that we want to 'show to the world' when we 'come in focus'. The eradication of these blind spots is intended to bring our self-image under control and make identity formation the object of strategic decisions with the ultimate aim of tearing down the restricting walls of tradition. The national border constructed and conceived as an epistemological barrier must be annihilated in order to achieve hyperbolic vision. In this context identity is no longer referred to in terms of genealogy and destiny but as a *project*, as something to be constantly adjusted and renegotiated in encounters with the outside. The prime capacity of a profile is its adaptability, not its continuity. Authenticity, which was the central notion of the national identity, is no longer discursively significant.

One problem that soon became acute in this line of argument was that of relativisation. If the single most important criteria for evaluating cultural forms is that of its potential visibility and ready consumption by strangers, the risk becomes acute for some, in that what are felt to be intrinsic qualities no longer apply. This dilemma was particularly evident in the committee within the LOOC responsible for preparing the programme for the folk arts (*Folkekulturutvalget*). They would normally be the most conservative and essentialist voice in the discourse on culture, an attitude that also emerged clearly in parts of their documents, insisting, for instance, that '[we want to] show the relationship between our folk culture and Norwegian nature, and thus link natural qualities and cultural qualities.[13] Further, it was insisted that 'Norwegian folk music and dance has a unique position in Western Europe, in that several districts in the country have unbroken, genuine and endemic traditions'.[14] Moreover, 'Why is the *springleik* [genre of fiddle tunes] from Nordfjord much faster than the one from Telemark? It has to do with influences and choices, something to do with the character of the people'.[15] As they stand these statements are paradigmatically essentialist and national-romanticist. Cultural expressions are understood as inherently connected to nature through the character of the people who live in the landscape.

On the other hand, a historical precedence was also found for the opposite view that culture has always moved in global space and should continue to do so, as in the following quotation: 'The concept of "the modern Viking" links up with cultural diffusion. The Vikings took their culture out to the world, to the North Sea countries and other continents. At the same time they brought home influences and impulses. Even today Norwegian folk culture is marked by this dualism.'[16] Thus, the marketing metaphors were also present even here. It was generally admitted that they had 'worked too little on communicating with the audience', and very soon they were also discussing how they best could 'present' their material strategically. The focus changed from preservation to dissemination as the perspective of the speaker oscillated from an intrinsic to an extrinsic orientation.

In an interview with the research team an informant, a prominent member of the committee, explained their position in the following terms:

The whole thing is about dissemination. One thing is what we present here (locally), quite another is how we must present it to be able to disseminate what we want to disseminate. There is a difference between presenting a programme for a Norwegian audience, which knows parts of the material already and are anticipating what they are about to hear – they already know it in a way and can relate to it – and presenting folk art on a level with all other art forms to an ignorant audience.

Here the problem of dissemination, i.e., that some editing of the authentic material is necessary, is accepted apparently because of the fear that the national folk art will lose its unique and endemic value when attended to by an audience of strangers. Nevertheless, the essentialist and the relativist attitude were combined in what could be called reflexive nationalism, as indicated in the following statement:

In foreign countries Norwegian folk music is often met with enthusiasm, interest and awe. These are positive reactions one should develop and utilise in the marketing. We therefore want to emphasise that the traditional expressive forms both in music and dance are important to use and should be emphasised in the selection of folk music material.[17]

This shows that even the most essentialist voices in the Olympic discourse were re-orienting their concept of tradition in relationist terms to be able to become 'visual' and attract the attention of 'the world'.

Conclusion

As Peter Brooks says of melodrama, the Olympic rhetoric is 'centrally, radically hyperbolic'. We find these rhetoric figures and graphic designs as a basic configuration throughout the ceremonial repertoire and as distinctive features in the 'Olympic process'. We also find them as the basic structure of the ideological narrative on all levels and fields of discourse.

I have suggested that these grandiose references to the open space beyond the restricting limitations of local tradition have a pragmatic discursive base in the processes of the marketplace. The hegemonic voices in the organising committee and the political establishment all saw the Games as instrumental in the general development of the country and especially in dismantling the barriers of communication between Norway and the global marketplace. The metaphoric relationships between the athletic achievements, the ceremonial symbolic forms, and the strategies of the marketplace were quite explicit throughout the Olympic process. Thus for the first time in Norway it became quite legitimate to evaluate cultural forms and performances in terms of their potential to attract customers and secure contract partners for Norwegian export industry, and not to see them simply as expressions of inherent identity. This relationship, I suggest, is a key to an understanding of the twin processes of instrumentalisation and reflexivity that became so apparent in the discourse on self and culture that was generated by the Olympic process.

It seems that the process of national reconstruction in Norway, with the XVII Winter Olympics at Lillehammer, has reached the moment at which the country discursively has been transformed from being a nation, i.e., an idea of an abstract community based on the shared feeling of particularity and difference, to becoming what Wernick calls a 'commodity sign' (1991:190). In line with the ideas of commodity aesthetics (see Haug 1986), he holds that a transformation occurs in a phenomenon the moment it is designed specifically to be circulated on the market and not just happens to circulate on the market. When the promotional strategies take over and supplant all other motivations concerning the phenomenon, the promotional devices are no longer decorative embellishments – additions – but become its new character. The indications are that the centuries-old national ideology of culture is being gradually supplanted by a strategy of self-promotion in a rhetoric of hyperbole; for many actors the country is no longer thought of as a nation, but increasingly seen as a site of consumption with itself the prime commodity.

Notes

1. From the brochure *Offisiell leverandør* published by the LOOC in 1991.
2. Address held in Lillehammer February 1995 by Gudmund Hernes, then minister of education.
3. *Norwegian Olympic Design,* published by Norse Form, Centre for Design, Architecture and the Built Environment, Messel Forlag, Oslo 1995, in conjunction with the exhibition *Norwegian Olympic Design.* Arranged by Norsk Form on behalf of the Royal Norwegian Ministry of Cultural Affairs.
4. *Kulturplan for De XVII Olympiske Vinterleker på Lillehammer* (Plan for the cultural programme of the 17th Olympic Winter Games at Lillehammer) Chapter 1, section A: 'Mål for virksomheten' (Aims of the activities).
5. The address was entitled 'Was it megalomaniac?' on which he answers an unhesitating 'Yes!'
6. Lit.: 'the skin on our backs started tingling with warmth', which is a pun on a standard saying in Norwegian: 'the skin on his or her back started tingling with cold', meaning to tingle with fear. By substituting 'warmth' for 'cold' the speaker indicates the opposite emotion.

7. This is an intertextual reference to a song in the power patriotic tradition, well known to Norwegians. The adult generation learned it at school and it is about the advantages of sports in the life of young boys: 'Courage in heart, sense in head, and steel in legs and arms. That's the kind of boys that Old Norway wants.'

8. Interview with the American speed-skater Dan Jansen on *Dagsrevyen* (Daily News), NRK television, Sunday 5 December 1993.

9. 'Bikkja i bakken' (The dog on the slope) is a standard Norwegian saying that expresses the spontaneous nature of the skiing event. All kinds of unpredictable things happen and even the animals want to participate.

10. From the brochure 'Lillehammer '94. Offisiell leverandør', LOOC 1991.

11. 'Typically Norwegian' has a particular meaning in this context, and the formulation is no doubt chosen consciously. During the 1980s and early 1990s there was a public debate over which features were 'typically Norwegian'. The globalist voices used the term in a negative sense, referring to everything in Norway's traditional way of life that the speaker found obtrusive to international contacts, be it in arts, industry, education or other fields. Saying that something was 'typically Norwegian' was a way of distancing oneself from restricting traditions and, accordingly, establishing a cosmopolitic and progressive identity for the speaker. In other words the term 'typically Norwegian' was used as a rhetorical vehicle for a globalist ideological drive. Everything that was hampering international integration and the general course of modernisation was called 'typically Norwegian'. In her New Year's speech to the nation in 1993, with an explicit reference to the upcoming Olympics, the Prime Minister turned this discourse around by saying that it is 'typically Norwegian to be the best.' Following this, the expression was adopted by the self-styled cosmopolitans as definite proof of the inner-oriented and self-content narcissism of the 'locals'.

12. *OL-Status*, no. 2, 1991, p. 25.

13. *Innstilling frå Folkekulturutvalget* (Recommendation from the Committee for Folk Culture) 4.3: "Mennesket, Naturen og Maktene", (Man, Nature and the Powers), p. 12. Lillehammer May 15, 1992.

14. Ibid.: p. 6.

15. From an interview with an informant/member of the Committee on folk culture.

16. *Innstilling frå Folkekulturutvalget* (Recommendations from the Committee for Folk Culture). Lillehammer 1992: 7.

17. Ibid.: p. 6.

References

Aristoteles Retorik (1991) Museum Tusculanus Forlag: København

Brooks, P. (1985) *The Melodramatic Imagination. Balzac, Henry James, Melodrama, and the Mode of Excess,* Columbia University Press: New York.

Cupido No 8, (1994) Hverdag A/S: Oslo

Eide, T. (1990) *Retorisk leksikon,* Universitetsforlaget: Oslo.

Haug, W.F. (1986) *Critique of Commodity Aesthetics: Appearance, Sexuality and Advertising in Capitalist Society,* Polity: Cambridge.

Hernes, G. (1998) 'Mellom husmannsånd og stormannsgalskap' In *Kultur og OL '94,* LOOC-Rapport: Lillehammer

Hernes, G. (1995) "Var det stormannsgalskap? In *Fikk vi det vi øns-ket oss? Klarer vi å utnytte effekten?* Unpublished Conference Report, Municipality of Lillehammer: Lillehammer.

MacAloon, J.J. (1984) 'Olympic Games and the Theory of Specta-cle in Modern Societies' in J.J. MacAloon (ed.) *Rite, Drama, Fes-tival, Spectacle. Rehearsals Toward a Theory of Cultural Performance,* Institute for the Study of Human Issues: Philadelphia.

MacAloon, J.J. (1988) 'Double Visions: Olympic Games and American Culture' in Jeffrey O. Segrave and Donald Chu (eds) *The Olympic Games in Transition,* Human Kinetics Books: Cham-paign, Ill.

Sinding-Larsen, H. (1976) *Med pressekort. Reiser og mennesker,* Aschehoug & Co: Oslo.

Wernick, A. (1991) *Promotional Culture. Advertising, Ideology and Sym-bolic Expression,* Sage Publications: London.

Chapter 5

THE TORCH RELAY:
Reinvention of Tradition and Conflict with the Greeks

Arne Martin Klausen

Introduction

This chapter is a detailed description of how the Olympic torch relay was exploited by official Norwegian agencies, various local communities and other interest groups. Both the international, national and local parts of the relay were important public events. The strategy of one local community in particular, Morgedal, 'the cradle of skiing', caused an interesting conflict with the Greeks in its attempt to reinvent the 1952 flame and make it an international symbol of the Winter Games.

The Olympic ceremonies, as codified in the Olympic Charter, can be compared with the rules for rituals of all sorts of church-related activities found in the service book. Few other secular institutions have a corresponding codified set of rules for the carrying out of its arrangements. In this light the Olympic ceremonies are 'secular rituals' par excellence (Moore and Meyerhoff 1977).

The torch relay is, however, one ceremony which is not mentioned in the Olympic Charter. The Olympic flame is referred to in rule 60 as follows: 'The Olympic flame is formally lit in Olympia. The Olympic flame, the Olympic torch and the entire Olympic ceremonial belong to the IOC.'

Herein lies the grounds for the growth of the economic power of the IOC. Their monopoly over the symbolic capital which the Olympic Games represent has proved to be highly convertible into sponsorship contracts and exclusive advertising deals.

In rule 60 it is stated that it is the national organisers who are responsible for 'bringing the Olympic flame from Olympia to the stadium'. It does not specifically state that it is to be in the form of a relay, only that all arrangements *en route* are to follow Olympic protocol and must be free of advertising. This has not, however, affected the publicity which the official sponsors gain from their co-operation with the IOC. Furthermore, the national publicity and profiling which the organisers reap from the torch relay is not normally hindered by the formulation in the Charter.

The plans for the Norwegian torch relay appeared at first to be accepted without reserve by the IOC. Once the details concerning the two Norwegian relays became known in Greece however, it stirred up a storm of protest. The following clause from rule 60 concerns this theme, which was to become a source of conflict between Norway and Greece: 'There shall only be one Olympic flame, except by special leave of the IOC.' It is clearly stated here that the IOC is free to accommodate alternative ceremonies, and it has to a great extent done this since the relay was first arranged in 1936.

When Oslo hosted the Winter Games in 1952 the IOC agreed that a separate torch in Morgedal could be lit and that this flame could be brought into the arena and used to light the cauldron in Bislett Stadium. The IOC did, however, set clear conditions, which were worded in the official report from the Games as follows:

> It was specifically stressed that this was no Olympic flame being carried from Morgedal to Oslo, but a torch greeting ... a natural form of greeting ... as torches have been used for centuries in Norway for skiing in the dark. *(VI Olympic Winter Games Oslo 1952)*

In the Norwegian text in the report there is a sentence which, interestingly enough, was not translated into English:

> The idea behind it [the Morgedal-Oslo torch relay] was a parallel to the torch relay of the Summer Games, which goes from Olympia in Greece to the venue for the Games, which was first undertaken in connection with the Berlin Games in 1936.

It was precisely this idea which the IOC expressly reserved itself against in 1952.

In 1952 then, no flame was brought from Olympia. The torch from Morgedal nevertheless became the special flame symbol of the Winter Games. Subsequent Winter Games have, in contrast, used the 'true' Olympic flame, at the same time as there have been several

Norwegian attempts to promote the Morgedal flame to the same Olympic status as the Greek one. Nonetheless, the IOC has been defiant in its claim that there is only one 'true' Olympic flame. In a brochure published by the IOC for children about the Olympic symbols it is stated that:

> The Norwegians decided to promote a run similar to those organised for the Summer Games. However, they drew their inspiration from their own traditions. For them, skiing had been born in Morgedal, in the province of Telemark. They kindled the flame in the chimney of the house of the 'God of skiing',[1] the famous Sondre Norheim, who, in 1868 had achieved a prodigious jump of 18 metres without sticks. The flame was then carried to Oslo by skiers.
>
> The flame was kindled in the same way a second time for the Games in Squaw Valley. In fact, it should have come from Olympia, but the Greeks were informed too late by the Americans and the sun did not deign to shine on the citadel of the gods.
>
> Now, everything has returned to normal and the flame is regularly kindled in Olympia for the Winter Games as for the Summer ones. (*The Olympic Flame* 1986)

Despite such clear statements from the IOC, once again plans were made prior to the Games in Lillehammer to attain equal status between the Morgedal flame and the Greek flame. There is much that indicates that the leadership of the LOOC was not acquainted with the conditions laid down in 1952. The plan was to use two flames, one from Morgedal and one from Olympia, and arrange two relays, a national one from Morgedal and an international one from Olympia. These two flames would then meet and the flames would be mixed and united to a single flame in Oslo, and then continue on to light the cauldron in the arena in Lillehammer.[2] This time the Morgedal flame travelled around all of Norway, accompanied by ceremonial arrangements far more extensive than those in 1952.

This was a re-invention of the semi-tradition invented in Oslo back in 1952. This time, however, the torch ceremony would also emphasise the overriding Norwegian objective with the Games, i.e., to display to the rest of the world a modern country firmly rooted in solid old Norwegian traditions. The international relay was the arena of the modern business world, with the state-owned oil company as the main sponsor, and the Ministry of Foreign Affairs and the Export Council of Norway as co-arrangers along with the LOOC. The national relay, by contrast, was the arena of nature, culture, and market-oriented tourism, arranged by the General Post Office, the LOOC, the local cultural administrations and local sports clubs.

These plans turned out to be far more difficult to implement than the organisers could ever have imagined. Below we shall present some of the main features of the national torch relay, the development of conflict and the compromise which was the final solution.

The Practical Arrangement

As has been the case in many other countries, it was the national postal service (Post Office) which shouldered the responsibilities for the practical organisation of the national torch relay. Thanks to its well-developed transport system and its central position in all Norwegian local communities, the Post Office was particularly well-suited to this task. In addition to the flame symbol, the runners also bore a message to the Norwegian people from the president of the LOOC in the form of a *budstikke*, an ancient Norwegian means of communication. The oldest form of this was a wooden stick with a carved message; later it was transformed into a wooden cylinder, within which a written message was sent from farm to farm in order to summon people to public meetings or military activities. The Olympic *budstikke* was carried by the torch-bearer's escort who was always a member of the Post Office's local sports team. The management of the Post Office played up the role of the postal institution as a mediator of culture and nation-builder, and used the relay successfully to develop its corporate identity.

The team which accompanied the national torch on its grand tour of Norway consisted of sixty people and thirty cars. They worked continuously for periods of two weeks at a time, and were then relieved by another team. For seventy-five days torch-bearers ran for twelve hours a day from Morgedal, criss-crossing the entire country, with detours to the oil rig Gullfaks C in the North Sea and to Svalbard in the North of the Arctic Ocean. Approximately 7,500 runners took part in the 8,000 km long relay. The semi-governmental oil company, Statoil, was responsible for the provision of fuel and other pyrotechnic effects, and thus also had the right to profile itself as a company.

Roughly 2,500 cultural performances were staged in connection with the relay, most of which were small local arrangements of five minutes to half-an-hour's duration. Each evening there were larger events at the hotels where the team was staying, and each Saturday evening there were nation-wide television shows including a national talent contest. The event which became known as the torch ceremony took place at 7 p.m. precisely and was hosted by a local postmaster and the mayor of the town or village. The local head of culture was usually responsible for the cultural arrangements in connection with the ceremony, often in close collaboration with local sports teams.

An open competition was held for the design of the torch and it received 138 entries. The winners were the designer André S. Marandon and the architect Paal J. Kahrs. They had developed a long, staff-like torch holder, which broke with traditional conceptions of a torch. 'The idea behind the torch was inspired by man and the way in which he took control of fire by dragging a branch out of the fire', said the designer.

The LOOC had also arranged a nation-wide competition, the aim of which was to see who could kindle a flame in the least time using only Stone-Age tools. The winner was to receive the honour of lighting the Morgedal flame in this manner at the start of the relay outside Sondre Norheim's house, Sondrestua. This ceremonial element was yet another attempt to make the Morgedal flame more authentic, and thus better able to compete with the Olympic flame which is ignited by the sun's rays. In response to a question asked by a television reporter, the flame champion said that the wood he was using as tinder was, in fact, materialised solar energy as well! In 1952 it sufficed to bring fire from Sondre's hearth which had been lit with modern matches; this time it was deemed necessary to use an even more original flame – a flame kindled by nature itself. This was a new symbol which fitted in with a Norwegian symbol complex in which natural phenomena always play the leading role – a fact which was observed in many of the themes presented in the torch ceremonies.

The international relay was originally planned as a vast, continuous run from Greece to Norway. The unrest in former Yugoslavia, co-operation problems between the various Norwegian bodies and the difficulties with the various nations' Olympic committees resulted in a somewhat amputated relay. The flame was driven by car in oil lamps from Olympia to Athens, and from there flown to Germany. Here there were short relays around twelve cities there, including Stuttgart, Düsseldorf and Hamburg. The torch also visited the three Scandinavian capitals before arriving in Oslo on 11 February, and in Lillehammer the following day for the opening ceremony. Top Norwegian politicians were present at all the events abroad, as well as representatives of the large companies and tourist organisations and various Norwegian artists.

Despite the amputated form of the relay, the organisers were nevertheless very happy with the marketing of Norway abroad during the relay. At home, however, people were most interested in the fate of the Morgedal flame after the Greeks had taken up the gauntlet against what they perceived as an improper mixing of the flames – a contamination or pollution of the pure Olympic flame by an impure one from Sondrestua.

Before we look at this conflict and its solution in more detail, we shall first dwell on the most important symbolic messages in the national relay.

The Main Messages in the National Relay

During the planning stages of the Olympics several Norwegian towns had applied for the right to start the relay. Skiing is the national sport of Norway and, as such, is surrounded by all sorts of myths. There are a number of places which claim to be the birthplace of the sport, basing their claims on anything from archaeological finds to more recent historic sporting events. The history of Morgedal is linked to Sondre Norheim, the man who became known for his daring skiing feats in the form of *slalom*, an old Norse word which has become part of modern sporting terminology. Accompanied by other people from the village, he skied to Oslo in 1868 to take part in a skiing competition which the 'outdoorsy' city-dwellers had organised. Through time this particular competition grew to become the famous Holmenkollen race, Norway's secondmost important national ceremony. The torch relay in 1952 had followed the route taken by these people from Telemark almost a hundred years earlier. Sondre's journey did not stop in Oslo however; he then emigrated to United States and introduced modern skiing to the New World.

In 1952 the idea of a torch relay from Morgedal in 1952 had been put forward by the nephew of Olav Bjaaland, the Antarctic explorer whom Roald Amundsen, the expedition leader, had allowed to go first and plant the Norwegian flag in the ice at the South Pole in 1911. The elderly Olav Bjaaland, who in 1902 had won the royal cup in the Holmenkollen race, sat in Sondre Norheim's cottage in 1952 and lit the first torch from the hearth. In this way the Morgedal flame also became linked to another important element in Norwegian nation-building – the various Norwegian expeditions to the North and South Poles.

Morgedal is situated in the heart of Telemark, a county which holds a special position with regard to nation-building in general in Norway. In the nineteenth century folk tales and folk songs were gathered from the villages here, and the folk music, and folk arts and crafts still flourish. Many modern visual artists visit the county regularly, and many of Norway's major poets are from this region.

In light of the history of the area and the successful invention of tradition which the inhabitants of Morgedal had achieved in 1952, no other local community could have had much hope of competing with Morgedal in 1994.

The people of Morgedal, led by their mayor, had carried out a solid lobbying programme. They had built a modern amusement park related to the history of skiing. Outdoors, on a small lake in the centre of the village they had also built a stone beacon with a built-in gas burner. When the flame from Sondrestua passed by on its way to the start of the relay proper, the gas flame was lit and was to burn continuously as a marker of the place known as the 'cradle of skiing'. The tourist industry and other businesses in Telemark were also important actors. This time the myths about skiing were clothed in a modern guise. The two-day ceremonies in Morgedal which were to mark the beginning of the torch relay were a post-modern blend of folklore and modernism.

The LOOC's main objective with the torch relay was to create a positive public attitude towards and enthusiasm about the Winter Games. This was the essence of the message contained in the *budstikke*, which was read aloud at all major receptions. During the planning period there was no general consensus in Norway that hosting the Games would be a blessing for the country; indeed, opposition to the Games was clearly articulated. In various contexts the leadership of the LOOC sought to rouse excitement and enthusiasm about the Games. To achieve this kind of nation-wide enthusiasm in Norway it is essential to base work on co-operation at the local community level. It is also necessary to emphasise the significance of sport as a mass organisation and a means to create 'a good society'.

This was the background for the initiation of the campaign 'Shape up for the Olympics', a typically Norwegian all-out effort with the aim of getting as many Norwegians as possible to start exercising. Many of the torch-bearers were subsequently recruited from this project.

The LOOC official responsible for the torch relay emphasised that the relay would provide the various local communities with a unique opportunity to present their individual character, and thus together display contemporary Norwegian culture in 1993/1994.

As it turned out, there was fierce competition between communities to be included in the route of the relay. It was impossible to pass through every village in Norway, so the problem was solved by arranging so-called branch relays. A second torch lit from the main torch could thus be carried to a remote community, so that the inhabitants there could take part in the ceremonies.

In the original plans for the relay, a standardised framework was formulated for the main elements in the ceremonies. The expression 'standard ceremony' was employed. Typically, there were many objections from the local communities to this kind of standardisation. The local organisers did not want to have anything to do with this kind of central organisation. Later on, the expression was replaced with 'torch ceremony'. Although there were common elements in these torch ceremonies, the local communities now at least felt that they had more control over the design of the ritual.

The most important element in the torch ceremony was the 'hand-to-hand line', which consisted of a group of specially selected people forming a line in front of the stage. The torch was then passed from the last runner along this line to the local cauldron which was to be lit – usually by a local sports personality. The choice of people and how they were presented to the spectators was often quite revealing of local and national values.

Since the relay started in Morgedal, 'the cradle of skiing', national skiing champions and all sorts of myths relating to skiing became a strong and decisive theme in the ceremonies throughout most of the country. It is not, however, possible to muster enthusiasm and creativity about skiing in places that hardly ever see snow, i.e., along the southern and western coastlines. Two alternative themes were dominant here: firstly general local heroes, and secondly the Olympic messages of peace and tolerance. An example of the first was seen in the coastal village Grimstad where Henrik Ibsen had spent his youth as a pharmacist's apprentice. Here they held a torch-lit meeting between Henrik Ibsen and a mythical hero, Terje Vigen, about whom Ibsen wrote a vast epic poem, which is known and loved by all Norwegians. It was Terje Vigen who rowed to Denmark to fetch grain when the British blockaded Norway during the years 1807-1814. A person dressed up as Ibsen read a prologue and carried the torch down to the harbour where it was passed on to a Terje Vigen character, who then rowed the torch across the harbour in the town.

In some local communities Bosnian refugees staying in the area were included in the artistic elements and there were appeals for solidarity. Recent immigrants to Norway were otherwise scarcely involved in the torch ceremonies. In northern Norway by contrast, the old and, to some extent, traditional multi-culturalism was employed systematically in the ceremonies. The ethnic elements found among the populations in this part of Norway are the Lapps (Sami), Finns, immigrants from Østerdalen in central Norway and other ethnic Norwegians. The torch ceremonies held in the north of Norway demonstrated almost every conceivable ethnic relation, from the more dramatic displaying of ethnic conflict, via multi-cultural co-existence, to pure creolisation.

In Mortensnes, where the oldest pair of skis ever to be found have been excavated, we witnessed a very dramatic mix of modern ethnopolitics and the battle over the right to claim to be the place where skiing originated, a spectacular challenge to Morgedal. The Sami population had put together a performance which portrayed how skis were invented. The play was performed outdoors, in a traditional Sami settlement, a *siida*. The torch arrived and was placed outside the *siida* while the play was acted out. The local eccentric showed up with a primitive-looking piece of carved-out wood and tried to use it as a ski. At first the people laughed at him, but after several attempts he succeeded. The people understood that they had witnessed an important event. At that moment there was a huge noise and a snow scooter rushed into the *siida*, the driver – a Norwegian – stole the ski from the Sami inventor, grabbed the torch and disappeared into the darkness. The audience was surprised and at first had no idea what was going on. It then became clear that this was an Olympic dramatisation of the old ethnic opposition between the Sami people and Norwegians.

In Nordreisa the circumstances surrounding the development of a local costume were included in the ceremony. This costume has caused controversy within the state body responsible for approving local national costumes, as it has mixed formal elements from all the ethnic traditions found in the community, and is as such an example of creolisation.

One characteristic common to the local ceremonies was that local and national mythical themes were mixed and matched and, in a highly creative way, reconstructed to a surprising extent. Local myths and other traditions were not always perceived from an essentialistic perspective. Our observations revealed that even in regionally peripheral local communities post-modern creativity and reflexivity are well developed (which may or may not come as a surprise), indicating that the invention of tradition is also inherent in folk knowledge and conscious practice.

In a village in Gudbrandsdalen, in the neighbourhood of Lille-hammer, two historical local personalities were portrayed meeting each other (with a sovereign disregard for chronology, being sepa-rated by roughly 300 years) and discussing how foreigners should be treated. One was the Scottish officer Sinclair who was cunningly killed by peasants in the valley when he, along with a couple of hun-dred mercenaries, arrived to assist the Swedes in the battle against the Danish-Norwegian state in 1612. The other character was Kristin Lavransdatter, the most famous protagonist in the medieval novels by Nobel Prize winner Sigrid Undset. The part of the foreigners depicted all the guests expected to visit the valley during the Olympics in Lillehammer in 1994.

The sheer numbers of local and national heroes who were given a new lease of life in the ceremonies, and the ways in which they were put to use, correspond well with central characteristics of what many believe to be the Norwegian ethos. In keeping with the emphasis we place on equality, our heroes must never distance themselves from their roots. The greatest heroes are those who go out into the world and win fame and fortune, but who nevertheless always return home again and do not consider themselves to be bet-ter than their neighbours. The cross-country skier and folk hero Veg-ard Ulvang, who took the Olympic oath, and who a few days previously had very provocatively criticised the IOC, was a proto-type of this kind of hero in his home community in northern Nor-way. The downhill skier Atle Skårdal from Telemark was used in a similar way in connection with a television programme about the start of the torch relay in Morgedal.

In many of the artistic elements in the ceremonies, the unknown and unsung volunteers were praised as heroes. They are the ones who made it all possible. By making coffee and clearing up after the festivities, they constituted an idealistic driving force in an otherwise modern and commercialised world of sports.

The local ceremonies thus confirmed a whole series of stereo-types about the Norwegian ethos. Nevertheless, it was still surprising that there was so much formal and communicative variety in the cer-emonies. The messages emerging from these performances were also aimed at various types of recipients. In some places the com-munity communicated internally, in others the message was directed at the macro-community, and in some, even to the world at large.

It is in this perspective that we must view Morgedal's battle to get its flame elevated to Olympic status. The two-day ceremonies in Morgedal clearly had two different aspects and two different recipients. In Sondrestua, at the hotel and in the Skiing Centre we saw the modern Morgedal promoting itself as a tourist attraction to the rest of the world by means of the Olympics. But in the community hall on Saturday night the villagers gathered together to celebrate their local traditions and watch artistic, national-romantic performances while local politicians, the LOOC elite, the media and foreign visitors celebrated at the tourist hotel.

The Conflict with the Greeks

In the description of the role played by Morgedal in the Norwegian Olympic ceremonies we showed how much importance the Norwegians attach to the right of ownership of the skiing tradition. It would appear that it is even more important to the Greeks to mark their right of ownership of the Olympic flame, even if the IOC sees itself as the most important party in negotiations concerning all things Olympic. If we are to understand the conflict that arose between the LOOC and the Hellenic Olympic Committee prior to the torch being lit in Olympia on 16 January 1994, it is important that we bear this perspective in mind. The conflict between the 'pure Olympic flame' and the 'impure flame from Morgedal', and Greek opposition to the 'mixing of the flames' is more than merely an entertaining soap opera, although many have found this type of burlesque drama in it. It is first and foremost a power struggle about meanings, in which the symbolic flames are an expression of deeper and more widespread tensions.

As far as the flame from Olympia is concerned, there seems to be a certain amount of disagreement between the IOC and the Hellenic Olympic Committee as to what rights the Greeks actually have. In recent times the relationship between Greece and the IOC has been fraught with problems. The IOC decided to build the new Olympic museum in Lausanne rather than in Olympia, which is already home to the Olympic Academy, one of the main administrators of the Olympic ideology. The choice of Sydney over Athens for the Games in the year 2000 also gave rise to much dissatisfaction in Greece, although not as much as the decision to give the centennial Games in 1996 to Atlanta, home of Coca-Cola and CNN. These events, combined with a generally strong Greek nationalism, as well as the complicated interrelationship between Greece, Turkey and Macedonia, comprised good enough reasons for why the conflict with the LOOC became so serious.

The conflict can also be understood as an expression of an old theme in the Olympic ideology. In his view of things, Coubertin distinguishes between patriotism as an asset and nationalism as a hazard. During the first modern Olympic Games in 1896 Coubertin was already greatly concerned about the pan-Hellenic movement. He had hoped that the Greeks would become patriots through the noble, revitalised Olympic sports, but only one year later they were at war with Turkey (MacAloon 1981).

The conflict between Greece and Norway was first made public in Norway in a small article by Jan Erik Smilden, a correspondent for the Norwegian national daily paper *Dagbladet*, on 30 October 1993. According to this article two LOOC representatives had aired the 'merging' of the Morgedal flame with the Greek one during negotiations in Athens. When the Greeks heard about these plans they vetoed them. In Greece it also became known that the Morgedal flame had been referred to as 'the Olympic flame' in some of the LOOC's documents.

The vice-president of the Hellenic Olympic Committee made the following statement to *Dagbladet:*

> It will ridicule the whole idea of the Olympic flame. All previous organisers of the Olympics have accepted that there is only one Olympic flame and it comes from Olympia. Norway is a civilised country and cannot act differently... The Olympics will be held in Atlanta in USA in 1996. What would happen if there was one Olympic flame for the Indians, one for the cowboys and one for New York? (*Dagbladet* 30 October 1993)

In the last week of October 1993 a circular was sent out by the director of information in the LOOC to 700 employees, giving instructions on how the term 'Olympic flame' was to be used. This circular does not seem to have had much effect. Once the Morgedal flame had been kindled and the Norwegian torch was on its way round the country, it was time and again referred to as the 'Olympic flame'. The message which accompanied the flame – signed by the president of the LOOC, Gerhard Heiberg – also used the expression 'the Olympic flame of the torch'.

On 18 December 1993 *Dagbladet* ran a new main story with the following headlines: 'The Greeks are threatening to boycott: The Olympic flame up in smoke?' and 'Greek newspapers badmouth Norway'. At this time the Morgedal flame had been touring for over twenty days and was still being referred to as the Olympic flame. In his article Smilden quoted Greek newspapers as saying, 'The one true Olympic flame is under attack from people with no understanding of history'. Greek journalists also used words such as 'sacrilege' and 'theft' about the conduct of the Norwegians. We can recognise the motive of theft from the Sami dramatisation during the torch relay described above. As a political comment, Smilden added that 'On 1 January the Greeks will take over the presidency of the EC. We will have to deal with the Greeks when discussing our application for membership of the EC'. As can be seen, the most important political issue in Norway at that time – whether to join the EU or not – also became associated with the Olympics.

What provoked the Greeks most of all, however, was the thought that the two flames would be united. Smilden maintains that the two LOOC representatives had, in mid-October, already assured the Hellenic Olympic Committee that the flames would not be mixed, and the Greeks gave the impression that they had this assurance in writing. This view was not reciprocated by the two LOOC officials in question. In other words, there were serious communication problems between the LOOC and the Hellenic Olympic Committee. The LOOC press officer said to *Dagbladet* that 'We were perhaps a little misguided in our choice of terms to begin with'.

As it turned out there were more parties involved in the conflict than the LOOC, the IOC and the Greeks. The Post Office felt itself contractually obliged to take the Morgedal flame to Lillehammer; any other solution might be seen as a breach of contract by the LOOC. The citizens of Morgedal were, of course, most interested in seeing their flame united with the Greek flame, or that the Morgedal flame alone was used to light the cauldron in the Olympic arena in Lillehammer. In their eyes a Greek boycott of the Games was perhaps not so dramatic.

The Ministry of Foreign Affairs, and the Export Council of Norway, in contrast, felt a Greek boycott would have very serious consequences. As already mentioned they had planned to use the occasion for, and had already invested large sums of money in, a vast profiling campaign for Norway in Europe. If this were to go down the drain the damage to Norway would be far greater than petty local complications on Norwegian soil.

The president of the LOOC, Gerhard Heiberg, said in an interview with *Dagbladet* on 19 December that he had been authorised by Samaranch to decide the case, but that he, at that point, could not guarantee that the Morgedal flame would end up in Lillehammer. Heiberg also claimed he completely understood the strong reactions of the Greeks to the Norwegians calling the Morgedal flame Olympic, and, according to the paper, he said 'They have the historic flame from Olympia and have for that reason been making a lot of noise for a long time over this matter'.

Heiberg's choice of words indicates that the administration of LOOC was still not taking the battle about symbols completely seriously at this point. In fact over a month passed before the final solution was worked out – after a lot of drama and with considerable help from politicians at the highest levels.

In the meantime the Morgedal flame continued its triumphant journey through the towns and villages of Norway. The reaction to the fate of the Morgedal flame among Post Office employees and the runners was mixed. The pragmatists among them saw the whole thing as a 'transport task' and were not particularly interested in the symbolic content of the job. Many of the runners were, however, critical of the LOOC for not having managed to sort out these problems at an earlier stage. There was a tangible feeling in the convoy that the emotional aspect of the relay, which most people felt was the main driving force, had suffered a blow.

The media spent a lot of time and effort pointing out the ironies in this conflict. The historical background, the German, Nazi origins of the torch idea from Berlin 1936, were brought up to stigmatise the entire initiative.

The LOOC president claimed on 21 December that 'there is no hurry' and that a decision would not be made before the New Year. The Greeks mobilised their embassy in Norway, and the Norwegian ambassador in Greece assisted in the consultations over various possible solutions. Heiberg kept referring to his authorisation from Samaranch, that it was the IOC which owned the flame and that the Greeks could not make demands once the flame had reached Norwegian territory.

The flame-merging ceremony in Oslo had originally been intended as a grand event. The Oslo municipality had gone to great lengths to stress its position as the capital of the country – and what it called 'the gateway to the Olympics'. It also emphasised the connection to 1952. The Greek minister of culture, Melina Mercouri, was invited to Oslo to participate in the torch celebrations on 5 February. This would politically sanction the equal status of the two flames. In Athens the Norwegian ambassador and the Greek minister of culture met to discuss the programme for the Norwegian minister of culture's visit in connection with the torch-lighting ceremony in Olympia. If a compromise could not be reached regarding the journey of the two flames to Lillehammer, these plans could risk total failure.

The Post Office had by now decided that it could accept two flames in Lillehammer. 'We will not extinguish the Norwegian flame before it has reached Lillehammer', the project manager for the torch relay said to the daily newspaper *VG* on 22 December. It was clear that the fate of the Morgedal flame was of primary interest to the Post Office. Lillehammer town was the magical destination, but where it ended up after that, for example at the Paralympics, seemed to be of lesser importance.

On Christmas Eve, fifty days before the start of the Olympics, *VG* ascertained that Gerhard Heiberg had announced that the agreement reached with the Greeks ruled out the possibility of the merging of the two flames. The Greek flame would be used to light the main torch in Lillehammer. Thus, two of the Greek demands had been met. According to the newspaper, Heiberg was still taking the whole matter very lightly:

> We are working on finding alternative uses for the Morgedal flame. This issue is not a priority for us. The racket started when the Greeks read Norwegian papers, where both I and Åse Kleveland, the minister of culture, referred to the Morgedal flame as the Olympic flame. This was perhaps not quite correct'. (Newspaper *VG* 24 December 1993)

New Ceremonial Constructions

The LOOC president, his advisers and the various interest groups involved were trying to find potential uses for the Morgedal flame. The president of LOOC, and LOOC's head of culture, made an extra trip to Athens on 6-7 January, and once again it was believed that a final solution had been reached. The meeting of the torches was to proceed as follows:

The Morgedal flame would arrive at Oslo City Hall on 5 February at 6 p.m. The Olympic torch would arrive at the same time by aeroplane from Stockholm and be transported by ship from the airport to the City Hall jetty. In order to distinguish the two relays and flames the torch bearers on these legs would wear different uniforms. They would meet in front of the City Hall, face one another and exchange torches. In this way the Morgedal runner would have taken over the Greek flame and 'the Greek' would be holding the Morgedal flame. Both would then turn to the cauldron used in 1952 and light a new flame with their torches.

The flame in this cauldron would burn in Oslo for as long as the municipality wanted. The torch relay runner who now had the

Greek flame would then continue the journey to Lillehammer. The other flame would be extinguished by covering the torch.

This solution had been suggested by the Greeks, according to the LOOC president, after a meeting with the Director General of the IOC and three top executives from the Hellenic Olympic Committee. This new solution, which was now called 'the meeting of the flames' whereby 'the Olympic flame consumed the Morgedal flame', was quite acceptable to them. In this way the Morgedal flame had come one step closer to becoming an Olympic tradition, a ritual element on a par with the Olympic flame. The people of Morgedal had opposed the proposed solution by which the two flames would make their way to Lillehammer separately and the Morgedal flame would then either disappear or function only as a Paralympic symbol. The president of LOOC told the press that this new solution entailed 'mutual respect of the two flames', and that 'a symbolic bridge has been built' between them and that there would be no break in the continuity of the torch relay.

New problems of interpretation and more drama were to arise however. At a press conference somebody asked whether the solution did not in fact entail that the two flames would be mixed in the cauldron. Heiberg insisted that it did not, they simply met. He was also adamant that this was the final solution.

At this press conference Heiberg said that he understood the persistence of the Greeks, as the issue was of such importance to them historically and culturally. He had now accepted the gravity of the situation, at least to the parties involved, instead of dismissing it as a rather amusing and unnecessary affair. He expressed now for the first time an acknowledgement of the fact that this was an important battle about the right to symbols and the right to create new traditions: 'Both the Greeks and the people of Morgedal are fighting for a position and to maintain traditions in an Olympic context'.

We have now come to Thursday 13 January. A large Norwegian delegation was ready to leave to observe the torch being lit in Olympia on Sunday 16 January. The correspondent covering the Olympics for the Lillehammer newspaper *Dagningen* had already arrived in Athens. Here he met the Secretary General of the Hellenic Olympic Committee, Dionysos Gangas, to whom he related the philological discussions that had taken place at the press conference in Lillehammer. Thus, on the day that the notices of the press conference reached the pages in other newspapers, *Dagningen* was able to report on the furious reaction of the Greek Olympic administration to what it had read in the minutes from the press conference:

'This is shocking. This is not what we agreed on. What Heiberg has said means that the flames will be mixed after all. It does not matter what you call it'.

When the official Norwegian delegation, consisting of twenty-three members, arrived in Athens to attend the kindling of the Greek flame, their confusion was apparent. There was a rumour that the Greeks were once again threatening to boycott the Games and were demanding new assurances that no meeting or mixing of the flames would take place in Oslo. Throughout the afternoon and evening before the lighting of the flame there were hectic diplomatic efforts to find an acceptable solution to these problems.

An impromptu press conference was arranged at 10 p.m., at which the Norwegian ambassador, the LOOC president and the Norwegian minister of culture were the main actors.

The president now suggested the following procedure: the torch bearers would meet in Oslo and exchange torches. Then the Morgedal runner alone, who would now be carrying the Greek flame, would light the cauldron. Afterwards the Morgedal flame would then merge with the Greek flame in the cauldron and then the torch would be extinguished. In this way agreement was reached about the following formulation and interpretation: 'The spirit of the Morgedal flame lives on in the Olympic flame'.

Only one Greek journalist attended the press conference, which was held in Norwegian. He asked after a while, 'Is there any chance whatsoever that the two flames will be mixed?' He was assured that this would not happen. At the end of the press conference Heiberg was asked if the Post Office and the people of Morgedal had been consulted about the changes to the ceremony. His reply was that they had been 'informed' about the changes earlier that evening and that their reactions had not been particularly strong, in his opinion.

But at the public festivities in Bodø, where the Morgedal flame had now reached, a board member of LOOC and a representative of the torch relay administration in the Post Office said that this 'information' had seriously dampened people's spirits and enthusiasm.

There was no longer any threat of a boycott and everything was ready for the traditional ceremony in Olympia the following day. During the speeches in 'Pierre Coubertin's Grove' subsequent to the igniting of the torch there were attempts to play down the seriousness of the conflict. The president of the Hellenic Olympic Committee did not mention the conflict. The mayor of Olympia, by contrast, who greeted the Norwegian delegation with religious overtones as 'honoured pilgrims to Olympia', issued a discreet warning towards the end of his speech: 'We have now passed on to the organising committee and Norwegian people this unique and holy flame and the ideals it radiates with the conviction that they will treat it with due honour and respect'.

The Greek minister of culture and sports was even more explicit. Clearly addressing the issue he said, 'Although we fully understand the need of every nation to articulate its civilisation and its traditions, we cannot accept that any tradition should be allowed to contribute to distorting the contents and symbols of the Olympic Games.'

The Norwegian minister of culture praised the stylish ceremony and the noble Greek traditions. She assured the audience that the Norwegian government acknowledged and accepted the ensuing obligations and the honour of administering the Olympic flame, and that they would take the Olympic symbolic heritage to Norway with great pride. The Norwegian Olympic president made a very short speech in which he avoided all controversial topics.

Back in their hotel in Athens the Norwegian delegation was told that the reactions to the proposed new solution back at home in Norway were strong. We have thus reached the final act of the conflict, which was played out on the domestic stage.

The mayor of Morgedal accepted that the Greek flame alone would be used to light the cauldron in Lillehammer, but he demanded that the Morgedal flame should also travel to Lillehammer. In an interview with *Aftenposten* he said that it was unacceptable and disgraceful that the torch, having started its journey with the blessing of the monarchy, should 'end in an embarrassing anti-climax 200 km from its destination' (*Aftenposten* 17 January 1994).

The Post Office was more relaxed about the affair. Their arrangement – the national relay – was now on its way south through the county of Nordland, and was an unparalleled success. For them, the symbolic content was no longer the Olympics and the flame, but the 'transport task'. This expression had been used by the Director General of the Post Office in his speech at the commencement in Morgedal, and had in that context seemed profane and unpoetical. In the corporate culture and vocabulary of the Post Office, however, this expression had more noble overtones.

On Tuesday, after their arrival home from Athens, the top management of the LOOC had a meeting with the Post Office, the Morgedal Foundation and the minister of culture. Once again the people of Morgedal demonstrated their tenacity and persuaded the LOOC president to try to find a way of allowing the Morgedal flame to end up in Lillehammer too.

The mayor of Morgedal went to the Storting (parliament) to initiate a lobbying process and sent letters to the prime minister and the minister of culture. In the Storting it was a member of the Centre Party who was most positive towards these efforts. 'We must depend on our own resources' was his patriotic comment, interpreting the torch conflict as typical of Norwegian servility to foreign parties in negotiations. The EU debate can be glimpsed lurking in the shadows.

The mayor also toyed with the idea of arranging an illegal relay to Lillehammer. The county governor of Telemark told *Dagbladet* that he did not want the Morgedal flame 'to be extinguished in a bucket of water in Oslo'. In that case he would rather that it returned to Morgedal from Oslo, and he even offered to run the first leg himself.

These reactions caused much consternation in LOOC about what might happen during the opening ceremony in Lillehammer. Booing of the Greek team, sabotage, or demonstrations would be highly embarrassing. This is probably the reason why the LOOC president kept the possibility for change open right up to the last minute.

In the meantime, plans were being made for an alternative ceremony in Oslo, since it now was clear that the original plans of a merging of the two flames would have to be scrapped. It was at this point that the present author came into the picture as a participating observer, a form of fieldwork which we had not been involved in up to that point. The LOOC official in charge of ceremonies had been assigned by the LOOC president to work out an outline for an alternative ceremony – within forty-eight hours. The ceremony manager wanted advice from a theatre manager and an anthropologist, and travelled to northern Norway to meet the present author, who was following the national relay.

With a certain amount of professional curiosity as to whether it was possible to act as a kind of 'rituals consultant' in this sort of case, we started a collective brainstorming session.

Our main goal was to create a ceremony in the Olympic spirit which transcended the interests of the two conflicting parties, rather than sweeping the conflict under the carpet, and pretending it did not exist. Since the world is full of ethnic and national conflicts we thought we could use the occasion of the Olympics to manifest this in some way.

We perceived the main parties involved to be the Greeks on the one hand, and the people of Morgedal and other highly nationalistic people in Norway on the other. Our idea was to create some kind of sacrificial rite, in which both parties had to make a sacrifice. What was to be sacrificed was the 'nationalistic' component in the conflict, symbolised in the artefacts used in the ceremony. In the case of the Morgedal flame, this could be the pine taper used to light the torch at Sondrestua, and for the Greeks it could be the olive branch used during the ceremony in Olympia.

In order to express these ideas symbolically we suggested that the two torches meet in a ceremony in Oslo, in front of the City Hall. A prominent person – a representative of the monarchy, an Olympic champion, or the minister of culture – could act as a kind of high priest. A pile of wood for a large bonfire could act as an altar. These ideas could be achieved symbolically by the Greek flame being accompanied by an olive branch on the last leg of its journey. At the altar the master of ceremonies would take the Greek flame and light a Norwegian pine taper from it, which in turn would be used to light the fire on the large altar. The taper and the olive branch would then be put on the fire to be consumed in the flames. The 'denationalised' Olympic flame would then continue its journey to Lillehammer.

This main ritual would be emphasised by means of a number of other symbolic components: children from all over the world bearing international flags forming a lane leading up to the altar, four flags behind the altar: the UN flag and the Olympic flag on two tall poles, and the Greek and the Norwegian flags on two much shorter poles.

The ceremony official accepted the main ideas and wanted to present them to the LOOC the following day. During the course of that Tuesday, however, events changed. The LOOC president had once again approached the Greeks and the IOC, and had obtained permission for the Morgedal flame to complete its journey to Lille-hammer – but without having contaminated the pure flame from Olympia en route. The plan for the ceremony on the quayside thus remained no more than a rough outline of ideas.

All the parties involved had now accepted a solution whereby the Morgedal flame would be received in the centre of Lillehammer on the day before the opening of the Olympic Games. When the ceremony took place it was attended by the mayor of Sarajevo and his wife, amongst others. Indeed, this improvised ceremony was distinguished to a great extent by the organisation Olympic Aid, a Norwegian initiative to make more concrete the humanitarian content of the Olympics.

Later that evening the Greek flame arrived by helicopter at a mountain village near Lillehammer from where it was taken into Lillehammer during the opening ceremony the next day. The ceremonial reception of the Greek flame in the mountain was contemplative, with a smack of general religiousness and few elements which were particularly national or Olympic. The atmosphere was described by many as being 'new age'.

The Morgedal flame kept burning in Lillehammer until the Paralympics, and was used to light the main torch in the stadium during the opening ceremony of these Games.

The people of Morgedal eventually gave up the idea of achieving acceptance of their flame as an official Olympic symbol, but they did not give in to the IOC entirely. On 3 April 1995 the mayor, with the support of the prime minister, sent an application to the IOC requesting that the Norwegian *budstikke* be introduced as an official element in the torch relay of the Winter Olympic Games. In the letter the mayor had written:

> Morgedal and the Morgedal Foundation regret, but respect the decision of the international Olympic Committee that the Olympic Flame shall be kindled in Olympia only ...
>
> We propose that the 'Olympic Budstikke' would be part of an official ceremony at the opening day of future Winter Olympic Games, and that the Budstikke contain a greeting from Morgedal to be read out as the messenger reaches the Olympic City.

Notes

1. The IOC here gives Sondre Norheim the status of a God. In Norway he is not a God, merely a mortal historical hero. The Norse God of skiing is called Ull.
2. As mentioned in Chapter 2, John J. MacAloon warned the director of ceremonies in the LOOC against the idea of merging the flames, referring to the Seoul Games at which the two flames used were kept completely separate and thus avoiding any conflict with the Greeks.

References

MacAloon, J.J. (1981) *This Great Symbol. Pierre de Coubertin and the Origins of the Modern Olympic Games,* The University of Chicago Press: Chicago.

Moore, S.F. and B.G. Meyerhoff (eds) (1977) *Secular Ritual,* Van Gorcum: Amsterdam.

Newspapers: *Aftenposten, Dagbladet, VG(Verdens Gang)*

Olympic Charter 1990, International Olympic Committee: Lausanne.

VI Olympic Winter Games 1952, Official Report of the Organissing Committee: Oslo

The Olympic Flame (1986) Olympic Museum and IOC: Lausanne.

Chapter 6

PRODUCING NORWEGIAN CULTURE FOR DOMESTIC AND FOREIGN GAZES:
The Lillehammer Olympic Opening Ceremony

Roel Puijk

Culturally, Norway is the homeland of Ibsen, Grieg and Munch. Its population is one of the world's most literate and well travelled. But the Olympic opening and closing programs have been built around the kitsch of reindeer and nomads, trolls and folk magic. (*Time*, 14 February 1994)

We were inside the gates of Heaven. We were in the magical winter realm created by God and Bentein Baardson [director of ceremonies]. Never has the world seen anything more beautiful. Each and every one of us was a piece of Norway. We had a feeling of pride that gave us goose flesh, even at minus 10. But this had nothing to do with the temperature. We participated in the winter fairy tale itself. And the snow crystals formed the most fitting backdrop to our deep pride and unlimited love for this country, while a golden winter sun blazed through a break in the clouds before darkness fell and the vetter emerged from beneath the earth. For those of us who were in Lysgårdsbakken yesterday, heaven was somewhere we could be while still within this mortal coil. (The largest Norwegian newspaper *VG [Verdens Gang]* 13 February 1994)

Introduction

When the Olympic Games were reinvented at the turn of the century, they were intimately connected with the modernisation process that was taking place in the Western world at that time. The Games contributed not only to a specific institutionalisation of sports, but were also closely connected to the construction of nation-states and international relations. Sporting and Olympic achievements were both a sign of, and contributors to, the rise of a general notion of 'progress'.

One of Coubertin's aims was to create a 'humanistic' religion based on the worship of the human body (MacAloon 1981: 266). In addition to the educational effects of sports, the Olympic Games were meant to celebrate the unity of humankind. Within this project of creating an alternative religion, the notion of the nation was problematic. Coubertin saw cultural differences as a pre-condition for true internationalism and he was opposed to a cosmopolitanism in which cultural differences would be eradicated. But too strong national feelings would also inhibit the fulfilment of the Olympic ideals. In Coubertin's eyes, love for one's country (patriotism) was positive, but combined with hatred for others (nationalism) it was considered negative.

Both society and the Olympics have changed greatly over the last century. Though the Games may also have contributed to this, one may see the changes in the Olympics as a reflection of general changes to society at large. Growing commercialisation, a fading ideology of amateur sportsmanship, the advent of the drugs problem and the huge media coverage are traits that connect the Games with what might be called 'late-modernity'. The question of nationality is still an ambiguous one within the Olympics – it is the structural basis of the organisation of the National Olympic Committees; it is also the most important factor in the relationship between the spectators and athletes. Nevertheless, the athletes do not, in fact, represent their country of origin during the Games. Rule 9 in the Olympic Charter states that, 'The Olympic Games are competitions between athletes in individual or team events and not between countries.'

The question of national representation and promotion is particularly moot for the host country. From the start, the Olympics have far from served only humanistic and idealistic ends. Often mentioned in this context are the Berlin Games of 1936, but also the Moscow Games, for example, have been accused of using the event for national/political ends (Hazan 1982). The question of the national emotions of the host country goes back to the very beginning of the modern Games. Descriptions from the first Olympics in Athens 1896 show how effective the Games can be in uniting the people of the arranging city/country; MacAloon even raises the question whether the national feeling created by the Olympics may have played a role in the eruption of the Cretan war (1981:259).

A direct link between the Games and a war would be an extreme situation. And, of course, it is difficult to 'prove' such an allegation. The question as to whether the war would have taken place without the arrangement of the Games is impossible to answer. The relation between the Olympics, the host country, and its internal and external representations is also interesting in less extreme cases. Even though the situation has changed greatly, all Olympic host cities and countries have been occupied with their images to varying degrees (for Seoul see Dilling 1990; Larson and Park 1993; for Barcelona see Moragas 1991; Moragas and Botella 1995).

As far as the meaning of public and media events like the Olympic ceremonies is concerned we may expect it to be multi-layered. Directed towards and broadcast throughout the whole world, they have to 'work' in many different cultures. Even though the organisers of the event[1] may have explicit communicative intentions and provide a clear exegesis and guidance, the results are dependent upon the media personnel who communicate and interpret them for the millions of individual spectators. This situation is, of course, quite different from 'traditional' public events in which there is a 'clergy' to explain the meaning of the event and rituals according to some 'holy book' and/or ideology.

In comparison with the opening ceremony in Albertville, the opening ceremonies at Lillehammer can be characterised by their extensive use of traditional cultural elements. This raises a question as to whether the ceremony was an expression of an essentialistic and homogeneous conception of Norwegian culture or whether what appeared as essentialistic and homogeneous was in fact intended and/or received in a much more reflexive way by the various actors. Having said this, I would like to raise the question of the status of the opening ceremony of the Lillehammer Games in terms of different intentions and responses to the image of Norway and the presentation of Norwegian culture.

This task entails the consideration of three levels of analysis. The first deals with the relation between the production process of the ceremony and Norwegian culture at large. Even if there exists something like a specific national culture, a one- or two-hour show cannot present everything. The production process implies that the organisers have to choose certain elements as typically Norwegian, and then find acceptance for their choice. Of course, such processes may very well imply cultural struggles, outright conflicts and discussions about what to show and how to show it. Secondly, as most people see the event as it is broadcast (live) on television, the television mediation of the event requires a special analysis – not only because television as a medium transforms the event, but also because different television channels mediate the same event differently. The third level of analysis is, of course, the reception of the ceremonies in different contexts by different people. As the number of viewers are in their hundreds of millions[2] at least, it goes without saying that such a task is impossible. But it is possible to elicit some interpretations by analysing how the event was treated by foreign commentators and in the printed media afterwards. Here, the differences between the Norwegian and the foreign press are crucial for our understanding of the ceremony as a public and global event.

Opening Ceremonies as Public Events

The Olympic Games differ from most sporting events in two ways. Firstly, as a coming together of many countries and many sports disciplines. Even though many sports are practised world-wide, many countries have a special affinity to some sports. The 'trick' of the Olympics is that these sports are assembled at one place, thus receiving a world-wide attention that no other sports contest can boast of (see Puijk 1997). Secondly, the Olympics differ from other sports contests by virtue of their elaborate ceremonial aspects. Both the opening and closing ceremonies have grown into two-hour long public and artistic events, watched simultaneously by hundreds of millions of television viewers throughout the world. MacAloon (1996:32) argues rightly that the Olympic ceremonies are unequivocal – there are no public rituals that compete on this scale. The only organisational body that could match the IOC would be the United Nations, but this organisation has not developed the same kind of rituals.

If we concentrate on the opening ceremonies, these may be regarded as a public event on the national and international level. Some parts of the ceremony are carried out in accordance with IOC rulings, while other parts are devised according to the wishes of the local organisers. In terms of symbolic representation, opening ceremonies represent humanity, sports, the host country and a multitude of other entities. In Handelman's (1990) terms they consist of a combination of *presentation* and *representation*, and sometimes even *modelling*, i.e., public events that not only show the existing order directly (as in presentations) or indirectly (as in representations) but that affect the order and at least lay a germ for change (modelling).

Producing Opening Ceremonies

Dilling (1990) mentions three principles that the organisers of the opening ceremonies in Seoul worried about: 1) Is the script universal enough? 2) Does it show the specific character of Korea today? 3) Does it have the fresh shock of avant-garde? These three questions are probably basic questions for every Olympic opening ceremony. Being a global ceremony and ritual watched not only by an international audience in the stadium where it is performed, but also covered live by television stations throughout the world, one of the basic preoccupations of every organiser is to construct a ceremony that can be understood universally. Of course many of the 'obligatory' elements laid down in the Olympic Charter will provide globally accessible symbols and rites (Olympic rings, flags, heads of state, oaths, etc.). But most countries want to present something more, they want to create a performance proper to their country, representing their culture. This involves identifying useful national cultural elements that are generally accepted as such nationally, and presenting them for an international audience in a digestible way. In addition to being an arrangement full of tradition, it also is a very modern television show whose aim it is to present tradition in a creative, new and refreshing way without duplicating previous ceremonies.

MacAloon (1996: 36) distinguishes between three different ideal-type models of ceremony production. One model he calls *the impresario model* in which companies experienced in television/entertainment production are in charge of the ceremonies, e.g., Los Angeles 1984 and Barcelona 1992. In *the cultural experts model* (e.g., Seoul 1988) the ceremony is a result of the co-operative effort of cultural specialists so that it is impossible to attribute the ceremony to any one single person. *The auteur model*[3] describes the production process in which the ceremony may be said to be the result of its director, in the way that the Albertville ceremonies in 1992 were, to a large degree, the product of Decouflé's visions. Although the ceremonies certainly expressed some national cultural elements of the host country, MacAloon rejects the idea that the production model in some way or other was 'typical' of the country. Instead, he suggests that more thorough research should be done on actual ceremonial productions in order to find the cultural codes of meaning which the actual designers and producers work with, and the reason why certain production models are chosen. I want to follow up this point and turn now to a description of the production processes as they unfolded in Lillehammer.

Production of the Lillehammer Opening Ceremony

The Lillehammer Olympic Organisation Committee (LOOC)[4] started working on the ceremonies in January 1991, inviting four production groups (choreographers, producers, etc.) to prepare a synopsis of their visions for a possible opening and closing ceremony. The LOOC's document drew up some general directions, summarised by the LOOC in the following three points:

1) The ceremonies shall harmonise with the intentions that are the basis for LOOC's main organisational aims nationally and internationally. Because of the huge media focus and international attention the international public will clearly be the main target group.
2) The content of the ceremonies will show Norwegian culture and national character. The Norwegian image will follow the same standards and prerequisites as in the Lillehammer Olympics otherwise. The ceremonies shall be characterised by high artistic quality, precision and professionality.
3) The artistic content shall be founded on the ceremonial intentions and therefore contain the Olympic symbols and ideology.[5]

Based on this document four groups prepared their ideas for the ceremonies:[6]

1) The Stein Roger Bull group probably best represents the impresario model. It consisted of a group of people with experience from large television and theatre productions. In addition to these, it included a specialist in the history of skiing, in visual presentations and a person centrally placed in local Norwegian theatre revues. Even though this group was considered the 'safest' in terms of professional spectacle arrangement, television production and financial control, it was not chosen. The artistic concept of the group was based on the slogan 'Norway in the world', with ice, snow and wood as basic elements and the Olympic rings and the Northern lights as the main symbols. The script consisted mainly of a series of tableaus (one historical, one built around Roald Amundsen, Sonja Henie, and Norwegian trolls/Peer Gynt). It was specifically noted that the individual should not be forgotten and one tableau features one of Norway's most famous Olympic participants, the figure skater Sonja Henie. In addition, more spectacular elements were envisioned. It was proposed that the finish of the Birkebeiner cross-country ski-race[7] should be a part of the opening ceremony. It was also sug-

gested that people from different parts of the world could play a musical piece together, live – each playing in their own country but brought together in the arena on a big screen.

The main reason why this group did not get the job was scepticism about the focus on tableaus and individuals (Sonja Henie may not be so well known internationally). According to the ceremony supervisor in the LOOC, the script was a summing-up of what Norway is renowned for, but lacked artistic vision. The concept also lacked a ceremonial awareness and the international musical piece was considered an expression of unsophisticated internationalism rather than universalism.

2) Norsk plateproduksjon AS, included a famous television presenter who is also one of Norway's most well-known record producers and a former television producer. The group had contacted the biggest (pop) concert impresario in Norway, the film director Nils Gaup, and a composer. In many ways this group could also be said to be organised in the form of the impresario model. Their concept included a prefatory video introducing Norway through two people (a traditional Norwegian country-girl and a Sami boy) as they approached Lillehammer in seven-league boots. The opening ceremony in Lillehammer was to include skiers skiing down the ski-jump slope, a ski-ballet, a performance of the Olympic 'hit-song' in addition to the obligatory elements. A spectacular surprise element was to be an arranged confrontation between spectators pretending to 'storm' the arena and guards/police, evolving into a human text: 'Welcome to Lillehammer'.

This concept was not chosen partly because it was thought to have been conceived as too much of a show made specifically for television, partly because it lacked an artistic vision, but also because of financial and organisational reasons.[8] The group's budget was only 43 million Norwegian kroner (while the LOOC had reckoned with 85) which resulted in LOOC doubting the realism of the concept (and the group).

3) Filmeffekt A/S. The LOOC's cultural department got this group together after the other three groups were established. The theatre director Bentein Baardson headed the small group with the film producer Petter Borgli as its producer. Baardson insisted that the main focus in this phase should be ideological and strategic, not concrete ideas. The group argued that the ceremonies should be seen in the context of the total cultural programme the LOOC was preparing for the Games, and that the ceremonies should 'mirror' the whole arrangement. In their conception, folk culture, fairytale characters and

winter sports were in focus. Key elements in the artistic part of the programme were to be formations of abstract graphical patterns and symbols, movement and costumes in addition to fairytale characters. As the design department in the LOOC the group found inspiration in abstract patterns in nature. In addition, this group also looked for inspiration in traditional Norwegian handicraft (e.g., knitting patterns).

As the group rejected the idea of working out concrete ideas in this preliminary phase, the concept they delivered remained very much on an abstract level compared with the concepts presented by the other groups.[9]

4) Polyvision. The group that won the contest in the autumn of 1991 consisted of a small production company (Polyvision) in cooperation with the choreographer Kjersti Alveberg. In this concept the obligatory ceremonial elements were mixed with more artistic ones. The beginning of the opening ceremony was modelled around the old Norwegian (Norrøn) genesis myth: first there was the earth, then an explosion, then the Yme-troll. After this, a section on Norway as the birth-place of skiing, including well-known persons such as Nansen and Amundsen, the Sami people and mythological figures would be presented. After the parade of the athletes there would be a rural wedding procession and formations, followed by the opening of the Games. Then the 'modern' (Viking) gods (especially the male god Tor and the female Frøya) would arrive, followed by the Olympic flag, the release of doves, before an ecological tableau. The Olympic flame and the oaths were to precede an element called 'spider of fate' and the Norwegian national hymn.

The concept was chosen mainly because of the unified artistic grasp, and because it presented Norway as a mythical country, even though the ceremonial elements of the concept were considered weak and the chief of ceremonies in the LOOC also feared it might be difficult to comprehend for a world-wide audience.

In many ways this group represented an auteur model for the opening ceremonies with the choreographer at the centre. As the production company was rather small, an experienced film producer, Gunnar Svendsrud, was engaged who was to act as a 'controller' and middleman between the cultural department in the LOOC and Polyvision. The group first prepared the Lillehammer element in the closing ceremony of the Albertville Games in February 1992. It combined a fairytale figure (an ice princess riding on a bear)[10] in a combination with Vikings and a Viking ship.

After this work was done the group concentrated on the opening and closing ceremonies. Nothing more than a sketchy outline was available at that time. In addition, the choreographer had not yet signed her contract with Polyvision. During the summer of 1992 the problems with creating a final script and budget for the opening and closing ceremonies came to a climax, and the association with the choreographer was terminated.[11]

This once again opened up the whole question of the ceremonies. The Polyvision producer argued that even though the choreographer had not signed a contract with his firm, his contract with the LOOC still existed and he was therefore free to produce another script. He mobilised a new group to write a completely new script which he presented to the president of the LOOC in October 1992.[12]

At the same time as the conflicts between the LOOC, Polyvision, and the choreographer Kjersti Alveberg were culminating, Bentein Baardson was contacted for advice. As a result of the subsequent process Bentein Baardson, who had previously been involved in the Filmeffect A/S group, was asked to take over altogether. He had the advantage of being able to build on his previous work on the ceremonies. He was currently involved with Dag Alveberg in a production of *Peer Gynt* for Norwegian television.[13] In the autumn of 1992 Baardson was hired as head of ceremonies, and, in cooperation with the dramatist Bodil Kvamme, he developed a new script.

Gunnar Svendsrud, the controller, was first appointed as producer for Bentein Baardson's version of the ceremonies, but Baardson was not satisfied with the organisation and Dag Alveberg came in as co-producer. The new concept was officially approved in a LOOC board meeting on 18 February 1993 – only a year before it was to be realised. In the meantime, LOOC's director of culture Bente Erichsen had resigned because in the organisational structure the new group became – in line with its own wishes – answerable directly to LOOCs leadership, thus by-passing the director of culture. Also Svendsrud, feeling pushed to the side by Alveberg, resigned in February 1992.

The Baardson Concept

Bentein Baardson had contributed to one of the concepts (Filmeffect A/S) in the first round. Returning to work on the ceremonies Baardson was able to use his initial thoughts and develop them further. Looking for unique Norwegian cultural expressions he found them in the so-called folk-culture programme outlined already by the LOOC as part of the total cultural programme for the Games. The first script, written in collaboration with Bodil Kvamme, was completed in December 1992, while new revisions followed about every two months. Of course, many changes were made, but the basic concept and some of the elements stayed almost unchanged throughout the whole production process.

The first script shows that the opening ceremony was supposed to start with a welcoming section (ski-ballet in the air, welcome to the winter festival), continue with a demonstration of Sami culture, Norwegian folk culture and the arrival of the Norwegian royal family. The next section included all the obligatory ceremonial elements: the parade of nations, the opening of the Games, the Olympic flag, the lighting of the Olympic flame (after the torch had arrived carried by a ski-jumper in a leap off the jumping hill), the release of the pigeons, the oath and the Norwegian national anthem. The script also contained some unconventional elements. After the parade of nations it was suggested that the Declaration of Human Rights be sung.[14]

In addition to the official ceremony with all its prescribed elements the most recent ceremonies also have offered an artistic element. From the beginning it was obvious that Baardson and his collaborators regarded this artistic element as the most important and it was subject to more extensive reflections in an introduction to the script.

In his search for something through which to express Norwegian culture, Baardson turned to folk culture, not only for the Norwegian costumes, but also as a source for inspiration for the artistic element. In the script it is argued that 'low mythology' (mythical creatures living underground) is a living tradition in Norwegian folk culture, in contradiction to the Viking gods that have been replaced with one Christian God. Baardson introduces the term *vetter*[15] for these creatures, and refers to a modern fairytale as a source of inspiration (Ingulstad and Solem 1992). The fairytale describes how the mythical beings (*nisser*) each year perform their own inauguration of the ski-jump at Holmenkollen (Oslo) the day before the humans have their World Cup. This idea became Baardson's point of departure – the artistic part would be a mythic paraphrase of the human opening ceremony. At this juncture the artistic part is referred to as follows: 'Ski-jump is inaugurated with feast and joy' (see Table 6.1 for an overview of the changes in the concept).

The artistic part starts with the Band of the Royal Guard. After a while feminine, sensitive *vetter* mingle with the formal military drill. Throughout the performance the five *vetter* clans, representing the five continents, carefully exploit the arena. Using large innovative musical instruments and winter transportation equipment the *vetter* gather in five stations lighting five bonfires. Then five large medals (three to four metres in diameter), are brought into the arena and the *vetter* light their own Olympic flame. The medals disappear underground, and the end is marked by a 'fireworks' of snow (with the use of snow canons) and pyro-fountains.

A Simple Adventurous Fairytale Country

During his first meeting with the LOOC's employees Baardson declared that his all-embracing aim for the Olympic ceremonies was to establish Norway as 'a wonderland fairy-tale country'.[16] The two main elements that were to establish this image were enduring Norwegian folklore and Norwegian fairytale characters. With presenting the *vetter,* Norwegian culture and folklore are presented. The *vetter* are supposed to represent some 'typical' Norwegian traits.

Closeness to nature. Being mythical underground beings, the *vetter* represent the natural forces, but the director stresses the likeness between the *vetter* and Norwegians and their relation to nature:

> Like us, the *vetter* have always had to struggle with the natural elements like ice and snow (...) The *vetters'* activities tell about Norwegians' special relation to winter activity. Our leisure time is closely connected to nature. Catchwords like play, joy, health and collectivity are associated with physical activity. (Baardson and Kvamme 1992/93, First Script:13-14)

The *vetter* are supposed to live in balance with nature, and so are Norwegians:

> The harmony lies in the balance between nature and culture – a balance that, possibly more than anything else, characterises our Norwegian uniqueness. (Baardson and Kvamme 1992/93:20)

The choreographers also underlined the Norwegian closeness to nature as one of the traits they wanted to bring to the fore. Here they pointed to the fact that many of the preceding ceremonies had not been on snow or ice. Moreover, they designed the show in such a way that many movements would be near the ground with *vetter* lying, sitting or creeping on the snow to express a closeness to the natural elements.

Care for each other. Baardson stated that he would build on pairs and formations: 'not individuals wandering around like in Albertville'. The couples dancing would express affection for each other, while the formations would express the comparison of the individual versus the collective.

For many, individual presentation and collective manifestation can seem like a contradiction, but this interplay is in many ways an important part of Norwegian identity. (Baardson and Kvamme 1992/93:17)

Even though the ceremonies used many traditional elements, it was very much a contemporary artistic show. 'Movements, costumes, light and music must be presented in contemporary form, but with an echo of yesterday' (Ibid.:16). The different parts of the *mise-en-scène* thus had to live up to two different – and at times conflicting – expectations. 'Traditional folkmusic will, in this part of the ceremonies, be presented in a creative and innovating way.' (Ibid.:15) The music is supposed to be 'universal and timeless, but, at the same time, Norwegian in form.'

Bentein Baardson incorporates elements of both the auteur and the cultural experts model. Even though he co-operated closely with others, the script was very much an expression of his own ideas, and it was he who had most control during the preparations. In this sense the Lillehammer ceremonies were organised according to the auteur model. But at the same time Baardson also functioned as a cultural expert – with his own analysis of Norwegian culture. He was also a cultural expert in the sense that his loyalty was not primarely to his own creative ambition, but in a role as a guardian of Norwegian culture.

In his treatment of 'the typical Norwegian', his reasoning may, in many ways, may be characterised as reflecting Norwegian culture as both homogeneous (i.e., shared by all Norwegians) and essentialistic. His stress on the tension between binary conflicting pairs (nature-culture; individual-collectivity; tradition-modernity; informality-formality) as elements of Norwegian culture gave him some room for manoeuvre and saved the programme from being based on well-known stereotypes and clichés alone. The script provides for both presentational and representational aspects. While the first part may be said to present (a restricted part of) Norwegian culture, the artistic part *re*presents Norwegian culture. It does not seem as if there are any pretensions to create a modelling event that surpasses existing reality.

Changes in the Script

The script was accepted just one year before the ceremonies were to take place. During the twelve months of preparations many changes were made. The first part – based on folkloristic elements and the prescribed IOC rites – changed only little. The parachutists in the first script were supposed to be dressed as *vetter*, while in the final video[17] they were dressed in red, white and blue, the colours of the Norwegian flag. Another major change in the manuscript was that the two *vetter* children announcers were replaced with what was called the 'Olympic family', consisting of Liv Ullmann, Thor Heyerdahl and six children, dressed up like an 'ordinary Norwegian family on a Sunday skiing trip'. The Human Rights element was later moved to the closing ceremony.

The artistic part of the opening ceremonies changed more substantially during this period (see Table 6.1 overleaf). Several of the envisaged elements were cancelled because they could not be realised – for either practical or financial reasons. For instance the snow fountains turned out to be too expensive and were – at least partly – replaced by fireworks (but restricted, both in space and time).

But the main worries concerned the spectacular climax of the event. Several changes were suggested and rejected. Instead of gigantic medals, five icebergs, combining into one big egg, were suggested. The construction was supposed to be used in the closing ceremony too. Slowly the idea developed of having an egg being drawn from the underground room. The egg represented life and its rebirth. The *vetter* were to form a protective nest and the egg was to turn into a globe representing the earth (Tellus-Egg). The globe was to open and a flower to appear, but later a gigantic pigeon was substituted for the flower.

The dramatic concept of the artistic element was also changed. The *vetter* disappeared from the early sequences and were introduced as a proper fairytale. Thanks to this introduction, the *vetter* could more easily be conceived as fantasies rather then existing beliefs among the Norwegian population. As Bentein Baardson wrote in the script:

> The *vetter* are peace-loving creatures who live in harmony with the natural environment. Nature would be less exciting and our existence poorer if faith, poetry, and fantasy were not allowed to be a substantial part of our way of life. (Baardson and Kvamme 1992/93:11, also quoted in the official programme.)

During this process of readjustment some of the elements and symbols that appeared in the first manuscript were weakened. In the final manuscript the use of Olympic symbols was heavily restricted,

Table 6.1: Changes in the artistic element of the opening ceremony

Title	January 28	Undated	July 14	August 27	October 19
Discipline and Play*	The royal band's formality against feminine *vetters'* fantastic movements	(This part missing from the manuscript)	The royal band's formality against feminine *vetters'* fantastic movements		
Anxiety and Courage	5 pairs of *vetter* dance and approach each other	*Vetter* emerge from underground; *vetter* slide down the slope; 5 *vetter* clans, *vetter* and snowball	*Vetter* emerge from underground; *vetter* slide down the slope; many *vetter* appear from underground; from centre to Sun-formation	*OHM:* *Vetter* emerge from underground; *vetter* slide down the slope	*OHM:* *Vetter* emerge from underground; *vetter* slide down the slope
Expectation and Preparation	*Vetter* come from the tribune into the arena. Form 5 clans around 5 bonfires	*Vetter* enter with skis, sledges and (very large) chair sledge, towards the centre of arena	*Vetter* enter; *vetter* from the slope with snow runners (drop-shaped)	*SUN/DROP:* More *vetter* from underground; sun-ray formation; *vetter* in drop-form down the slope	*SUN/DROP:* More *vetter* from underground; sun-ray formation; *vetter* in drop-form down the slope
Alone and Together	All *vetter* into the arena; winter sports; meet at their stations (bonfires)	5 ice mountains together form shape of the earth (Tellus egg)	Ropes from middle, pulled towards tribune and slope, midnight sun, Tellus egg.	*ROPE:* *Vetter* form sun-ray, ropes from middle pulled towards tribune, midnight sun, Tellus-egg	*ROPE:* *Vetter* form sun-ray, ropes from middle pulled towards tribune, midnight sun, Tellus-egg

Title	January 28	Undated	July 14	August 27	October 19
Ceremony and Victory	5 big medals, ribbons, the *vetter* torch is lit	Ribbons form a protective nest.	*Vetter* move toward the egg, form protective nest, looks like Monolitten statue	*EGG AND NEST:* *Vetter* move toward the egg, form protective nest, looks like Monolitten statue	*EGG AND NEST:* *Vetter* move toward the egg, form protective nest, looks like Monolitten statue
Life and Future				*EARTH:* *Vetter* raise the egg, chief *vetter* dance a victory dance	*EARTH:* *Vetter* raise the egg, chief *vetter* dance a victory dance
The Beginning and the End are One	Snow canons and fireworks, moving pictograms	Egg moved towards slope, ropes become Olympic rings, 400 children in choir join their clans, pictograms; fireworks (snow canons?)	Egg rises while chief-*vetter* dance a victory dance, 400 children in choir join their clans, pictograms; fireworks (snow canons?)	*PIGEON:* Flower and live pigeons emerge from the egg that opens, 400 children in choir join their clans, pictograms; fireworks (snow canons?)	*PIGEON:* Artificial pigeons emerge from the egg that opens, pictograms; fireworks (snow canons?)

Note: * The texts in italics are actual titles as used in the manuscript. Roman text refers to a summary of the main action in the script. The term OHM refers to the title of the music played during this sequence.

as were most references to sports. This also implied that humanity as an abstract category was no longer expressed mainly through Olympic symbols but through the *vetter* and more general entities (egg, globe). As the *vetter* part developed, the paraphrase of the human Olympic ceremony was also de-emphasised, which also resulted in a de-emphasis on the sports aspect of the ceremonies.

Conflicts with the Norwegian environment

While the final version of the ceremonies was being developed, several conflicts arose. A few of these conflicts were of a mainly internal character. Of course, it is to be expected that conflicts would appear in a fast-growing organisation such as the one under consideration, these involved conflicts among the ceremony staff and between the staff and the volunteers (e.g., amateur dancers and musicians). I will not elaborate upon these more organisational conflicts here, but concentrate on the conflicts that in one way or another had larger repercussions concerning the representation of Norway.

In the vacuum that was created after the news broke of the first production group leaving, several voices suggested that the ceremonies should, perhaps, be kept to a minimum and the rest of the money used for humanitarian purposes, for instance ex-Yugoslavia.[18] One of the Norwegians who was sceptical about using 85 million Norwegian Kroner on the ceremonies, an active left-wing politician in Lillehammer, was quoted in one of the newspapers as saying:

> What I react to concerning this opening ceremony is that it is a one-time event in which in the course of twenty minutes fireworks will be set off costing an amount of money that could save thousands of people. (Tove Lehre in *GLT*, 14 September 1992)

The national newspaper *Dagbladet* also raised the same issue in a two-page spread where several well-known Norwegians were asked if they agreed that so much money should be spent on the ceremonies. In particular it seems that the well-nigh gigantomanic ceremonies in Barcelona with their long-lasting fireworks had created a negative impression[19] – at least it was felt by some that this would not fit in with the Norwegian ethos.

Several objections to the Baardson concept came from religious circles in Norway. Sami *joik* singing has for a long time been conceived of as an expression of animism by Norwegian Christians.[20] As the plan for the opening ceremony, including the *joik* to be performed by Nils Aslak Valkepää, became known, it was criticised by one Norwegian priest in particular. The same priest also condemned the use of *vetter,* trolls etc., as being anti-Christian and his view found support among several Norwegian bishops.

Another conflict arose around the Olympic hymn. The hymn was translated into one of the Norwegian languages (*Nynorsk*), and as its content became clear there were loud protests from religious circles in Norway accusing it of being worshipping of Zeus and thus anti-Christian. Several bishops were active in the protest, and the question was widely discussed in most religious newspapers, but to no avail.

During the parade of nations each team was to be headed by sign bearers, carrying a sign with the name of their country. It was decided that Norwegian couples wearing traditional Norwegian costumes should carry the signs – each couple dressed in a costume from a different region in Norway. One of the costumes (from the Sunnmøre region) was disallowed because the official council approving all traditional costumes refused it on the grounds that it had been newly created. There was a lively debate in the local media, but the costume was not to be found among the signbearers during the parade – even though a local newspaper reported that at least one was observed during the folk-dance number.

As had happened in several previous Olympics, the LOOC organised a competition for an official Olympic pop song – a competition won by Svein Gundersen and Jan Vincent Johansen and sung by the Norwegian singer Sissel Kyrkjebø (who also participated during the Lillehammer element in Albertville). Kyrkjebø's manager/record company demanded that the song be played during the ceremony, but Bentein Baardson refused, arguing that he was not aware of the tradition of an Olympic pop song, and that there was no room for it in the manuscript which was already been accepted by the LOOC's board. It is unclear what happened, but the manager threatened with a lawsuit. In the event, as it was Sissel Kyrkjebø who actually sang the Olympic hymn, one might conclude that this was part of a compromise.

Media influences

These conflicts show that the opening ceremonies were being scrutinised by various actors in Norway. Baardson told me that his basic strategy was to accommodate as many wishes as possible, but some of the conflicts were unavoidable. Details of the ceremonies were kept hidden from the general public in order to avoid, for the organisers, a frustrating media debate about the presentation of Norwegian culture where almost every group would claim their right to be represented.[21] Compared to the LOOC a more open information strategy was chosen and the ceremony organisation avoided the partly hostile media critics with which its mother-organisation was faced . Nevertheless, the release of information about the ceremonies to the general public was restricted, partly because journalists accepted the argument that some of the elements should be a surprise. As the information trickled out this had the effect that representational issues were debated separately while the overall concept was never discussed in public. Most of the elements chosen were approved of, but the director still received an offer for a typical Northern Norway fishing boat to be shown during the ceremonies.

In addition to criticism from various Norwegian actors, there was one more powerful actor who tried to exercise influence. Just two weeks before the opening ceremony was to be staged Bentein Baardson had a meeting with CBS – a meeting he refers to as the most grotesque of the whole period. The executives from CBS had been informed about the content of the original script, but when they came back they learned that the most spectacular elements (ice-mountains and large medals) had been cut from the script. Baardson was heavily criticised during the meeting, but nothing was changed.

The Performance

Let us now see what kind of national signs and symbols were used during the actual performance. In the folklore part of the ceremonies people from different parts of Norway contributed. The Telemark skiers (Sondre group) came from the province of Telemark, the wedding group from Hardanger (Voss) while the dancers and fiddlers came from the region north of Lillehammer (Gudbrandsdalen). The different regions of Norway were even more fully represented during the parade of nations, which, because the sign-bearers were dressed up in regional costumes from all over Norway, also became a 'parade of regions'. Here we may characterise the exposition of Norway as mainly presentation. It shows Norway as composed of different regions and a people with deep respect for their king. The Sami element may also be characterised as presentational. The artistic part, based on the fairytale figures known as the *vetter*, had a much more representational character. It was explicitly announced as a fairytale. At the same time it also contained the comparison between Norway and the world (*vetter* representing simultaneously both Norway and humanity in general).

The presentation combined traditional and modern elements. The Telemark skiing group is essentially a modern phenomenon, and its skiing style, though based on a traditional style of skiing, has recently been re-invented and become popular, in particular among wealthy urban youngsters. The apparel, also based on traditional elements, was one of the fashions inspired by the design developed by the LOOC. The music used during the ceremonies was also a combination of traditional and modern music (Berkaak and Lie 1996; Lundby 1997).

Nevertheless the different elements essentially presented a homologous version of Norwegian culture – the 'original' Norway as it was defined by the nation-builders at the end of the nineteenth century: rural (Telemark) Norway, the Hardanger fiddle, folk costumes, folk dances. In spite of the fact that the fiddlers and dancers were from Gudbrandsdalen, regional identity was not prominent. This was also clear from the fact that the dancers not only performed their own regional dances, but also those from other parts of Norway.[22] Only the Sami section of the opening ceremonies established a clearly different identity. In this way Norway was presented as a pluralistic society – a society in which different ethnic cultures co-exist within one nation. But at another level the Sami element fitted in very well with the folklore of the Norwegians – there was a parallel in traditional dress, skis and old-fashioned means of transportation.[23]

Even though regional differences were recognisable (at least for those familiar with Norwegian culture), the general image of Norway was rather one-sided. It was the image of a Gemeinschaft, based on likeness between the elements. It was also of a people close to nature, simple and unspoiled. This notion of simplicity was well-suited to the ideal of 'bringing the Games back to basics', an ideal widely adhered to in Norway. Simplicity was one of the elements Bentein Baardson stressed and much effort was made to have things look simple and natural. For example not only were the audience camouflaged by wearing white capes, but technical equipment (cameras, loudspeakers, and wires) were disguised as well as possible. In addition, concrete walls were sprayed with water in order to create thick layers of ice, which were lit with blue lights to produce an icy effect. Many elements were introduced to make the stage look 'cosy' – Christmas-trees were assembled, small 'Christmas-tree lights' were hung up, etc. Of course, this also cost money as Bentein Baardson pointed out: 'It is not less expensive to make things look simple.' The simple appearance was also meant to keep the complex organisational apparatus in the background – its effectiveness would show through the right functioning of what was shown.

But intermingled with these intentions to communicate a specific image of Norwegian culture were other interests. For example, the choreographers stated that they wanted the dancers to be sitting and lying on the ground to express Norwegian closeness to nature. Working with dancers close to the ground is a prestige-enhancing professional challenge in choreography. The same is true for pair-dancing, which is also more prestigious than individuals just 'wandering around like in Albertville.' The professional interests became so interwoven with the aim of showing Norwegian culture that isolating them becomes difficult.[24]

Commercial interests also came into play. Most striking was the use of 'snow-runners' (skiing shoes with the sole formed as a mini-ski) by the *vetter* running down the ski-jump slope, and the use of mini Maglites during the closing ceremony. The snow-runners were supplied free of charge by the American factory that obtained the right to use its participation in the Olympics in its promotion of this new product. The Maglites provided to all the spectators during the closing ceremony were donated by the owner of the Maglite factory (who himself originates from Bosnia) as a gesture to promote the Sarajevo cause.[25]

The opening ceremonies may be interpreted as a genesis myth, even though Baardson tried to avoid making a statement about how things had originated.[26] As for the actual opening itself, he explained that it seemed to be an Olympic tradition that something should take place in the air.

Another aspect of the ceremony can easily be misinterpreted. The changes that were made from the first script to the final one implied that the number of Olympic symbols and symbols representing sports was diminished. The explanation for this was not, according to Baardson, that they made the show more Norwegian at the expense of the other aspects, but primarily because they had so little time to produce the first script that they added these self-evident aspects just to have something to start with.

Opening Ceremonies as International Media Events

In the course of the last century there has been a steady increase in international contacts. International television coverage and global communication networks are just two of the factors in this changing situation. Increased commercialism, international trade, and tourism also contribute to increasing globalisation. This tearing down of national state boundaries results not only in a global village, but also, paradoxically, increases the need for the actors on the world stage to become visible. From the individual actor's (whether this is an individual or a nation) point of view, as the world expands so does the need to present a specific image to attract the attention of more and more actors of relevance to one's situation. In this context we can see the urge to use the Olympics as a promotional vehicle for the nation.

During the Olympics many television companies place the competitions at the centre of attention – changing their regular schedules and often providing the viewers with live broadcasts from the Olympic arenas. In many countries these broadcasts also attract large audiences and the events at the Olympic venues are followed up by the print media. In this sense we can characterise the Olympics as media events (Dayan and Katz 1992). In their discussions on media events Dayan and Katz differentiate between three different kinds: *contests, coronations* and *conquests.* The sports competitions as such are typical examples of contests – they are played according to rules fixed in advance and 'miniaturise and humanise' conflicts. Whether the ceremonies should be characterised in the same way is not equally evident. In many respects the ceremonies function rather as coronations, celebrating both the IOC, the Olympic ideology, and the hosting country.

Dayan and Katz argue that the live media coverage of the event is in the hands of television companies and thus beyond the direct influence of the organisers of the event. This gives the media a certain autonomy in their coverage – even though Dayan and Katz observe that they normally stick to the organisers' definition of the event (1992: 83). In the case of the Olympics, the host broadcaster, contracted by the local organising committee, normally produces the so-called international feed (visuals and sounds from the arena), while national broadcasters provide commentaries. While the international feed is supposed to be free of national angles, the national broadcasters use this material, their commentators, and sometimes extra visuals, to give their coverage a national angle. Only the US broadcasters have the freedom to produce their own coverage in near total independence from the host broadcaster as a compensation for the huge amounts they pay for the exclusive rights to cover the Games in the US.

This type of media organisation implies that although numerous television channels cover the same event, viewers throughout the world do not necessarily get the same message. Several publications have stressed the differences in interpretations in broadcasts in different countries (see Larson and Rivenburgh 1991; Larson and Park 1993; Moragas et al. 1995; Puijk 1997). One version stands apart: the national broadcast in the hosting country. Here, especially during the ceremonies, the commentators identify with the (re)presentation of *their* culture on behalf of their viewers.

Mediation of the Ceremonies

Responsibility for the international coverage of the Lillehammer Olympics was given to ORTO 94, a subdivision of the Norwegian State Broadcasting Corporation (NRK), which, in turn, subcontracted other broadcasters to cover parts of the Games for them. ORTO 94 had reserved the prestigious opening and closing ceremonies for NRK itself, even though not all of the television staff that worked for ORTO 94 were Norwegian.[27]

The role of television in the Olympics is multifaceted. Television is both a mediator and an interpreter of the event. Of course, the way the event is covered will give a specific view of the performance, a view different from that of any one spectator at the event (see Puijk 1997:15). On the other hand, as noted before, the television audience was considered the main target of the Games and from the beginning there was close co-operation between the ceremony production group and the ORTO 94 television crew.[28] From this perspective the ORTO 94 feed – the pictures and the accompanying sounds – may be considered a mere mediator of the organisers' intentions to spectators all around the world.

In addition to the pictures, all national broadcasters provide commentary from their own commentators. Even though they are an integral part of the television broadcasts, these commentators may be considered important foreign receivers. Although they take part in live broadcasts, they act as instantaneous interpreters of the event. Here they function more on the reception side, like newspaper articles reviewing the event the day after.

Most television rightsholders picked up the ORTO 94 signal, provided it with commentary, and distributed it live to their viewers at home. CBS, however, had an entirely different coverage. Representing the single largest income source for the IOC and the local organisation committee, the US television network which obtains the exclusive rights to cover the Games has a privileged position during the Games. For Lillehammer, CBS had paid $295 million, and had 1,100 accredited personnel. During the opening ceremonies they also had privileges other television companies did not have: not only did they produce their own broadcast using the signal from ORTO 94 cameras, in addition, they had 15 cameras of their own. CBS also had their own commentary position – a cabin built in one of the light towers on the arena. CBS's coverage was not sent live, but was delayed for several hours so as to coincide with 'prime time'. This gave CBS the time to edit the ceremonies – at least to shorten them. In addition, CBS – not unlike many other commercial broadcasters – added the main programmes in accordance with their source of revenue: advertisements.

ORTO and CBS *coverage*

In this section I will compare the CBS coverage of the opening ceremonies with the coverage broadcast on Norwegian television (that is, NRK's broadcast using the ORTO 94 signal). The main differences are summarised in Table 6.2.

1) While all the ORTO 94 broadcasts included the – Norwegian – presenters of the ceremonies, CBS had edited the Norwegian presenters out and replaced them with their own presenters. Thus the Olympic family (Liv Ullmann, Thor Heyerdahl, and the six children) although not completely absent, was truncated. Thor Heyerdahl was shown only once and the children presenting the countries were shown only briefly in two short sequences. The main focus in the CBS coverage was on their own presenters – Greg Gumbel, Andrea Joyce, Ed Bradley and Charles Kuralt. Not only could we hear them as well as the NRK commentator, they were also shown on the screen from different parts of the arena where they commented on what was going on.

2) Altogether, CBS broadcast 30.5 minutes of advertisements during the opening ceremonies, making the US coverage much more fragmented than the ORTO 94/NRK one hour and forty-four minutes of uninterrupted transmission. The CBS broadcast was intercut both by advertisements and features. During the parade of nations 12.5 minutes were given over to advertisements, at the expense of the countries in the parade. As a result, only fifty-six countries were introduced on CBS as against a total of sixty-six on NRK.

3) The CBS broadcast had several small sequences that did not follow the linear coverage of the ceremonies by ORTO 94. Sometimes these were national items which the international broadcasts

lacked. During the first part of the ceremonies President Bill Clinton had a one-minute speech directed to the participating US athletes. CBS also had 'reports' from the rows of the athletes. They had provided the Norwegian free-style skier Stine Lise Hattestad with a radio transmitter and she was 'interviewed' by Greg Gumbel while she walked in the parade of nations. The US athlete Picabo Street was also equipped with portable camera and radio and gave a short account during the artistic programme.

When IOC president Juan Antonio Samaranch asked for a moment of silence for Sarajevo, CBS inserted a short sequence from Sarajevo. It started with a picture from a bullet-pierced window, then panned to a family sitting and watching the Olympic opening ceremony. An inserted text read: 'Sarajevo tonight'.

4) CBS's coverage was also more individualised than that of ORTO 94/NRK. In particular, during the parade of nations, individual athletes were more focused on by CBS. Some of the Americans had their names superimposed on the screen as they were shown in the parade. A few special foreign athletes (Alberto Tomba, Jayne Torvill and Christopher Dean, Katarina Witt and Sanda Dubravcic who had ignited the Olympic flame in Sarajevo ten years before) had short (thirty second) presentations inserted as their countries passed CBS's cameras.

The superimposed subtitles presenting the different countries also varied between ORTO 94/NRK and CBS. While ORTO 94/NRK inserted the country name, its abbreviation and the colours of its flag together with the common elements, the LOOC-designed pictogram of the torch bearer and fonts, CBS had its own logo, the nation's name, flag and abbreviation for each delegation, plus the name of the athlete carrying the flag, and his or her discipline. The inevitable human interest story was added to the presentation of the American flag-bearer who was said to be 'thrilled', but 'whose thoughts are with her brother Tim who is out of the hospital for the first time in six weeks today'.

5) Not only did CBS replace some of the ongoing events with advertisements and other items, they also shortened sequences. In this way, not only were parts of the traditional Norwegian folk dance sequence and parts of Samaranch's speech left out, but several sequences were absent: Gerhard Heiberg's speech, (the president of the local organising committee) and the parade of the Royal Guard. Also the *vetter* section was heavily edited and cut down by approximately one half. On CBS, the *vetter* sequence was a clear and uncomplicated narrative: the *vetter* popped up from underground, they

Table 6.2: ORTO 94/NRK and CBS coverage of the opening ceremony

Mins	ORTO/NRK	Mins	CBS
1'	ORTO's logo		
28'	Norwegian folk culture Parachute – flag * Olympic family (Liv Ullmann, Thor Heyerdahl and six children) Sami singer (Nils Aslak Valkepää) * 3 Norwegian folk dances Entrance royal family	26'	Norwegian folk culture Parachute – flag Sami singer (Nils Aslak Valkepää) 2 Norwegian folk dances Entrance royal family *Inserts of:* CBS presenters President Bill Clinton's address to the US Athletes *6.5 minutes commercials*
30'	Parade of 66 nations *10 countries more than CBS* * (Andorra, Argentina, Brazil, Bulgaria, Georgia, Iceland, Cyprus, Krygystan, Romania, Turkey)	39'	Parade of 56 nations *Short inserts of:* Alberto Tomba Sandra Dubravcic (torch bearer in Sarajevo 1984) Jayne Torville and Christopher Dean Katarina Witt Interview with Stine Lise Hattestad *12.5 minutes commercials*
18'	Olympic Ceremony * Thor Heyerdahl introduces: * Speech Heiberg Speech Samaranch Opening: King Harald Olympic flag Olympic hymn Torch Oaths Norwegian national anthem * Band of the Royal Guard	28'	Olympic Ceremony Speech: Samaranch (shortened) Opening: King Harald Olympic flag Olympic hymn Torch Oaths Norwegian national anthem *Short inserts of:* Serajevo today CBS reporters *9 minutes commercials* *6 minutes Olympic news*
26'	Artistic programme * Liv Ullmann introduces fairy tale: Anxiety and Courage * Expectation and Preparation * Alone and Together * Ceremony and Victory Life and Future The Beginning and the End are One	16'	Artistic programme Anxiety and Courage Life and Future The Beginning and the End are One *Short inserts of:* Picabo Street's point of view during the programme *2.5 minutes commercials*
1'	ORTO logo (short)		

*Note: * Elements not present in the CBS broadcast.*

assembled in the middle, drew up the egg that changed into the globe. The egg opened and out came the doves. Fireworks ended the show.

Of course, it is unreasonable to expect American commercial television to have the same coverage as a European public service broadcasting. As Barnett argues, 'It is invidious to compare two completely different television environments and try to evaluate which best serves the sports viewer' (1990:78). The main aim here is not to evaluate, but to document the differences in the transformation processes involved and the possible consequences of this on the representation of Norwegian culture.

Taken together the American coverage was more *segmented* (i.e., divided into different short segments). While the NRK coverage was a continuous broadcast of the entire performance, the CBS coverage was intersected with advertisements and other items. The intersection of advertisements is not unique to CBS though, all commercial channels insert commercials during Olympic ceremonies (see Rivenburgh 1991; Moragas et al. 1995). In addition to segmentation, the CBS broadcast was more *dramatised* and *personified* than the NRK coverage. Personification is part of a conscious attempt at making the broadcast more familiar and it is obtained both by using well-known commentators and by focusing on the athletes. The effect of this, and also of other traits of the CBS broadcast (the often nationally anchored small features), is that the coverage had a particular *national* American angle, more so than the broadcasts based on the ORTO 94 feed where the national angle only emerged from the commentary.

In terms of the (re)presentation of Norwegian culture, one CBS transformation stands out as different from the ORTO 94-based broadcasts – the introduction of the artistic section. As the introduction of Liv Ullmann was omitted, so was the formal introduction of the *vetter* sequence as a fairytale. Although the commentator support system carried Liv Ullman's introduction, CBS introduced the *vetter* in a very different way:

> [What you see now] introduce[s] you to the mythical beliefs of these people, the Norwegians. *Vetter* are an integral part of what Norwegians believe. They will not build on land until they have consulted the *vetter*. These mythical underground beings are now inaugurating the ski-jump and inaugurating the Games for all of us. They are said to be knowledgeable, wise and honest and watch constantly over the activity of mankind. That's because they are good *vetter*, as opposed to evil *vetter*. Much like the Mother Goose story and Andersen's fairy tales, these *vetter* make up the bulk of the Norwegian fairy tales. Children grow up learning all about them.

This introduction of the artistic section of the opening ceremony may be seen as a reification of Norwegian culture from CBS's side, by turning the sequence intended as a representation of Norwegian culture into a presentation.

Reception of the Ceremonies in Norway

In general, the opening ceremonies were positively received both in Norway and abroad. Nevertheless, reception was also differentiated. In this section I will give an overview of the reviews in the Norwegian media, of the elements that contributed to a positive evaluation of the ceremony and the criticism that was levelled at it.

Representing Norway

One of the aims of the opening ceremony was to use it as a showcase for Norwegian culture. Some of the newspapers commented on the content of the presentational aspects:

> A correct presentation of Norwegian culture. (...) The opening ceremonies reflected the variety of our traditional cultural heritage. (*Porsgrunns Dagblad*, 14 February 1994)

The catchwords in most Norwegian newspapers were *simplicity, dignity* and *popularity*. A widely held view was that the opening ceremonies were simple, in accordance with the Norwegian egalitarian view that previous ceremonies had been pretentious and overdone. The back-to-basics strategy that had been one of the local organisers' aims seems to have gained huge support in Norway:

> Both for Norway and the Olympic movement it was a blessing that Bentein Baardson and Dag Alveberg did not fall into the Hollywood trap and make excessive use of computer technology to mount a television show with digital sound and picture editing and all kinds of casino effects. Everything was simple and plain (...) it was nature that acted. (*Finnmark Dagblad*, 14 February 1994)
>
> Many feared an outlandish artistic content, but the master of ceremonies Bentein Baardson & Co. had chosen the plebeian and simple instead of the pompous and professional. (*Porsgrunns Dagblad*, 14 February 1994)

Keeping the ceremony plain and simple, without any overdoing was seen as positive. The previous ceremonies, in particular those in Albertville, served as a (negative) contrast:

Master of ceremonies Bentein Baardson and choreographer [sic] Dag Alveberg have put their bets on an authentic and unadulterated Norwegianness. There is not much high tech and technological hanky-panky here. (*Oppland Arbeiderblad*, 14 February 1994)

Being proud

Although emotions are seldom written about in Norwegian newspapers, the reports from the opening ceremonies were an exception.[29] Many of the reviewers expressed their being emotionally carried away with the ceremonies. The NRK announcer's first comment after the end of the ceremony was one of pride. Citing a six-year-old boy he said, 'I am so proud, my heart is smiling inside me'.

Under the heading 'strong experience' *Oppland Arbeiderblad* wrote, 'The opening ceremony turned out to be an experience powerful enough to call forth tears and a throbbing heart' (*Oppland Arbeiderblad*, 14 February 1994).

Pride and emotional involvement sometimes resulted in euphoric descriptions as in the report in Norway's biggest newspaper (*VG*) cited at the beginning of this article. Although not as euphoric as *VG*, other newspapers also made a connection between the strong emotions and national sentiments.

Most Norwegians probably felt national sentiments rise as a lump in their throat when Øystein Rommetveit started to play 'Fanitullen' on his violin, when the telemark skiers zipped fearlessly down the landing slope, and when 250 folk dancers demonstrated vivid Halling and springleik dances. Sissel Kyrkebø's crystal-clear voice also caused pleasant ripples to shiver down one's spine – however Greek the Olympic Hymn might happen to be. (*Nordlands Framtid*, 14 February 1994).

Reception abroad

An oft-cited cause underlying the commentators' positive evaluation of the opening ceremonies was the positive reception the ceremonies received abroad. Foreign journalists were cited, often those interviewed by the Norwegian press agency (NTB). The fact that the ceremonies had been positively received by 'the world' was a major argument in many Norwegian newspapers and indicates the reflexivity of these newspapers' attitude towards Norwegian culture. Here the argument is not so much about whether the ceremonies reflect Norwegian culture in a 'representative' way, but whether the Other approved of what was shown. This reaction to what might be called 'the foreign gaze' was probably a fundamental element of the whole involvement of the Norwegian population during the Olympics,

> The American CBS describes the opening ceremonies as a cosy neighbourhood party with a royal couple as part of the neighbourhood. (*Avisa Trondheim*, 12 February 1994)
>
> 'Gripping, charming, genuine, natural, and simple, the Olympic ceremony is on the right tracks after all the excesses' – these are the characteristics foreign journalists send back home. (*Stavanger Aftenblad*, 14 February 1994)

Presentation, representation and modelling

In terms of presentation, representation and modelling, the above-mentioned reactions in the Norwegian media show that all three elements were present.

Sometimes essentialistic terms were used as in the following example from NRK's commentary during the folk-dance sequence, when one of the commentators claimed that 'This is, then, the Norwegian sequence of the opening ceremony. The proto-Norwegian'. The other commentator, who had a more sober attitude to what has been presented, immediately adds the rejoinder: 'At least from the end of the last century.'

Presentational aspects were present in the reviews and commentaries although they were not particularly emphasised – the focus was more on representation. While the main sentiment of the coverage was positive, some aspects of the ceremonies were the target of criticism. Several newspapers, for example, criticised the television production in particular for not being good enough:

> While I am grateful for the substance and the artistic performance, I didn't like the NRK side of it. The picture editing was too diffuse. (*Bergens Tidende*, 14 February 1994)

The numerous 'people in the street' interviews also showed a great variety including which parts of the performance were most liked and disliked, and people's interpretations of the event.

Modelling was also present as a way of interpreting the ceremony, mostly in connection with the reactions of the foreign press. The success of the ceremony abroad was described in several papers as showing that Norway (in spite of pessimistic predictions) had climbed onto the world stage with dignity, thus proving that it was capable of producing a first-class programme.

The opening set the tone which indicates the level of ambition of the Lillehammer Olympics. This is going to be a dazzling Winter Olympics which will be repaid abundantly in PR value and goodwill abroad, in increasing self-esteem, community spirit and daring among the people. (*Bergens Arbeiderblad,* 13 February 1994)

As far as I am concerned, the opening ceremony will be able to be used in all future time to add moral conviction to our ability to rely on ourselves. (*Glåmdalen,* 14 February 1994)

'After this, Lillehammer will never be the same', the television commentator Kjell Kristian Rike said with an emotional voice when the whole thing was over. In our opinion, neither will Norway. (*VG,* 14 February 1994)

These kinds of assessments indicate that at least in parts of the population there was a conception of a changed world – a world where Norway had left its inferior place and was now participating on equal terms with the well-established nations (like the United States, France and Great Britain). Of course, this is exactly what Blain et al. highlight as the reason for peripheral countries to apply for international events like the Olympics: 'The Olympics are primarily a media event in which the hosts aspire to world-wide prominence.' (1993:186)

Alternative interpretations

Most Norwegian newspapers wrote on the basis of what might be called a national perspective and judged the performance from a national angle, sometimes adding a few lines about local participants. In some cases the local angle became more dominant, but this was mostly in articles subsidiary to the main text.

Even though the Olympic opening ceremony was largely well received in Norway there was also one clearly alternative interpretation. The conservative Christian newspapers (e.g., *Dagen, Sogn Avis*) that had denounced the ceremonies for being a worship of Zeus continued on the same track and repeated their criticism of the ceremonies as anti-Christian:

It is beyond doubt that it was a New Age ideology which determined the identity of the various segments. In addition, the ceremony preached a peace pathos that did not search for hope for peace in the Creator of heaven and earth, but made mother earth the source of peace. And that is pantheism. *(Dagen,* 14 February 1994)

Evaluations in the Foreign Media

While CBS had their own coverage of the ceremony, the other foreign countries depended for their broadcasts on what ORTO 94 had to offer. The commentators were given background information – they had a separate monitor that provided information about the sequences (what was to come, background and short biographies of the participants, etc.). This information was generally used by the commentators, but to varying degrees.

One item about the *vetter* caused a good deal of confusion. As a general description it was stated that the *vetter* were both good and bad. This was loyally mentioned by several commentators, but when it came to interpreting the actual sequence they became confused because the bad *vetter* were not present (they did not appear until in the closing ceremony).

After the dress rehearsal some of the foreign newspapers were less impressed than the Norwegian ones:

> Spare us, spare us. After Albertville brought us the women in the bubbles Lillehammer brings us the babes in the balaclavas with 400 singing children, 200 goose pimpled folk dancers, two skydivers and maybe some dancing reindeer. (*Irish Times*, 12 February 1994)

The words 'kitsch' and 'cliché' were also used. Several newspapers refer to this in their reviews of the opening ceremonies, such as the *Time* quotation at the beginning of this chapter.

In spite of some critical comments, the general foreign reaction to the opening ceremonies was positive, even though the kitsch aspect was recognised. Under the title 'Norwegens schöner Weg zurück zur Natur. Überzeugende, schlichte Eröffnung', the German newspaper *Die Welt* writes: 'A kitschy postcard, a cliché? Maybe. But nevertheless beautiful and seldom over-the-top.'(14 February 1994) The organisers seem to have succeeded in their aim of convincing the foreign media that they wanted to bring the Games 'back to basics', reducing its commercialised profile.

> There is absolutely no doubt about it: The Winter Games have returned to their cradle. They belong in Norway, and the whole world can see this for itself over the next two weeks. (*Die Welt*, 14 February 1994)

Also *Le Figaro* underlines the simplicity and non-commercial image of the ceremonies. In the heading they wrote:

They have gone for authenticity. A feast reflecting the country: simple and traditional. The Norwegians have recounted their history, and turned their back on exaggeration and commercialism. (*Le Figaro,* 14 February 1994)

Several times the foreign media suggested that Norway had revealed its secrets to the world.

Lillehammer had opened its temple. The ritual could begin. Then, during two hours, Norway showed the world its nature, its history, its secrets, its simplicity, its legends. (*Le Figaro,* 14 February 1994)

Also *The Times* reporter refers to this sharing of secrets:

In the most enchanting Olympic opening ceremony I can recall, Norway shared its secret with the rest of the world. It was as though they were lying on the consultant psychiatrist's couch, and the television cameras had crept in the door. Norway bared its heart, and what we saw was not funny or embarrassing or silly, but one of the fundamental truths of mankind: that we share this earth with creatures and spirits of which we know not, of which Prospero spoke to us. (*The Times,* 14 February 1994)

Not only did the foreign press have a positive evaluation of the opening ceremonies,[30] they also seemed to agree with the simplicity, back-to-basics and peace message that was intended by the producers.

Conclusion

For two weeks in February Norway had inherent newsmaking power, normally only granted to elite countries like the United States. As a peripheral country it had the opportunity to get on 'all' of the world's television screens and front pages without having been visited by some kind of catastrophe, war or disaster. This situation enabled the Norwegians not only to break in on the usual US-dominated flow of entertainment programmes within the United States, but also to reach other (also often peripheral) countries with which there normally is only a minimum of exchange of television programmes.

The production process of an Olympic opening ceremony may be viewed as a selection process by which certain elements from the national culture are chosen. This choice was primarily one between readily noticeable elements – material culture (costumes, musical instruments, artefacts), music, historical events, famous persons, etc.

But the different scripts also intended to show what were considered typical traits (Norwegian egalitarianism, Norwegian closeness to nature, Norwegian love for sports, Norwegian children, etc.). The description of the different phases makes us realise that the ceremony might easily have been quite different – and probably still be called 'typical Norwegian'. If the concept that originally was chosen had been realised, the ceremonies would have been different – among other things they would have been based on a (pre-)Viking tradition.

Despite the differences between the concepts, they had in common a focus on traditional Norwegian elements, ignoring the more modern aspects of Norwegian society and culture. None of the concepts paid any attention, for example, to Norway as an important oil-producing country. The reason this angle was chosen can be explained by the fact that the sporting context in Norway is associated with rural traditions (in particular cross-country skiing) and former national sports heroes. In addition, the stress on employing the Games as a showcase for Norwegian culture and uniqueness also opened up the use of tradition – the modern aspects of Norwegian society are not as amenable for the production of a distinct identity and media image on the international arena. The local organisation committee had used this connection with tradition actively and in this way prepared a common conception of the Games. In the next phase they preferred to use mythical concepts, depicting Norway as a tourist destination.

Norwegian culture provided the organisers of the ceremonies with an almost unlimited source of artefacts and symbols to use in their work. It would be impossible to discuss why certain aspects were included or omitted, but I will mention one feature. In connection with the Olympic Games, one might have expected the local organisers to actively use the fact that the Nobel Peace Prize is awarded by Norway each year. Several times this theme was raised, both within the LOOC and from the outside, but the LOOC was reluctant to use the connection, precisely because it was too obvious. It seems that those in charge in the LOOC felt that using the Peace Prize would fall outside the economic discourse in which the Games were embedded. Talk about peace was felt to be unfitting and hypocritical. In contrast to the LOOC's reluctance to incorporate peace as a separate theme for the organisation, many observers interpreted the opening ceremony as a powerful request for peace. It must be remarked that the peace message of the opening ceremony was intermingled with an ecological message (care for the world) and that Bentein Baardson received much help from IOC president Samaranch who called on the actors in Yugoslavia to put down their weapons. The peace message was thus reinforced and stood out as one of the clearest messages.

We have noted that Norwegian cultural elements used in the opening ceremony were chosen from local, regional and national levels. From being local, regional or national they changed their status and became international. This change implies, of course, changes in space relations – the elements are lifted from their traditional context and used in another. Staging traditional cultural elements in an international television context changes their meaning – at least by adding another meaning level to the original one.

In terms of decontextualisation and delocalisation the change is perhaps less dramatic than it might look at first glance. Many of the elements that were used already circulated in wider contexts – both as elements in national Norwegian culture and media industry, and as elements in the tourist industry. For instance, Norwegian folk music and folk dress have been used since the beginning of this century as entertainment for tourists (Bårdtvedt 1984). Thus one may consider the circulation of localised Norwegian cultural elements in the international television culture rather as a question of magnitude. Now more people, including those who had never been to Norway, came within reach of these elements. Even though the use of traditional cultural elements in wider contexts is not new, there is another level on which changes may seem to be more profound. Many of the Norwegian cultural elements normally have a localised meaning; at least they are connected to the rural areas. In the international context of the Olympics these Norwegian cultural elements functioned as markers for Norwegian identity for many Norwegians, even those who normally would not identify with the rural identities that were displayed. Here, the level of identification – whether at a local/regional (urban versus rural) or a national level (Norway versus the rest of the world) – determines the meaning of the different symbols. During the Olympics a vogue of nostalgic traditional Norwegian culture swept the country. This nostalgic vogue must also be seen in the context of the whole period of the Games, which, it might be argued, functioned as a *liminoid* (Turner 1977) period for most Norwegians (see also Puijk 1997:42-53).

For two hours on 12 February 1994, the world's attention was focused on Norway. But even though 'the whole world' had tuned in to one and the same event, did it receive the same image of Norwegian culture? The question is, of course, rhetorical and the answer obvious: no, there were many differences – the television viewers did not see what the on-site audience saw. The Norwegian viewers watching a two-hour-long continuous performance while American viewers saw a number of extracts intersected by features and commercials.

But, can we try to be more precise and point out the main trends in this question of the image of Norway? In order to do so we can start by pointing out a fundamental difference between the functions and interpretations of Norway, internally and externally. In Olympic ceremonies there is often an opposition between the general humanistic values inherent to Olympic ceremonies and nationalistic values of the hosting country using the world's attention to profile itself.

The balance between these opposing values is precarious, as both sides have powerful proponents. Internally the ceremony had to unite the people, externally it had to make a statement that was understandable – either by focusing on readily recognisable Norwegian traits, traits that are easily comparable with traits from other countries,[31] or by representing universals. Both strategies were followed by the organisers of the opening ceremony.

During the first part of the ceremony Norwegian traditional life was displayed, providing an easily accessible way of showing something 'typically' Norwegian. Of course, there are many parallels and resemblances between the folkloristic costumes and dances displayed here and those in other parts of Europe – in fact they are the results of international cultural exchanges in former centuries. In addition the royal entrance provides an easily understandable theme.

We have also seen several examples of the second strategy – presenting universal 'human' traits and values. The ecological message was an example of this. We also noted that on several occasions the universal/global was intimately mixed with the Norwegian – the *vetter* that represented Norwegians represented at the same time humankindness; the parade of nations mixed with the parade of Norwegian regions. Even the Olympic hymn sung in Norwegian may be seen to sort under this strategy.

I have used the terms presentation, representation and modelling as concepts to describe not so much the different expressions of the ceremony, but rather the different attitudes towards the various elements of it. Instead of concentrating on the performance itself, I have concentrated on the views of the diverse actors. Unlike public events that are performed repeatedly, the Olympic opening ceremonies are unique in the sense that they are performed only once. They maybe are recorded and shown again (as in Norway), but these recordings are mere copies of the unique original performance. The

uniqueness of these public events contributes to the fact that there is little public discussion and no crystallisation of one dominant meaning.
Television commentators have to rely on themselves during the live
broadcasts, which, in turn, makes them vulnerable and dependent on
the information provided by the organisers. Journalists from the print
media of course have more time to discuss the performance with colleagues and adjust their comments to the reactions of the others.[32] As
for public opinion, opening ceremonies are the introduction to a series
of sports competitions that occupy the headlines once the first reviews
are published. This inhibits a more general public signifying process
where one or a few clear alternative interpretations might crystallise.

The main conclusion as to whether the ceremony presented, represented, or modelled Norwegian culture is that it contained all
aspects, but that there was a different emphasis in both Norwegian
and foreign media. Although there were nuances, the main trend in
the foreign media was to take a presentational view of the ceremonies. There was a certain contradiction between those who saw
the ceremonies as stereotypical and those who saw them as going
beyond stereotypes, presenting the core of Norwegian culture, but
the foreign interpretation of the opening ceremony was rather essentialistic – many statements about '[typical] Norwegian traits' were
made without qualification. What the critics asked for was a more
artistic and reflexive interpretation of Norwegian culture, but the
actual show was evaluated in presentational terms.

The Norwegian evaluation of the opening ceremony was less
focused upon presentational aspects: few newspapers mentioned the
just or unjust presentation; there were no allegations that some
regions were profiled too much while others were invisible, etc. In
fact, most comments stressed form rather than content – the dignity
of the ceremony and the good impression made on the foreign
media. Many of these comments created the basis upon which the
statement that the state of affairs for Norway had been changed, was
based. Norway's position on the world map was changed.

In sum, while the interpretations in the foreign media had a tendency to be submitted in presentational terms, there was a tendency
to interpret the ceremonies more in representational, and even modelling, terms within Norway. These kinds of differences – where the
meaning of an event depends on an ability to see the differences and
on identification – are probably quite common in our age of global
media. This implies that global-media products can function simultaneously as rich and reflexive and as simple stereotypes.

Notes

1. In the case of the ceremonies, the organisers may consist of several acting bodies (the IOC, the local organising committee, and often a special unit responsible for the ceremonies), not to mention the personal visions and viewpoints at stake in such an elaborate production.
2. The exact number of viewers is difficult to estimate, but for the Summer Olympics, they were estimated to be between 1 and 2.5 billion people world wide (for a discussion of the numbers see Moragas and Botella. 1995:209-21).
3. This model is named after *teori d'auteur* which was developed by the New Wave filmmakers in French film during the 1960s which stresses the responsibility of the individual director in film.
4. During its short life from 1988 to 1995 the organisational structure – and its name – changed several times. In this chapter I will use 'LOOC' whatever the 'official' name of the organisation at the particular time.
5. Internal memorandum to LOOC director Ingar Flugsrud written by the LOOC's chief of culture, Bente Erichsen and ceremony supervisor Olemic Thommessen, 22 September 1991.
6. In the field of arts the traditional approach is to arrange an open competition among artists. This approach reflects egalitarian values in Norwegian society as much as strong organisation of the artists' interest groups (Vaagland 1993). One of the consequences of not defining the LOOC as a public organisation was that it could (and did) act more according to other criteria. The groups were chosen by the LOOC for their potential – the composition of one group (Filmeffect/Baardson) was influenced by LOOC itself. One additional constellation of persons LOOC tried to get together was not realised.
7. A popular annual cross-country ski-race between Rena and Lillehammer (57 km) in which thousands of people participate (it can be compared with the Swedish 'Wasaloppet', the Dutch/Frisian 'Elfstedentocht' in speed skating, or the New York Marathon).
8. The concept included a description of the organisational model of responsibilities/reporting and a budget. The organisational model was criticised by the LOOC because it had conflicting financial and reporting channels.
9. In the LOOC's cultural department the group's lack of concreteness was ascribed to the fact that Bentein Baardson was too occupied with other projects. Another interpretation, by the department's ceremony supervisor, was that the group was searching for a coherent idea for the cultural programme as a whole to anchor the concept for the ceremonies. As they did not find such an idea, the group withdrew, delivering their concept only in order to obtain the 200,000 Norwegian kroner accorded to each group.
10. The princess figure was played by the popular Norwegian singer Sissel Kyrkjebø.
11. Several versions of what went on circulate; there is no need to go any further into the matter here.
12. The second Polyvision concept was not taken into serious consideration.
13. This production was shown on NRK during Christmas 1993.
14. In the script this musical piece is called 'Olympic slager'. As the heading reads 'Declaration of Human Rights', it is possible that this song was intended to be launched as the musical theme tune of the Games.

15. Although the common term *vetter* is rarely used in Norway, mythical beings like *troll, nisser, nøkken* and *fossegrimen* are well known by Norwegians and relatively often used in fiction.

16. The expression used in Norwegian is *'eventyrlig eventyrland'* which makes it even more fairytale like.

17. The original script states that the parachute sequence preferably should be live. As live coverage would take too much time the sequence was filmed (in the Alps) and reworked for special effects. Two parachutists jumped with a large Norwegian flag during the ceremonies and were covered live when they flew over the arena.

18. In Lillehammer people working for the the LOOC started a fund-raising organisation – Olympic Aid. Liv Ullmann made a speech right after the closing ceremonies in Barcelona which was offered to all the television rights-holders, but it does not seem that many countries actually broadcasted this speech.

19. The Barcelona closing ceremony was shown on a large screen in Lillehammer. Being present to observe people's reactions to what was shown I was surprised to see no reaction at all by the group of people sitting around me. The only utterance I noted was someone saying to his neighbour when the fireworks in Barcelona had lasted some minutes: 'What a waste of money'.

20. The same criticism had been raised when the Norwegian and Sami Norwegian singers Sverre Kjelsberg and Mattis Hætta performed a *joik* ('Samiid Ædnan') at the European Song Contest in 1980.

21. Numerous groups and organisations had presented themselves to LOOC during previous phases in the hope of getting international attention through their participation in the Olympic project.

22. The dancers complained during the rehearsals that they were not allowed to dance their own regional dance first.

23. The prominence of the Sami section represents the real emancipatory process that has occurred over the last decennia.

24. During the rehearsals, while the choreography was still being developed, one could often observe the interrelation between practical problems (e.g., how to move a group of dancers from one part of the arena to another), choreographic principles (e.g., let them move in a certain way) and ideology (finding a proper ideological rationale for the movement as in: 'this movement can express taking care of each other').

25. The small torches – bearing the inscription 'Remember Sarajevo' – were turned on by the spectators in a 'peace' sequence during the closing ceremony. The 40,000 small lights harmonised well with the 'Christmas-tree' decorations.

26. Such an interpretation would, among others, imply a distinct relation between Norway (as symbolised with its flag), the Sami population, and the Norwegian population.

27. Specialist help was hired to operate the wireless camera system (England), the helicopter camera (Netherlands), and the remote controlled camera (South Africa). NRK did little to attract publicity about this.

28. Even though the two groups were in contact with each other from the beginning, several (serious) conflicts arose on the way. Still, in general, one may consider the international television feed a result of the joint effort of both groups.

29. We encountered the same emotional style in some of the newspaper reports on the torch relay in advance of the Games (see Klausen et al. 1995:216).

30. Closing ceremonies are usually only mentioned with a few lines as they 'drown' in the general evaluation of the Games and each country's national achievements.

31. In connection with ethnic struggles for recognition, Eidheim (1971) uses the terms 'complementarisation' and 'dichotomisation', i.e., showing symbols complementary to the majority's main symbols in the minority's culture.
32. Sometimes rumours spread very quickly within the journalistic community, resulting in an almost instant opinion-making process. On the other hand, especially on international occasions, the journalistic community may also be divided into several non-communicating sections.

References

Baardson, B. and B. Kvamme (1992/93) 'Åpnings- og avslutningsseremoniene til de XVII Olympiske vinterleker, Lillehammer 1994. Konsept og manus.' Manuscript, Several editions: Lillehammer.

Barnett, S. (1990) *Sets and Games. The Changing Face of Sport on Television,* BFI: London.

Berkaak, O.A. and M. Lie (1996) 'Norway. Oslo 1952, Lillehammer 1994', *Olympic Message,* Vol. II, April/May, pp. 70-4.

Blain, N., R. Boyle and H. O'Donnell (1993) *Sport and National Identity in the European Media,* Leicester University Press: London.

Bårdtvedt, R. (1984) 'Vor gode bræ også i sommer beskuet af høifornemme øine.' Møtet mellom turister og bygdefolk i Otta 1861-1914', MA theses, Department of Ethnology, University of Bergen.

Dayan, D. and E. Katz (1992) *Media Events. The Live Broadcasting of History,* Harvard University Press: Cambridge.

Dilling, M. (1990) 'The Familiar and the foreign: music as medium of exchange in Seoul ceremonies', in *Toward One World Beyond All Barriers. The Seoul Olympic Anniversary Conference.* The Seoul Olympic Sports Promotion Foundation: Seoul.

Eidheim, H. (1971) *Aspects of the Lappish Minority Situation,* Universitetsforlaget: Oslo.

Handelman, D. (1990) *Models and mirrors: towards an anthropology of public events,* Cambridge University Press: Cambridge.

Hazan, B. (1982) *Olympic Sports and propaganda games: Moscow 1980,* Transaction Books: New Brunswick, N.J.

Ingulstad, F. and S. Solem (1992) *Nissen. Den norske nissens forunderlige liv og historie,* Gyldendal Norsk Forlag: Oslo.

Klausen, A.M, O.A. Berkaak, E.K. Aslaksen, R. Puijk, I. Rudie and E. Archetti (1995) *Fakkelstafetten – en olympisk ouverture,* Ad Notam: Oslo.

Larson, J.F. and H.S. Park (1993) *Global Television and the Politics of the Seoul Olympics,* Westview Press: Boulder/London.

Larson, J.F. and N. Rivenburgh (1991) 'A comparative analysis of Australian, U.S. and British telecast of the Seoul Olympic opening ceremony', *Journal of Broadcasting and Electronic Media*, 35/1, pp. 75-94.

Lundby, K. (1997) 'The Web of Collective Representations', in S.M. Hoover and K. Lundby (eds) *Rethinking Media, Religion and Culture*, Sage Publications: Thousand Oaks/London/New Delhi.

MacAloon, J.J. (1981) *This Great Symbol. Pierre de Coubertin and the Origins of the Modern Olympic Games*, The University of Chicago Press: Chicago.

MacAloon, J.J. (1996) 'Olympic Ceremonies as a Setting for Intercultural Exchange', in M. de Moragas, J.J. MacAloon and M. Llinés (eds) *Olympic Ceremonies. Historical Continuity and Cultural Exchange*, IOC: Lausanne.

Moragas, M. de (1991) 'Spanish Television (TVE) and the Coverage of the Opening Ceremony of the 1988 Seoul Olympic Games', in F. and M. Landry and M. Yerlès (eds.) *Sport ... The Third Millennium*, Les Presses de l'Université Laval: Sainte-Foy.

Moragas, M. de and M. Botella (1995) *The Keys to Success. The social, sporting, economic and communications impact of Barcelona '92*, Centre d'Estudis Olímpics i de l'Esport: Barcelona.

Moragas, M. de, N.K. Rivenburgh and J.F. Larson (1995) *Television in the Olympics*, John Libbey: London.

Puijk, R. (ed.) (1997) *Global Spotlights on Lillehammer. How the World viewed Norway during the 1994 Winter Olympics*, John Libbey/University of Luton Press: Luton.

Rivenburgh, N.K. (1991) 'Learning About Korea – Or Did We?' in F. and M. Landry and M. Yerlès (eds) *Sport ... The Third Millennium*, Les Presses de l'Université Laval: Sainte-Foy.

Turner, V. (1977) 'Process, system and symbol: a new anthropological synthesis', *Daedalus*, 106/2.

Vaagland, J. (1993) *Kunstformidling i klemme*, Eastern Norway Research Institute: Lillehammer.

Chapter 7

A Place in the Sun:
The Vernacular Landscape as Olympic Venue

Odd Are Berkaak

When Lillehammer was selected to host the XVII Olympic Winter Games, work on the comprehensive plan for the area was speeded up so as to be able to integrate the arenas in the future outlay of the town. In a study undertaken by a regional architectural firm, the point was made that something would have to be done with the 'entrée' to the town. It was felt that Lillehammer was turning its back on the outside world and could only be experienced 'outwards' from the centre.

The experts pointed to the fact that after the main road had been reconstructed, so that heavy traffic could bypass the town on a long bridge along the river, the 'natural entry' to the town from the south had been obstructed. Up until the 1980s the main road had ended in the town square; it was the natural place for the traveller to arrive without having to look for a highway exit. After the reconstruction, it was felt that Lillehammer had ended up out of the way, quite literally. Visitors were no longer given the feeling of welcome on arrival. To reach the town from the main road one had to take a narrow, winding road up a steep hillside through a lakeside residential area, or, coming in from the north, drive a mile through an industrial area. The visitor/stranger was given the feeling of either intruding on private grounds or entering through the back door.

With the Olympics coming to town a transformation of this spatial relationship was strongly called for, and the municipal politicians and planners were advised to adopt an outsider's view and base the new development of the place on a non-subjective, 'global' conception of space.[1]

Raymond Williams's dichotomy between 'insiders', for whom place is a locus of being, and 'outsiders', who entertain an objective attitude towards it, was thus actualised by the planners as a main parameter of place construction (Williams 1973). Already in these early planning documents we see the deep dilemmas and ambivalences of the modern Olympic site, that of being simultaneously local and global, framing the place simultaneously as an inside and an outside. Through large-scale media performances the Olympics display the host city's unique and particular difference from all other places on the planet at the same time as making it universally translatable and accessible from radically different positions.

It has been repeated by a number of authors that modernisation has caused a 'disembedding' of social institutions and processes from particular localities with a corresponding 'emptying of place', i.e., a more abstracted and distanced sense of place has emerged (Giddens 1990; Harvey 1993). In Christopher Tilley's discussion of Western capitalist space, for instance, he says that landscape has become a 'backdrop to action' and is no longer the 'sedimented ritual form' it used to be in pre-capitalist, and still is in non-Western, spaces (Tilley 1994:20–21).

To discuss this modernist construction of spatial transformation I will take a closer look at the construction of the White Mountain downhill piste and the changes in practices and experiences that have occurred in its wake. It will become abundantly clear that a deconstruction of traditional meanings has taken place. In White Mountain a traditional agricultural area was modelled more or less directly on the more well-known central European alpine venues, creating what Harvey has called a 'serial replication of homogeneity' in space (Harvey 1993:8). On the early stages of construction a film was made presenting the project, in which it was stated: 'The Downhill course at White Mountain will be tailor-made and the most demanding in Europe. Well known venues like Wengen, Lauberhorn, Schladming, Val d'Isere, Val Gardena, Hinterglem, Krjanska Gora can not compete with "White Mountain, Norway", say the experts.'[2] This aspect of the process thus complies with the thesis of 'replication of homogeneity' in space, and with what Giddens identifies as the development of 'empty space' in modernity: 'the "lifting out" of social relations from local contexts of interaction and their restructuring across indefinite spans of time–space' (Giddens 1990:21). In the presentation above, White Mountain is taken out of its traditional spatial context and reconstructed as a replication of other places on a global frame of reference. This process, Giddens says, is linked to two related factors on the micro level: the tendency to represent space without reference to a privileged vantage-point, and the technological and economic factors making possible the 'substitutability of different spatial units' (Ibid:19). Both these factors are evident in White Mountain. First of all, we see that the building of the venue is carried out according to general requirements that apply universally and not locally, and those who form it and talk on its behalf, as we saw above, are the experts of the National Ski Federation (NSF) and not representatives of the local farming community. The venue was also regularly characterised in terms such as 'Norway's Kitzbühel',[3] and : 'You have to visit others to realise how you are yourself.'[4] In addition, even at the early stages of planning the members of the project group went to Central Europe to study the more famous venues in the Alps, as models for the reconstruction of White Mountain. In short, the White Mountain area has lost much of its local character and become 'substitutable' with other alpine centres and winter sports consumption spaces that can be found anywhere in the world; it has been 'disembedded', indeed.

However, it will become equally obvious that there is also a second step in this transformation process, which I will call here the reconstruction or reconciliation of place. When a place has been physically transformed ('developed'), as in the case of the White Mountain downhill venue, the old place names and their associated narratives are erased or recontextualised, which means that local traditional meanings are forgotten and the place, phenomenologically speaking, is rendered obsolete – an experiential void in the terrain. As Ann Game asserts in her analysis of Bondi beach in Sidney: 'To put a place on the market is to erase qualitative distinction and memory' (Game 1991:181). The personal histories that were discursively sedimented onto the landscape through those narratives, as well as the social relationships and identities they represented, are likewise rendered irrelevant and simply forgotten. In time, however, as becomes equally evident in the case of White Mountain, new sets of actors will appropriate and claim the area bringing with them new practices and interpretations; even some of the former users will reappropriate the place for new uses, new events will gradually take place, new collective memories and shared narratives will emerge which, with a twist on Malinowski's phrase, re-enliven the new place in new spatial-narrative contexts. This means that modernisation should not be regarded as a unilateral 'emptying' or 'erosion' of the meanings of locality, but as a dialectical process moving between deconstruction and reconstruction, reflection and involvement, commodification and being, the subjective and the non-subjective attitudes.

We are likewise sometimes given the impression by the phenome-nologist students of place attachment that relationships between self and place are somehow irreducible and irreversible, and that any change is traumatic and even pathological. This is most clearly articu-lated in the concept of 'dwelling', the experience of spiritual unity between persons, things and landscapes (Heidegger 1993; Seamon and Mugerauer 1985; Ingold 1991). The events described in this study, however, suggest a more processual relationship between people and their physical environment. Place attachment is obviously not only an unreflected 'condition' given once and for all in a standard form, such as nostalgic or commodified. Place attachment should rather be analysed as an on-going process that keeps changing and adapting as elements in the environment change and perceptions and narratives are transformed. Eric Hirsch (1995) makes a strong argument that land-scape must not be understood unilaterally as either an unreflexively lived-in space or a distanced and aestheticised vista, but as a continuous and context-driven shift between the two attitudes. There is always the dynamic and salient 'foreground' of factual everyday practice, but also, and often simultaneously, the envisioned 'background' of fixity and timelessness. The tension between these two modes of experience are never resolved in such a way that the 'foreground' of everyday life ('us the way we are') and the 'background' [of] potential social existence ('us the way we might be') (Hirsch 1995:22) become a congruent whole in a picturesque, idyllic unity of time and space.

Altman and Low make the related point that studies of spatial practices in the modern era have usually emphasised the deconstruc-tive aspect. The reason for this, they argue, is that 'the history of New World Western cultures has been one of instability, migration, and change, with research emphasising how people seek out and adapt to new situations, rather than focusing on how they affiliate and attach themselves to their new locales' (Altman and Low 1992:2).

In this chapter I attempt to analyse such an open and on-going process of spatial change at Myrlia, the construction area in the 'arena municipality' of Ringebu where the White Mountain down-hill course now lies.

The Wrong Side

Myrlia is situated some sixty kilometres north of Lillehammer in the Gudbrandsdal valley which runs more or less directly north–south. The direction of this valley is the single most significant ecological factor in the processes I am going to describe, because it means that there is one sunny side of the valley and one shaded side. At sixty-two degrees of northern latitude this makes a significant difference when it comes to average temperatures and general agricultural and social conditions. In the local dialect the east side is called 'the spring side' (*Vårsida*) or simply 'the sunny side' (*Solsida*), while the west side is called 'the winter side' (*Vintersida*). This difference is particularly pronounced at Fåvang where the valley is steep and narrow. During the winter there are significantly fewer hours of sunshine on the west side than on the east side, which makes it quite unsuited for agricultural purposes and less attractive as a residential area. The few farms and homesteads found here are situated on the river banks or at the mouth of tributaries and they are considerably smaller and generally less wealthy than the farms on the other side. At Fåvang, therefore, the shaded side is simply called 'the wrong side' (*Baksida*) which, naturally, carries very strong negative social-structural connotations for people on both sides.

This has been the socio-geographical structure of the valley for probably one-and-a-half millennium, at least as far back as the Early Iron Age, when the first farms were cleared and built in Ringebu. Throughout history the east side has had a much more cosmopolitan and dynamic character, while the Wrong Side in all respects has been more local and, quite literally, out of the way.

The river is thus a strong naturalised marker of social difference, or a qualitative difference in Ann Game's terminology, a fact which was reflected in the public reactions to the plan of turning the Wrong Side into an 'Olympic site' when it was first presented. It immediately revealed public attitudes to the power structures that underlaid the mental map shared by most people in the community. For those living on the Wrong Side the change was welcomed as a possibility to redefine the place, to escape local history, and finally to overcome the social stigma that seemed to have been imposed upon them by nature itself and reproduced by the hills for centuries.

> Every now and then they open a new bridge across the Laugen [the river]. The ... mayor's old dreams are fulfilled, the Wrong Side (*Baksida*) becomes the West side, and the Wrong-Side dwellers can reach other people whenever they want. (*Gudbrandsdølen/Lillehammer Tilskuer* [GLT], Thursday 20 October 1992)

The new bridge that was erected as a part of the Olympic plan is here used rhetorically to escape the power structures and social

geography of the traditional agrarian society and to neutralise mil-
lennia-old meanings sedimented in the landscape. The writer of the
above article hopes that the Wrong Side will now simply be like the
West Side, stripped of the burden of stigmatic connotations, and that
the east-west relationship will become a purely geographical distinction rather than a social co-ordinate. He strongly wants this qualitative difference to be erased even though it has been part of his
lived-in landscape. Tilley insists that: 'Landscape is the fundamental
reference system in which individual consciousness of the world and
social identities are anchored' (1994:40), but this should not be taken
to mean that the insider automatically holds a preservationist view
towards it, which has often been the case in modernisation studies.
The statement thus indicates that even though people 'dwell' in a
landscape in the sense that they have invested their sense of self and
their biography in it, the *whole* landscape is not 'sanctified' as a shrine
of their identity. The Olympic presence offers a new context in
which the simple inside–outside dichotomy does not seem to apply.
Some insider voices obviously do not feel at home in the whole
social geography as it is given in local tradition. The above quoted
writer uses the metaphor of the bridge to express his notion of the
Olympic project as a possibility to link up with the rest of the world
and escape local power relations sedimented in the landscape.

Already at this stage we see that the Fåvang Wrong Side is a
highly contested space and that most of the people who live there
have an ambivalent relationship to even essential parameters of the
'inside' construction of the place, and that some also have a desire to
distance themselves from it all together. It is not a situation where the
forces of change are external and the preserving forces are the internal dwellers. Change emerges in the alliance between the Olympic
organising committee and local interests driven by the desire to
overcome traditional socio-geographical structures. But simultaneously, when these structures are changed, as we shall see, it produces
in some contexts a nostalgic longing for the pre-Olympic landscape.

This dialogic and ambivalent relationship was expressed very
clearly on a seventieth-birthday card message addressed to an Anton
Rønningen from his friends at Mælum, a farmstead on which the
piste was constructed and which they owned. Rønningen himself
had been born on a small farm which still lies very close to the piste
and worked during the war years on the Mælum farm as a farm
hand. The card, which was inserted in the inside cover of a book
entitled *A Fairy Tale of Images. Lillehammer 1994* (Notaker and Johnsen
1994) – his birthday present – reads:

Dear Anton!
Here is a memory of The Olympics 1994.
That was the time when the unbelievable happened,
that *Stranda,* for a few days,
was the centre of the entire sports-interested world.
When the alpine elite, with Tommy Moe in the lead,
raced down from *Myrlikampen,*
along *Torevegen,* over *Løftet,* through *Klemma,*
down to a sea of cheering people from all nations.

First of all, the book itself is a celebration of the Lillehammer Olympics describing the transformation of the place and all its future possibilities. When given as a gift on such an important occasion in Anton Rønningen's life it is a strong indication of their positive attitude towards the White Mountain development. It is even referred to as a miracle – the unbelievable has happened. They cherish the memory as a counter-narrative to the traditional social scenario of the Wrong Side. It says on the back cover that 'The party is over but this beautiful book recreates the fairy tale for us.' The 'unbelievable' event that, at least for a moment, disengaged them from the predicament of the vernacular landscape in which the West Side is a nowhere outside of History.

However, the text continues:

It was the time when hundreds of buses
drove the winter road across the icy river.
This time Blackie[5] was only part of a historical procession
to show how things were in the old days.
How would father[6] and Olaf[7] have reacted
if they had seen the Olympic hustle and bustle?
Probably they would have said it was better
in the days when the pastures were for the cattle,
when you, Anton, took part
in the ploughing, sowing, and harvesting.
That was the time when Blackie and Brownie helped us
pulling the harvester and the hay cart.
That was an equally precious memory.

Here, in the last part of the greeting, the nostalgic longing for the old time and place with the old technology, the horses and the hay carts, and the traditional agricultural practices emerges with a strong emotional tone. Also the social relationships of the past are evoked through the reference to the forefathers and their imagined gaze on the present changes. The conclusion is that both memories are equally precious.

The Vernacular Landscape

The name 'Mælum' means the farm (or home) in the middle, derived from the old Norse *Medalheimr*. As the name suggests it lies between two other farms, namely 'Strande' and 'Berge' and belongs to the category of so-called *heim*-farms which means that it was probably built sometime between AD 300 and AD 500. The oldest class of farms are those which have names referring directly to topographical features. 'Strande', for example, means beach, and the farm is situated on the western bank of the river, Laugen, which name means water. 'Berge' means simply mountain or rock, and this farm lies beneath 'Storhaugen', i.e. 'The Big Rock'. 'Myre', south of Berge, means marsh, which again is a description of the local topographical conditions. All these farms date from the period prior to AD 600.

Mælum has been in the family of the present owner, Anders G. Fretheim, since 1873, when it was bought by his great-grandfather. Before that it was in the possession of a family line that probably originated at Rottås, also on the Wrong Side a mile or so to the north.

To give an impression of the historical depth and how local social memory and relationships are manifested at the Wrong Side we can take a look at the genealogies of the inhabitants of the abandoned homesteads in and near the piste. The family which lived at the small cottage farm *Bakfor* (lit. 'Behind[8]) just before the turn of the century consisted of Johanne and Emort Storhaugen. Johanne's maiden name was Myhrbakken, which is the name of another cottage farm (belonging to the Myre farm just mentioned above), a mile or so to the south. Storhaugen, Emort's family name, is a farm situated only some hundred yards to the west. It is also the name of the rock just above the farm where the people at Bakfor also had their hayfields. In the year 1900 the couple moved to Storhaugen. After that, Johanne's sister Eli moved in with her husband, Morten Brendhaugen, who came from the farm Brendhaugen about three miles to the north. Then came Amund Linviksveen, also from the Wrong Side but a little further to the north, and his wife Ahne, the daughter of another woman from Myhrbakken. Then followed Alfred from Bergsvea, the neighbouring farm a couple of hundred yards to the south. The people who last lived at Bakfor, who moved out as late as 1969, when it was finally abandoned, were also named Storhaugen.

For a documented period of nearly one hundred years, only one man from outside the immediate neighbourhood had owned the place. He was from Moelv, a small town eighty-five kilometres to the south, and he stayed for only one year. In the sources it is stated quite bluntly that he moved back to where he came from. He was obviously felt to be an outsider. Similar genealogies could be reconstructed for the other farms and cottages in the area, which should indicate that the naming discourse has been highly endogamous with very few references outside the time–space frames defined by still existing immediate consanguinal and affinal relationships. The place is thus highly 'embedded' in Giddens's sense of the word even though the area has been both 'modern' and 'capitalist' for several generations. Social and spatial relationships are irretrievably entangled in such a way as to form one very close-knit and narrowly localised discursive unit. To live at the Fåvang Wrong Side before the Olympic transformation, meant to have your genealogy and general social relations as well as personal history organically attached to the place.

The same was evident at Mælum where several of the micro-local place names have no relevance or meaning outside the household itself and are not in general use outside the Wrong Side. This is particularly evident at the lower parts of the piste where most of the traditional names have become irrelevant in the new alpine context and have not been carried over into the new history of the area as a World Cup venue.

As the racers come into view from the finish area, and enter what is generally called the finish 'schuss' in the alpine jargon, they pass a small hill that used to be called *Hemkuhaugen* (lit.: 'the home cow hill'), a name that has its origins in traditional agricultural practices. In the summer, when the cattle grazed in the mountains, the farmers always kept one cow at home to supply the remaining members of the household, specially the children, with milk and cheese for the season. The television cameras which follow the racers who are moving at speeds well above 130 kmph, do not even get the hill into focus, and it goes without saying that for the commentators to dwell on it would be felt by the television audiences to be utterly irrelevant and annoying when waiting for the next skiing hero to appear.

Below Hemkuhaugen are the still-visible remains of an old cottage farm locally called *Aschehaugen,* (spelt with the archaic German/Danish spelling -*sch* instead of the modern form -*sj*).[9] The only thing the current owner knows about the place is that it was built sometime during the eighteenth century. He has no explanation for the name other than that a man called Asle had been the founder. The history of the place, however, is that it was built by one of the sons from Mælumsvea, Asje Knutsen Mælumsvea, who was born in

1690 and died in 1760, who practised as a tailor in the district. It is interesting to note that this was the only place that the farmer specifically did not want to be disturbed by any Olympic construction activities or any installations. Even if he did not know the history behind the ruin, he felt it to be a sanctified place because of its old age. For him it was a symbol of historical continuity and time-depth at Mælum. When he was compensated financially he had no objections to the use of forty hectares of productive farm land down on the river flats, but on this particular spot he felt that it would be sacrilegious. The ruin now lies immediately behind the huge electronic display boards. In the winter, and particularly during races when the piste is fully rigged, it is not even visible.

Lower down was *Mælumgeilen* ('the mælum corral'), which also was retained by the naming committee but which is not included in the official map of the piste. It was mentioned once by the commentators on Norwegian television during the Olympics, but it seems generally not to have taken hold in the alpine discourse. A *geil* is a corral or a fenced-in cattle trail used to drive cattle from one pasture to another. Such corrals were characteristic features of the cultural landscape of the Gudbrandsdal valley until well after the Second World War.

What today is the Finish Jump used to be a small rock called *Håmårn* (lit.: 'the hammer') sloping directly into a large, dried-out pond (Tjønna) where the finish paddock, the spectator stands, and the reporters' booths are now. There used to be a ski-jumping hill at this point, where the children in the neighbourhood played in the winter evenings and where local competitions were sometimes arranged. The people at Mælum used to dump their rubbish in the pond. All this has been levelled to the ground and the pond filled in, much to the regret of the present farmer who now has to pay the municipality to get rid of his refuse.

A few yards to the south–west of the paddock, approximately where the technical staff building is today, there was a small field that used to be called *Rompa* (lit.: 'the tail' or 'the behind'). According to local etymology this name appeared as a result of the construction of the railwayline across the *Mælum* lands in the mid-1890s. At this particular point it runs on a high causeway. On the lower side just a small piece of land was left, but the railway company was contract-bound to erect a bridge across the line so that the field could continue to be cultivated. Since then the piece of land has been called *Rompa*. On the upper side of the causeway there is a field with the peculiar name *Gråtarmålet*. This might be derived from the Old Norse word for stone, *grjot*, thus meaning the stony field. The local folk etymology has, however, another explanation building on a literal interpretation of the word *gråt*, which in modern Norwegian means to cry. The farmer at Mælum says that on the upper side of the causeway a considerable piece of land is left in the shade which means that it does not dry up properly in the mornings or after rain. This flattens the corn and makes it difficult to cut. At harvest time it was the rule that each man had to cut one *mål* (a quarter of an acre) between each meal. The man who was allotted this field had a hard time finishing at the same time as the others, and this could cause bad feeling at times. The piece was therefore called the field of tears or the crying field.

At the northern boundary of the *Mælum* property, where the lower terminal of the ski lift and the new White Mountain railway station are now, there used to be a field called *Hunnbettet*, the dogbite or, paradoxically enough, *Synnstland*, the southern field. In the local etymology these seemingly absurd names refer to an episode in an unspecified past where a dog at Strande, the neighbouring farm on the north side, attacked and injured somebody of the Mælum house-hold. For this incident, the neighbours at Strande were sentenced by a local court to compensate the Mælum people with a portion of the southern part of their lands. Even though the field lies at the north-ern boundary of the Mælum property it is nevertheless still called the southern field. In the Gudbrandsdal valley, and even in other parts of the country, there are several fields lying on the borders between properties called the dogbite (*Hundbettet* or *Hunspet*), where the owners also claim the same story of compensation for a dogbite (see Rygh 1964).

Between the main buildings and the railway lines lies a place they call *Viftarbakken*, waving hill. This name also refers back to the 1890s when the railway came through Ringebu. The father of the present owner and his eight siblings, all born between 1898 and 1913, used to run down here when they heard a train approaching and wave to the passengers. His son says today, 'The trains went slowly in those days and there was very little else to do. Nothing was happening on this side.'

The social and narrative contexts making sense of these names and places are thus not only local but could even be understood as endog-amous. To share in the significance of these place names, even to know them, one had to be from *Mælum* and the neighbouring farms. When the present farmer relates the names he is referring to people of his own family, close neighbours, and the collective labour processes they were involved in. Using a concept from Brinckerhoff Jackson we could therefore call the Wrong Side a typical vernacular landscape. A vernacular landscape, according to him, is a subjectively centred but communally formed and encoded space, 'small (and visible) territory essential to its survival and to its kind of agriculture' (1986:69). 'The right to use these resources derives ... from membership in a family- or leader-centred community: a web of interpersonal relationships produces and preserves the vernacular landscape' (1986:75).

Such a vernacular time–space framing is, of course, not compatible with the non-subjective, global sense of space advocated by the Olympic movement. Let us now take a look at how this historically bounded place was transformed into an open space of international sports and media consumption.

New Names and Narratives

We can trace this transformative process through the renaming of the different places down the hillside. Interestingly enough, in the Olympic phraseology the individual places along the course are no longer called places but 'passing points'.

Perhaps the most striking change that has occurred is that the different zones of the hillside that the down-hill course cuts across are now looked upon as *one* place, in terms of being a 'venue'. Formerly they were used and perceived as several different places with different names and histories. There was actually no generic name for the hillside as a whole, apart from the deprecatory socio-geographic term the Wrong Side. The construction of the down-hill course has thus had a spatially homogenising effect by turning a landscape, which according to Tilley could be defined as 'a series of named locales, a set of relational places linked by paths, movements and narratives' (1994:34), into one place.

The organisers were aware of the power of placenames because at a very early stage a municipal 'naming committee', was appointed which not only found suggestions for new names, but also formulated new elaborate narrative frames and connotative contexts within which they wanted these names to be interpreted. I will explicate these frames as we proceed down the course.

The White Mountain

The place where the starting house now stands was formerly called *Myrlikampen* (marsh hill peak), which it still is on official topographic maps as well as in local naming practice. As we saw in the birthday greeting to Anton Rønningen this was the name they used. Some hundred yards to the south-west, across a little plateau, is *Segelstad-seterkampen* (Segelstad mountain farm peak), and a couple of miles to the north is *Kvitfjellet* (the white mountain), a small outcrop of quartzite only a few hundred yards across but highly visible in the high mountain environment because of its light colour. The name thus never referred to the hillside or a mountain in traditional, local name use but just to this small rock formation. In the first round of project planning, from 1984 to 1986, when Lillehammer was still in the bidding stage, the name Myrlikampen was used.[10] Later, when the local project group was looking for a name to present to the Lillehammer Olympic Organising Committee, the International Olympic Committee, and the International Ski Federation (FIS), they wanted to find a name that had the right alpine connotations to promote the place with the desired image on the English-speaking tourist and media market. This was discussed with Marc Hodler, FIS president and member of the IOC, who immediately saw the potential of the name Kvitfjell. Both Myrlikampen and especially Segelstadseterkampen are difficult to pronounce in English and, besides, were not felt to have the necessary alpine aura. They both sounded too local in the Olympic and World Cup context.

Sometime in the spring of 1986 the name of the project changed to *Kvitfjellet,* in the definite form.[11] The indefinite form *Kvitfjell* is not regularly used in the planning documents before sometime between March and June 1989, after Lillehammer had been awarded the Olympics. For a short period both forms occur in the same context before the definite form goes out of use altogether towards the end of 1989.

In the vernacular the name for the small white rock on the mountain plateau is always in the definite form singular: *Kvitfjellet,* with the suffix *-et,* while the new form *Kvitfjell,* in the indefinite form, is reserved for the new downhill course itself. The lexical distinction between the hillside, the piste and the small white rock is still maintained. In the new Olympic and alpine rhetoric no such distinctions are made. Already here, then, we see the general process of eroding local meaning as traditional practices and experiences become irrelevant in new global contexts. In local parlance the distinction between the definite and the indefinite form is also an important difference signifying whether the speaker is a local person from Gudbrandsdal, or a stranger, either a foreigner or a ski-tourist from the capital.[12]

Because of the reservations towards the sound of the name 'Myrlikampen' the naming committee also invented a new name for the starting point of the course. They wanted something that sounded impressive and alpine, and chose the name *Kvitfjelleggen*, the white mountain edge. They felt it sounded a bit dangerous and forceful and would give the kind of identity to the venue that they wanted to disseminate in the media.

Dølastil and alien bodies

The starting house itself was one of the physical installations that were felt most strongly to be out of place by the majority of the local community. It created a lot of conflict and debate when it was erected and was felt by most locals not to conform to what is termed *dølastil*, i.e., 'valley style'. The word *døl* is a generic term for a person from a valley, and the adjective *døla* something from or of the valleys. It marks a contrast to all things urban. It is used locally to denote something indigenous and authentic in a proud and positive sense implying that there is, in fact, an endemic cultural tradition in the valley. The starting house on the Kvitfjell Edge was conceptualised as a *fremmedlegeme,* that is, 'alien body', in relation to this tradition. This rhetoric brings out the political aspects involved in the appropriation of the Wrong Side by the agents of the Olympics. Local people, even those who were in favour of the piste, felt that the outside interests should show respect for the insiders by conforming to local aesthetic preferences.

In addition to being conceived as visual otherness in relation to 'endemic visual qualities' or 'the essence of things', it also violated micro-climatic and meteorological conditions by its positioning in the landscape. It was placed wrongly in relation to predominant winds, in such a way that instead of being a shelter it was accused of being a trap for wind and snow. There is a massive stone wall towards the south but only a shield of Plexiglas to stop the snow drifts from the north. The conditions at this spot, the very summit of the mountain, are so rough that the glass is said to have broken several times during the early winter months. To the locals this is taken as evidence of how things go wrong when those who build and change the landscape do not dwell in it, i.e., have not lived their lives there and do not know it through personal experience. The technical expertise of the architect does not compensate for this lack of legitimate presence in the landscape.

The aesthetic alienation has first of all to do with the building's flat roof. The traditional roof construction in the Gudbrandsdal valley is a so-called 'saddle roof' (*saltak*) which is used on mountain farm cottages. Early in the process the municipality issued a design guide to preserve local building traditions and they found that the starting house would be a splendid opportunity to promote the 'natural wood material' and local building traditions to the world. It says in the guide that the tourist venues must have a 'signal effect' and 'advertise themselves outwardly'. The insider–outsider dichotomy is thus, again, strongly present in the planning jargon, a key category being *stedskarakter,* that is, 'place character' which, according to the municipal planning unit, has to be preserved in the built-up environment.

The motives of the architects seem to have been diametrically opposed to the aesthetic preferences of the vernacular sensibility. They take as their point of departure the gaze of the stranger, i.e. the international television audiences, which brings them in direct conflict with the insiders. 'The house should be formed as an image seen from the camera angle and in relation to the format of the television screen.'[13] From this external position their basic design concept was developed as that of a 'launching pad'. The finished product has later been described by one of their supporters as 'a cairn-like sculpture'. It is obvious that they are not thinking in terms of tradition but of art, which also was made quite explicit: 'The starting house had, as all creative art, a thorny path to completion.' This rhetorical style implies that the genius of the artist has had to fight the narrow-minded, local philistines. In the art rhetoric of the Olympic planners the artist and the entrepreneur are clearly the heroes. The local representatives were sarcastically called 'state authorised missionaries of building tradition'. The project was subsequently turned down by the municipal building board which wanted the grass-thatched log cabins which, according to their view, 'belonged to the valley'. At this stage of the conflict the LOOC responded by redefining the whole project as a 'signal building' so as to avoid municipal political obstacles, and funded it instead under the budget post 'artistic decoration'. Then they re-hired the architects as 'artists' and by doing so rendered the whole debate of building traditions irrelevant. A compromise was finally reached whereby the building was erected but the flat roof would be changed after the Olympics. It was still there four years after the flame was extinguished, and there appear to be no plans for changing it.

This episode shows that even though some local voices wanted to transform the Wrong Side into a global space, and make it 'substitutable' with the more famous venues in Central-Europe, it was important for them to control the development to make the place appear as modern but with a difference.

The passing points

Immediately below the starting house there is a very difficult part of the course on which competitions are often decided. It consists of a steep slope that goes directly into a left, then a right curve and continues immediately into another steep slope before it comes down to a more moderately graded slope. The competitors who descend too far down to the right in the first curve lose valuable time and speed. The first steep slope is now called *Gaupereksla* (the lynx path). The naming committee wanted a certain number of wild animal names to emphasise the wilderness aspect of the 'profile' they wanted to create for the venue. One member of the committee who walked around the area with me said that 'I even think lynx *has* been spotted in this area'. It was obvious that the names did not have to be moored in the factual natural and historical conditions of the locality, but, rather were used as promotional signs in a global media context.

Perhaps the most famous part of the course is the second steep that is now called *Wintherhogget* (Winther's cut), named after the then mayor of Ringebu, Erik S. Winther, the man who took the initiative to build the course and who is credited with the honour of carrying it through the very difficult political process to its successful completion. In *Østerdalen* (the eastern valley) there is a famous place called *Jutulhogget* (the giant's cut) which reflects an old myth that dramatic topographical features were formed by the giants (*jutul*). Similar names are found several other places in the country. There is an obvious intertextual reference to this tradition in the name *Wintherhogget*. The association also metaphorically establishes Erik S. Winther as a political giant.

The name also evokes the most dramatic event of the construction period. Because the sponsoring bank and the LOOC had already invested considerable amounts of capital in Hafjell, the main alpine venue a few miles to the south, under the presumption that it would also be the down-hill arena, the White Mountain project group at times felt marginalised. Moreover, the political situation was difficult in relation to the central government and the Minister of Culture whose mandate it was to minimise expenses. In January 1990 the local group had planned the start of the deforestation in Myrlia. In February 1990 the conservative Government, in their white paper on the Olympics, proposed that Kvitfjell be built on a provisional basis with only temporary and limited technical installations. This led to massive protests from the Ringebu politicians, as well as the local community because it would mean the end of all their plans for developing a permanent tourist industry after the Olympics. Their vision of transforming the place would not be fulfilled. The argument advanced by the government was that there would not be a market for two big alpine venues in the same area. The local chamber of commerce in Ringebu, however, started a 'People's Movement' and Erik S. Winther, the mayor, performed some very intensive and eventually successful lobbying in the Parliamentary committee for cultural matters. In addition to all these local initiatives FIS expressed a very strong wish to have a first class downhill and super-G venue in Norway for future use in the World Cup.

The conflict came to a spectacular head on Wednesday 10 January 1990 when the White Mountain group, with Erik S. Winther in the lead, invited the national media to cover the start of the deforestation of the main course live on the television news. As they were gathering, a message arrived from the Minister of Culture saying that deforestation under no circumstance should proceed. It was then that Erik S. Winther took personal responsibility and defied the government by deciding there and then that they would use the municipality's own development funds to go ahead with the project. He resolutely ordered the men to start their chain saws and get to work. This made him a national celebrity and a local hero fighting for the cause of the small places in opposition to the economic and political forces from the capital.

In a regional newspaper a very significant turn of phrase was used in the reports of the event, namely, '*Taler* kulturministeren *midt imot*' ('Gainsays the Minister').[14] What makes it significant is the slightly archaic and poetic phrase *tale midt imot* (gainsay), instead of using the modern form *motsi* (contradict). The phrase actualises an intertextual reference to the legendary King Sverre of the old Sagas. King Sverre was excommunicated by the Pope for fighting against the clergy (*Baglerne*) and finally breaking their power in Norway in the early tenth century. He led the fighting group called the *Birkebeiner,* which was used extensively by the the LOOC to promote the deep skiing traditions of Lillehammer. In Norwegian historical mythology the phrase 'Kong Sverre *taler* Roma *midt imot*' ('King Sverre gainsays Rome') has established itself as a standard phrase for a person who stands up and defends the rights of somebody who is politically weak and marginal against a superior power. It also evokes an image of a person of outstanding courage and self-confidence. This aspect of Erik S. Winther's character was always emphasised and admired even by his political opponents.

There are even more mythological references attached to this story. A regional newspaper wrote: 'The Olympics have all the characteristics of the fairy tale. The alpine venue in Kvitfjell is the *Askeladd* in this fabulous tale. The one that nobody believed in, who was even made the laughing stock, but who succeeded at last. Splendidly!'[15] The *Askeladd* (lit.: 'the ash lad') is the undisputed hero of Norwegian folklore. He is the typical underdog that nobody believes in, not even his parents (if he has any), who is laughed at by his brothers and who is always depicted as sitting at home digging in the ashes of the fire place. By way of his great personal wit and cunning, and often also magical helpers, he always wins 'the princess and half the kingdom' in the end. Erik S. Winther and the whole White Mountain project were understood in the context of this heroic narrative tradition. When the naming committee was looking for a place to name after him the most dramatic point in the course was felt to be the most suitable, so that the story could be remembered and retold.

Tilley reminds us that 'If stories are linked with regularly repeated spatial practice the name and the place become mutually supportive, and when a story becomes sedimented into the landscape, the story and the place dialectically help to construct and reproduce each other. Places help to recall stories that are associated with them, and places only exist (as named locales) by virtue of their implotment in a narrative' (1994:33). This name, the historical event, and its mythological background are an example of how the venue is 're-enlivened' in its new form. Already, events have taken place and new collective memories are sedimented into the new modernised landscape. It is not emptied of meaning, as implied by Giddens (1990) but, figuratively speaking, refilled with new memories and narrative motives that resonates closely with tradition. In addition, the place chosen for the new name was in a section of the hillside that had not been of particular interest for traditional farming. The new narrative of the transformation of the landscape was thus attached to an empty slot so to speak, where it did not have to compete with previously sedimented myths. It became autochtonous, as it were.

After Winther's Cut the course moves into a calmer stretch which is now called *Sletten* (the plain) and the gradient is not as dramatic here. It is a point where the racers can 'rest' and concentrate on the last part of the course. The name is thus chosen to describe both the topography and the technicalities of the race itself. However, there is also a third context for the name. Arild Sletten was one of the pioneers of the Kvitfjell project who, among other things, selected the original site for the course. There are thus three contexts involved as interpretative frames for the name: the topography, the down-hill race, and the heroic tale of the transformation of the landscape.

This flat, traditionally called *Myrlisletta* (the marsh hill flat), that runs along the side of the ridge for a few kilometres north and south of the course, is today the place of the mid-station area where most of the tourist development is taking place. Here the farms of the Wrong Side had their mountain dairy farms and the area was thus a very important place in the traditional agricultural annual cycle and is still dense with history and meaning for the local skiers. Directly north of the course was the group of mountain farms called *Gammelsetra* and immediately on the south side was *Myrlisetra*, the mountain farm of *Mælum*. *Gammelsetra* was in use until the mid-sixties while at *Mælum* they stopped their mountain dairy farming a decade earlier.

At this place people in general but especially the youth, used to spend most of the summer relatively independent of the social controls that were so effectively enforced at home on the farms at the valley bottom. The mountains thus carry strong connotations of pleasure and freedom which are still quite real for most people in the valley. A lot of old legends and fairy tales of love and romance, *trolls* and *vetter*, are connected with the mountain farms in most parts of the country. Places like this were also the scenes of a very important part of the folklore that was used to create the image of Norwegian tradition by the nation-builders in the mid-nineteenth century. Especially the log cabins are today still strong positive symbols of Norwegianness.

This cultural–historical context is utilised in the development of the area around the mid-station of the ski-lift to create the image of historical authenticity in the alpine venue. A restaurant has already been operative for some years and a second hotel is under construction. Hundreds of plots for private cabins and cottages are sold on the open market. In addition, the main investor has built a private group of cottages in the same national-romantic style. Several of the other more modest cabins are also built in the traditional style of the mountain farm huts. The argument here is again that the cabins must 'belong' (*høre heime*) and not be something *fremmed* (alien). In the municipal design guide this area is called 'The High Plateau' and it is emphasised strongly that the new buildings should fit in with the traditional style. The hotel buildings should 'continue the hotel style [of] some generations ago', and the private cabins and cottages should be 'akin to the older mountain farm buildings'.

As a part of the 'Olympic process' the municipality constructed the *Kvitfjell Nature and Culture Trail*, marketed under the heading 'In the footpath of the mammoth'. The oldest remains of the 'Arctic elephant' in Norway were found in a quarry down by the river on the Wrong Side and this is used as a 'profile element' to attract visitors to

Kvitfjell. One of the motivations behind the culture trail was obviously the effort to authenticate the new development, to establish some concrete relations to unspoilt nature and 'real' history. It was opened in August 1993 by the Minister of Environment, who said in his opening address:

> A culture trail like this so close to an alpine venue with its life style, reminds people of the real life. Those who understand this see how important the environment is. Those who never understand this, we have to be aware of because they can be dangerous.

Here, then, is a vague hint to the barbarism of modernisation. The traditional conception of the area with its agricultural practices is referred to as 'the real life'. In a very direct and explicit manner the Minister addressed the feeling of oblivion and obsolescence in modernity, that a modern installation such as an alpine venue empties a traditional terrain of its memories and de-signifies the place. This is a concern also felt by the developers and through a project such as the Culture Trail they want to compensate and give the visitors a framework and some clues to read the traces and signs in the natural and historical environment outside the alpine scenario.

However, the concern for the end of history, apparently, is not as important in all parts of the piste. The design guide breaks down the Kvitfjell 'plan area' into six main zones which correspond more or less with traditional spatial categories. Area one is the 'valley floor' where the architects are encouraged to create 'unusual forms' and 'new interpretations' both in permanent and temporary structures. Area two is 'The Slope' (valley side) which is densely forested and where no buildings or physical development is planned. Area three is the 'mid-terminal area' where the hotels and various service buildings are being built, and where, as we have seen, a traditional style and explicit extension of tradition is encouraged. Area four is 'The High Plateau' where the old mountain farms used to be and here, again, the guide encourages private cabin builders to be true to tradition. At area five, 'The Top', however, the guide again recommends the architects to use a 'bold form language (with the sky as background)'.

These recommendations might at first glance seem inconsistent: to encourage the developers to transcend local conventions in area one and five but to build in accordance with tradition in areas three and four. An explanation could be, however, that the mid-station and the high plateau are not exposed to the TV cameras during races while the top and bottom terminal areas are intensely focused by the visual media. The cameras dwell for several seconds on each racer when they start and finish and these areas are thus exposed more than any other part of the course to the outside world. In addition, at these places the racers are not moving, which is a banal but important point which implies that the viewer rests his or her gaze more on the environment and less on the racer. When it comes to the possibilities for advertising, these places are the most suitable. Here the planners wanted, as we have seen, what they called 'signal buildings' and designed the places explicitly to conform with the expectations and desires of the imagined stranger audiences.

At the end of the Sletten the piste splits into two courses, one on each side of what now is called Lurhaugen, the take-off point for the Russi Jump. Lurhaugen is also a name invented by the naming committee, perhaps to evoke connotations to the traditional instrument *lur,* a long shepherd's horn that was blown by the dairymaids to communicate with the farms down in the valley. The open area between the courses is now used for performances and entertainment during World Cup events. There is often a choir of women from the municipality which are singing the *Kvitfjell Song* to the crowds. On the official map of the piste this place is called *Spellplassen,* which, in the local dialect, refers to a place where the capercailzie usually carries out its mating dance in the early spring. The word *spell-,* however, is also the generic term for play (music, games, jokes, and general fun), so again we have a name with a double meaning. On the surface it is a reference to a zoological event that anchors the place to natural processes and history. But it also refers to the social event of the World Cup festival itself. The name thus plays on the duality of nature and culture and simultaneously reveals and conceals the transformation of the landscape depending on the situation and the interest and knowledge of the audience.

Here, then, emerges a general pattern that will be confirmed as we move down the course. The traditional names refer to particular topographic features and historical events and concrete persons, while the new names have a much more abstract and general reference. At this particular place no 'spellplass' for capercailzie actually existed. The new name refers to a phenomenon that *generally* occurs at this *kind of places,* but not at this particular place. The hillside is thus semantically rewritten as a more abstract surface to be gazed at from more distanced positions. Furthermore, the new names are characterised by a multivocality and an openness that the traditional names did not have. This seems to be a strategic choice by the naming committee in order that the course will carry meaning for the heterogeneous audiences of the Olympics and the World Cup but at the same time emerge with an authenticity to the national and local viewers and users of the course.

On the north side of this divide is the other dramatic steep and perhaps the most media-focused point in the course. It is a seventy to eighty metres jump called *Russispranget* (the Russi jump),[16] named after the Swiss former downhill racer Bernhard Russi, who was the chief designer of the course. Again, one of the agents of change has had his name attached to an empty void in the landscape. This place did not have a special name and carried no particular significance in local tradition. The present farmer at *Mælum* says that 'It was all covered with wood'. But in the new media context it is a focal point, first of all because it offers a lot of spectacular drama and intensification, but also because it is here that the cameras pick up the racers live and follow them down for the rest of the course. Each new competitor more or less comes flying into view of the cameras at this point.

The whole hillside from Myrlia down is densely forested with fir trees which made it the most economically important area in the traditional agrarian mode of production. This was the most important part of the hillside as seen by the owners at Mælum but, as we have already seen, in the design guide and the comprehensive plan the Olympic developers do not focus on this area.

From this point on, the downhill course follows more or less the old track (*råk*) from Myrlia down to Mælum. Here, a lively transport of agricultural products took place, so even though it was not a built-up environment it was dense with meaning and memories for the local users. In the summer the farm hands used to bring up fertiliser for the mountain farms and take hay and dairy products back down, while in the late winter and early spring large quantities of timber were transported down in long 'chains'. Some of the old names representing these activities are preserved in the official map of the piste, but the continuity is often only phonetic. Either the terrain is changed and the names kept, or the interpretative context is changed to generate new meanings altogether.

An example of the first strategy is *Myrlihalsen* (the marsh hill throat), which is the first passing point after the Russi Jump. Here the old cart road went down into a deep ravine so narrow that some people insist that one could put a log of timber across on the top and drive a load of hay under it. The word *throat* denotes this deep, narrow passage. When the piste was constructed, however, the ravine was filled in while the name was kept on. The traditional reference is thus physically erased while the purely poetic drama of the word itself is kept. In addition, it is an example of the principal difference between the traditional naming process, with its concrete and experiential historicity, and the more abstract generalisations of the new naming practice. The old name is in this case reduced to an autonomous trope.

The straight passage following Myrlihalsen is today called The Elk Traverse. This is again a name created by the naming committee. The elk (e.g., moose) is very common throughout the Gudbrandsdal valley and the entire south-eastern part of the country and has nothing in particular to do with this spot. Again we see the change from a particular to a general relationship between the place name and its reference. It is thus another example of a renaming that is directed at the uninformed stranger, the ski-tourist or the television viewer, with the intent to create an image of wilderness and unspoiledness of the venue. The second part of the name, traverse, is a geometrical category which evokes connotations to demanding movements of the racer in the terrain. It is a technical alpine concept indicating that the line the racers have to follow between the gates cuts across the gradient of the terrain. After taking off at the Myrli Throat they have to make a turn in the air to avoid a too oval line and lose valuable time. Here the camera is placed directly in front of the racer to create a dramatic visual effect for the TV viewer.

After the Elk Traverse they reach the S-curve, which is the only point in the White Mountain venue where there is semantic continuity on all levels; both the name, the terrain and the meaning is kept intact. The horsemen and the skiers are facing the same difficulty: one left, then one right curve in immediate conjunction in a very steep gradient. This continuity is emphasised in the presentation brochure: 'From old times a footpath of this shape has run through this area, and therefore we have chosen to keep the original name.'

Ibsen as promotional sign

Two very demanding points of the course in the lower forested area have been given names from Ibsen's drama *Peer Gynt*. They are *Bukkerittet* (the buckride) and *Bøygen* (the snag). In the summer of 1862 Henrik Ibsen travelled through the Gudbrandsdal valley on foot and reported from the tour in the magazine *Illustrert Nyhedsblad*. One night he stayed at a farm called *Elstad* a bit further north from which there is a splendid view south down the valley. The central motive in this view is the Fåvang Wrong Side with Myrlikampen and the whole area of the present White Mountain downhill venue. Ibsen made a drawing of the hillside which was also published in the magazine in Christiania (which Oslo was called then).[17] The culture secretary of the municipality found this drawing in the Ibsen archives at an early stage in the planning process, and a reproduction was printed on post cards that were later sold with a first-day stamp at the official opening of the course. He also initiated the idea of naming points on the piste from Ibsen's works that would be known to the public nationally and internationally. Ibsen's drama was in this case utilised as a 'profile element' in the Olympic planning rhetoric. Something that is presumed to be known internationally and with strong, positive connotations is intentionally used as an interpretative frame to advertise the place as tourist product. The nature of the profile element is irrelevant for this function, skiing heroes, historical myths, folklore, environmentalist images and literature are all examples of such promotional devices.

A pamphlet presented by the Ringebu municipality to promote White Mountain brings extracts from the original texts to supply dramatic character to the places:

> Either side, if you look downwards,
> over glacier, scar, and hillside,
> you can see, across the ash-grey
> scree, deep into brooding waters
> dark as if asleep and more than
> thirteen hundred yards below!
> All the ridge's length, we two
> cut our way against the wind.
> Such a colt I never rode!
> There in mid-air straight before us
> seemed to hang the blazing sun.
> Halfway down before the waters tawny backs of eagles hovered
> through the wide and dizzy void,
> till they swung like specks behind us.[18]

Such literary texts are particularly well suited for international promotional strategies because no particular group can claim exclusive rights to them. High literature claims general human relevance and emerges in this context just as much as the 'heritage' of the American ski tourist as the locals. Ibsen is part of 'world' literature. By adopting such art strategic affiliation to the place can be established without the insider–outsider distinction becoming relevant. The place becomes universally accessible by establishing itself as the site of high art.

The point now called the Buck Ride is a place of relatively little significance in the traditional geography. It used to be the site of two hay fields called Upper and Lower *Svebakken* (swidden hill). It is now a stretch with a series of bumps like those usually found in the major downhill courses around the world like, for instance, the last part of Die Streiff in Kitzbühel.

The new name The Snag, on the other hand, glosses over and erases a part of local history that is felt to be important by the people from the Wrong Side. At that place there used to be a small cottage farm called *Bakfor* that both in its name and in its spatial situation epitomised the position of the Wrong Side as a whole. The two small houses and the three acres of cultivated land lay on a north slope under the long shadow of *Storhaugen* (the big hill) which meant that it received hardly any sunshine at all, regardless of the season. The farmer at Mælum, who had been a member of the naming committee, left the committee in protest at this point when the use of literature was suggested as a new interpretative frame to dislocate this memory. To him it was not replaceable. It seems that the rest of the committee felt that the name 'Behind' had too negative connotations to function as a positive 'profile element' in the Olympic context.

In the lower parts of the course, called *Hemskogen* (the home forest), are two of the most spectacular points essential to the TV coverage because of their dramatic effects on the screen: *Loftet* (the lift) and *Klemma* (the clamp). Both names have traditionally been in local use but are given radically new meanings in the alpine context. When used by the TV commentators they refer to the technicalities of down-hill racing. At the place called the Lift the racers are quite literally lifted from the ground before they go into a fifty to sixty metre jump down to the Clamp where their bodies are literally compressed before being shot into the finish schuss. Most World Cup downhill pistes have passing points like this and the TV commentators regularly use the name the Compression for the Clamp, referring to the topographical profile and the particular demands it places on the racer rather than the history of the place.

Both names, however, contain particular historical references to the times when timber was taken down this track by horses. Behind the horse they had a special sledge on which they put a few logs to give the driver the necessary weight to be able to manoeuvre. Behind this they linked together as many as ten, perhaps fifteen and even more logs in a string. To be able to control the speed of the timber string they had built artificial curves and fences to reduce the speed. The downhill course follows more or less this old timber track all the way down from Myrlia. The Lift was a critical place because of the speed they had picked up coming out of the very steep part passing Bakfor, now called Bøygen. As one informant, who had himself been driving timber, explained it, the danger was that the string of logs could at this point overtake the horse and actually 'lift up' behind the sledge and crush the driver. They had to have exactly the right speed and make the right bend to slow down the logs. Then, at the bottom of the hill, there was a huge rock lying very close to the mountain side, leaving only a narrow passage for the horse and sledge. Here the driver had to keep his nerve and guide the horse at exactly the right pace so as to reach the opening between the rock and the mountain-side to avoid getting stuck. To handle a horse with a string of logs or a load of hay down this area took quite a bit of courage and was considered very manly, just as the downhill racing is to-day.

There are, however, different folk etymologies which explain this name in different terms. The present farmer at Mælum had always thought of the name as meaning something like the Loft; something that was high up as seen from the houses of the farm. These different interpretations show how names and meanings are created in a conjectural and transitory manner in the vernacular landscape, depending on the physical positioning and concrete experiences of the person involved.

Regardless of the historically correct etymology of the name, the existence of multiple interpretations shows that there is no unified and singular vernacular landscape and that changes have occurred through reinterpretations, multiple positions and physical changes, as for example the construction of the railway line three generations ago. As Hirsch has reminded us, 'There is not one absolute landscape here, but a series of related, if contradictory, moments – perspectives – which cohere in what can be recognised as a singular form: landscape as a cultural process' (1995:23).

Naming principles

It is interesting at this point to try to summarise the different principles of reference and framing strategies that have been applied in naming the passing points on the White Mountain piste. The first and most obvious principle is the reference to topographical structure, like a plain, a rock, an edge or a steep. This, as we have seen, has been operative from the earliest settlements in the valley.

Secondly, local fauna has also been utilised as a world of reference but in a slightly different way. In the vernacular landscape we found two names that referred to the animal kingdom, the Dogbite and Home Cow Hill. In the first example the name is not just referring to any dog, but to a particularly dramatic and consequential incident involving a particular dog. In the latter, the name also refers to a special use of the cattle for a particular purpose that anchors the name in a concrete historical practice. The Olympic use of the fauna, however, as we have seen, abstracts and generalises its referents. Neither the Lynx Path, the Black Grouse Curve nor the Elk Traverse is tied to any concrete relationship between man and animal, but, as it is formulated in the official map, 'indicates the passage of wild animals across the course'.

Thirdly, the narrative context of the construction of the piste itself is used as a semantic frame. Its heroes and memorable events are catalogued in the names of several passing points of the course such as the Russi Jump, Winther's Cut and the Plain. All these names refer to the transformation of the locality from an agricultural landscape to an alpine venue. This shows that even though the planners want the piste to emerge as embedded in local tradition, they also want to remind the users of the piste of the transition of the landscape. Again, this naming principle has been in traditional use, such as in the case of Waving Hill, the Tail and other places that was radically transformed by the construction of the railway at the turn of the century.

Fourthly, we see that in some places physical traces of traditional agricultural practices continue to be used as moorings for the selection of names in the course itself. The Myrli Throat, the S-curve, the Lift, the Clamp, and the Mælum Corral are all examples of this. As we have seen, however, both the Lift and the Clamp are reinterpreted in the new context and the old narratives have become irrelevant, forgotten, or are only vaguely present in the alpine discourse. The phonetic surface structure of the landscape, so to speak, is kept intact while the semantic deep structure is erased or dislocated. A name such as the S-curve is unique in that it is the only name that represents continuity both on the phonetic and the semantic level and it is significant that it refers to movements through the terrain and not the terrain itself. The name gives meaning both for a horseman and a downhill racer. It is also the place where the physical modifications have been least dramatic.

A fifth context utilised for creating new place names has been classical literature. The naming committee applied some names inspired by Henrik Ibsen's classical drama *Peer Gynt*. The historical–legendary Peer Gynt lived at Vinstra, the neighbouring municipality to the north of Ringebu, and a tourist road through the mountains west and north of White Mountain is called the Peer Gynt Road. Each summer there is also a festival in the area trying to attract tourists. The Peer Gynt legend and Ibsen's play are emptied of their literary content and used to present the area with an attractive difference to the outside world.

The final parameter for renaming is the technicalities of downhill skiing itself, or the structure of the piste strictly as a racing course and not as a landscape. This is evident in such places as the Elk Traverse, the Tunnel Jump, and the Finish Jump. This is the category of new names that has the weakest relationship to earlier naming practices.

Also, concepts such as 'tradition', 'old times' and 'local people' are frequently referred to as verification devices in an attempt to authenticate the new names. The most obvious example is the S-curve where the connection to traditional practices and traces in the landscape are explicitly pointed out. Another case in point is Sletten, where it is asserted in the presentation pamphlet that, 'Popularly this area is called "The Final Rest" '. As the brochure was printed and distributed before the venue was opened, the place could hardly have been called anything at all, popularly or otherwise. Such uses of *vox populi* are therefore relatively straight forward instance of invention of tradition.

Voices and Positions

All these topographical changes and renaming strategies, of course, do not take place through the mysterious work of some cultural logic like modernisation or globalisation. As we have seen, it is planned and implemented and even enforced by concrete groups of actors as premeditated attempts to advance concrete interests as they perceived them in the particular historical situation that was established by the coming of the XVII Olympic Winter Games to Lillehammer. I will try to indicate some of these voices and positions to throw more light on the naming strategies.

At the very core of the initiative to build an Olympic arena in the municipality was the ambition of bringing change and growth to the area. Erik S. Winther, the then mayor who became a national celebrity, sees himself explicitly as an agent of modernisation. He compared the development of the downhill piste with the railway construction that took place one century earlier both in scale and in anticipated implications. As the railway brought radical changes in economic opportunities as well as changes in the landscape, he anticipated that the alpine venue would bring a new era to the central parts of the valley. For Erik S. Winther, the Olympic event was envisioned as an opportunity to break down the barriers between the place and the outside world, an indefinite global commercial space. In other words, his project was not to preserve its unique and particular character but, quite on the contrary, to erase qualitative distinctions to be able to open it up for outside investment and consumption.

Also the local Chamber of Commerce at Fåvang adopted the same style of utopian rhetoric that was used so extensively by the LOOC. A newspaper advertisement that was used in the promotion of the venue, emphasising its potential for tourism and business development, bore out this vision in graphic form.

In this fantastic image, the White Mountain piste is given the form of a launching pad into a future that seems to have liberated the place from the confinement of place and history all together. It creates the visual impression of a place quite literally taking off into the unrestricted space of global market possibilities. Local identities are envisioned as dissociated from geography and transformed to pure future. After the Games the company White Mountain Development has

Figure 7.1 The alpine racer as hero in the globalisation scenario *(Copyright: Ringebu kommune)*

been formed to convert this fantasy into real world politics, a project which three years later is still open and highly ambiguous. The company has several times been on the verge of collapsing because of a lack of fresh funds. It was 'saved' by a major private investor as late as 1996 who invested as much as 100 million Norwegian kroner, which has made him a local hero, the insider's outsider as it were. As an outsider, he brings necessary resources that are not available in the required amount locally, but at the same time commits himself personally to the place. He also expresses a dual attitude in the way he envisions the place in the future when commenting on the hotel that is under construction at the mid-station area: 'I wish to create a hotel with a high standard,' he says, 'that is "reeking" of quality, but with an informal and cosy atmosphere. The way you find it at the traditional Alp-hotels of Central Europe. The architecture is inspired by old Gudbrandsdal farms.'[19] On the one hand he is making the place substitutable with other similar spaces, but, on the other hand, he is insisting on the particular 'valley style'. He obviously wants his hotel to emerge as a hybrid of the inside and the outside.

The same duality is reflected in his own personal relationship to the community. Initially he was looking for an investment object in the Olympic region, but he did not find anything interesting enough at Lillehammer so he came to Fåvang. He says that he fell for the place and immediately built a luxurious cottage at the mid-station area. He always takes pains to stress that he and the family is attached to the place emotionally, that they spend their vacations there and do not regard it only as a commodity. As he says: 'It is important to take care of the softer values in life, and for me that is race horses and Kvitfjell.'[20] He has also invested a considerable amount of money in a local art gallery, actually the largest collection of the most famous contemporary Norwegian painter, Jacob Weideman. He even goes as far as explicitly stating that there is a realistic chance that he will lose all his investments which is a rhetorically effective way of committing his own destiny to that of White Mountain. After his last major investment in the fall of 1996, which 'saved' the project and, some say, the municipality, he became an even greater local hero. From this insider's outsider position he has accumulated a capital of legitimacy that clearly facilitates the progress of his development projects in White Mountain. The radical changes he initiates, like a golf course, an equestrian centre and several more ski-lifts, are received mainly positively by the relevant authorities and not regarded as alienating the vernacular landscape by the population at large.

Perhaps the strongest and most insistent agent of commodification of the place, though, came from within the LOOC system itself, expressed in a project called the Norwegian Culture and Environment Park. This was a development strategy for what was called the 'Olympic Norway', where the whole country was recast in a market-oriented and other-oriented perspective as a leisure consumption space. The central area of the eastern part of the country, with Lillehammer more or less as the geographical centre, was demarcated and renamed 'Troll Park'. This area was then reconstructed as a tourist commodity to attract the gaze and the desire of the imagined Other, the potential tourist. It was asserted that what the tourist buys and pays for is not an actual historical place as experienced by the locals but an expectation of what he will find in the actual area, i.e., a fantasy. This means that to sell the area on the tourist market, the lived-in character of the place is not even relevant, it is perfectly possible to establish what they call a 'profile' directly on the expectations and desires of the stranger gaze. As it is said in the documents, 'The nature and culture landscape is the backdrop or the side scene for movements and experiences in the area.'[21] This commodification strategy sees the Olympic venues as the main 'profile elements', and, as becomes evident, the locals and the insider position has fallen completely out of the picture. Initiatives like this, then, are clearly instances of what Tilley calls 'capitalist space' by constructing space as 'infinitely open', 'de-sanctified', formed and informed by economic process rather than cosmology, more or less 'stripped of sedimented human meanings', and 'open for exploitation and everywhere homogenous in its potential exchange value' (1994:20-21). This project, however, was not a success mainly because it was felt to be too 'alien' in its reductionist and almost clinical professional jargon.

The same landscape as seen by those who claim to belong to the place is, however, much more heterogeneous and transformative. Anders G. Fretheim, the present owner of Mælum, is clearly ambivalent in his attitude. On the one hand, he sold the area and disposed of it through a commercial transaction, and it seems that he is not nostalgic about the physical and social changes that have transformed his 'dwelling' so radically. He always stresses how he feels that the place is transformed in a positive way, that it has 'come to life', as he puts it, and finally has become part of history. He does not feel that history has slipped away from him or that the place is emptied of meaning. Quite to the contrary, as a 'locus of being' the place has been enlivened. 'These days there is always so much life around here', he says, when commenting upon the fact that in the peak season he has thousands of people virtually on his doorstep. From the position of the owner the experience of place has not been transformed from a subjective to a non-subjective one or emptied of meaning, but, on the contrary, its meaning and experiential content is radically intensified.

Nevertheless, his relationship to the place is still undecided. He sees it as a commodity when dealing with the White Mountain project group, but still feels that some moral limits were violated when the small cottage farm *Bakfor* was levelled to the ground and the name replaced with the fictions of classical literature. He also felt it sacrilegious to level down the ruins of *Asjehaugen*. In other contexts he is very much preoccupied with 'local culture and tradition',[22] he plays the traditional fiddle style and he has restored some of the buildings to rent out to tourists.

This dual relationship is also evident in the attitude of the local population in general. Far from being estranged from the new place, the people of the region are now attracted to the Wrong Side in a way and to an extent they never were before. It has become an arena of exciting new social practices, relationships, and possibilities of identity formation also for the people from the Spring side, which is an indication that the role of the river as a marker of social distinction actually has been reduced, at least in some contexts. On Sundays the people from up and down the valley gather at the restaurants at the mid-station area gazing at the tourists, commenting on their strange behaviour and costumes, condemning and condoning what they see. But they also take part in the new form of skiing, both alpine and snow board, that is becoming more and more popular, not only with the youth but also with the population at large gradually displacing cross-country skiing as the most symbolically circumscribed cultural practice.

Still, you can always tell a local *Gudbrandsdøl* (person from Gudbrandsdal valley) from a visitor. One such diacritical sign of 'insideness' is that the locals wear their beaver nylon suits in the piste, the same as they use when working on the farms. In other words, they are skiing 'valley style'. This is a conscious and very effective strategy to differentiate themselves from the general, international alpine style and an effective way of establishing a relationship of sameness between the venue and everyday local life. The dress code seems to imply that 'We don't have to change to use this piste, it's our home turf.' They strongly despise the slick, urban style so predominant in the alpine venues around the world. And even though they want White Mountain to be a high standard World Cup venue, they do not want it to be substitutable with other alpine 'spatial units' (see Giddens 1990:19). The difference and the particularity of the place are thus re-claimed in strategies of signification such as this. As they continue to use the place they build up a new stock of shared experiences and narratives that gradually marks the place off from other alpine venues and also give it the meaning and experiential substance in which, eventually, new social biographies will be moored. Three years after the Games the major newspaper in Norway writes that 'In the middle of it all sits the downhill venue. The soul of White Mountain, a landmark on which the place builds its identity.'[23]

One of the best and perhaps most striking examples of this re-appropriation is Anton Rønningen, the old farm hand who received the birthday greeting from Mælum referred to above. In his seventieth year he actively joined the world of alpine skiing and literally reconquered Myrlia for himself, and, as it were, re-inserted himself in the new place now called White Mountain. 'I just had to buy alpine gear when we got this venue on the home turf,' he says. With his decision to buy alpine equipment and actually learn the new way of skiing and using the course actively, he objectifies through his very person the collective process of reconciling the old and the new place. When he was a little boy he and his brother had to use skis when going to school in the winter mornings. Their track was down the steep slopes along *Torevegen,* a place which was mentioned in his birthday greeting, approximately where the Lift and the Clamp are today. With his body and through his biography he thus represents the pre-Olympic, 'inside' relationship to the place, but with his new equipment, new style and acquired skills he expresses the will and the ability to reconcile the two worlds. Tilley writes that places acquire meaning and history by virtue of the actions and events that take place in them, and that daily movements through the landscape are 'biographical encounters' for the individuals (1994:27). By acquiring the skill to move differently through the landscape, to ski the alpine way and thus experience a new form of 'daily passages' down from Myrlikampen, Anton Rønningen is taking part in the process of rewriting his own biography and, in the process, creating a new landscape.

Notes

1. The solution that was finally adopted was to build a tunnel from the highway which emerged in one of the central squares just in front of The Bank, a magnificent building that was refitted for the Olympics and used for festive and ceremonial occasions during the Games.

2. Television documentary produced by Arve Granlund, NRK Opplandssendinga, Lillehammer.
3. *Stavanger Aftenblad,* 27 November 1991.
4. Address held by the LOOC executive Petter Rønningen at the public presentation of the plans for White Mountain at Fåvang 19 February 1989.
5. Blackie is a horse which Mr Rønningen used when he was working at Mælum. He has been a horseman all his life and has very strong feelings for the animals.
6. The former owner of Mælum who was Anton Rønningen's employer during the war years.
7. Anton Rønningen's father.
8. The meaning of the word *Bakfor* is very difficult to translate into English without changing important connotations. Literally it means 'behind', which refers to its topographical position behind the hill *Storhaugen*. The connotations locally are of extreme poverty. Many cottage farms had names even more explicitly referring to social deprivation than this.
9. The first syllable derives from the name *Askjell* (mod. Norwegian *Eskil*), from Old Norse *ås* God + *kjell* helmet. The written form was changed during the Danish period to *Asche*.
10. Letter from Lillehammer OL-92 to the mayor of Ringebu Birger Sæther dated 2 October 1985.
11. A document from the planning unit in Ringebu municipality dated 6 May 1986 is titled: 'Development of an Alpine Venue in Kvitfjellet in Ringebu Municipality'.
12. The same is the case in *Hafjell* which is always articulated *Hafjellet* locally.
13. Excerpts from an article in *Byggekunst,* no. 3, 1994.
14. *Oppland Arbeiderblad,* 12 January 1990.
15. *Dagningen,* 31 March 1993
16. This is another intertextual reference to a name already established in public consciousness, *Ridderspranget* (The Knights Jump) which lies not far to the north of *Kvitfjell.* This link contributes to giving the name an additional poetic evocation.
17. At the Ibsen Centre at the National Library in Oslo, the experts are not able to ascertain the authenticity of the drawing as actually coming from Ibsen's hand.
18. Excerpt from Ibsen's *Peer Gynt,* translated by Peter Watts. Cited from the pamphlet *Kvitfjell* by Ringebu municipality. Undated.
19. *Dagbladet,* Tuesday 6 November 1996.
20. Ibid.
21. From the brochure *The Norwegian Culture and Environment Park. A Development Strategy for the Olympic Norway. An Introduction to a holistic Approach to Tourism,* published by Lillehammer Olympia-Vekst A/S (Lillehammer Olympic Growth Ltd.)
22. *Gudbrandsdølen/Lillehammer Tilskuer,* 26 February 1991.
23. *Aftenposten,* 15 February 1997.

References

Altman, I. and S. M. Low (eds) (1992) *Place Attachment,* Plenum Press: New York.

Bachelard, G. (1964) *The Poetics of Space.* Orion: New York.

Brinckerhoff Jackson, J. (1986) 'The Vernacular Landscape' in E. C. Penning-Rowsell and D. Lowenthal (eds) *Landscape Meanings and Values*, Allen and Unwin: London.

Elton, L. and P.T. Moshus (1995) *Norwegian Olympic Design*, Norsk Form: Oslo.

Game, A. (1991) *Undoing the Social. Towards a Deconstructive Sociology*, Open University Press: Milton Keynes.

Giddens, A. (1990) *The Consequences of Modernity*, Polity Press: Cambridge.

Harvey, D. (1993) 'From Space to Place and Back Again: Reflections on the Condition of Postmodernity' in J. Bird et al. (eds) *Mapping the Futures. Local Cultures, Global Change*, Routledge: London and New York.

Heidegger, M. (1993) 'Building, Dwelling, Thinking' in D.F. Krell (ed.) *Basic Writings. Martin Heidegger*, Routledge: London.

Hirsch, E. (1995) 'Introduction. Landscape: Between Place and Space' in E. Hirsch and M. O'Hanlon, *The Anthropology of Landscape. Perspectives on Place and Space*, Clarendon Press: Oxford.

Hovdhaugen, E. (1976) *Bygda vår. Lokalhistorie for Ringebu*, Ringebu Historielag: Ringebu.

Hovdhaugen, E. (1954) *Gardar og slekter i Ringebu*, Ringebu Historielag: Ringebu.

Ingold, T. (ed.) (1991). *Human Worlds are Culturally Constructed*, Group for Debates in Anthropological Theory: Manchester.

Kamfjord, G. (1990) *Den norske kultur og miljøpark. Utviklingsstrategi for OL-Norge. En innføringsbok i helhetlig reiselivsforståelse*, Lillehammer Olympia-Vekst A/S: Lillehammer.

Kleiven, I. (1928) *Ringbu. Gamal bondekultur i Gudbrandsdalen*, Aschehoug & Co. (W. Nygaard): Oslo.

Kolodny, A. (1975) *The Lay of the Land. Metaphor as Experience and History in American Life and Letters*, The University of North Carolina Press: Chapel Hill.

Marthinsen, L. (1974) *Agrarkrisa i Ringebu*, Hovedfagsoppgave i historie, Universitetet i Oslo: Oslo.

Meinig, D. W. (ed.) (1979) *The Interpretation of Ordinary Landscapes. Geographical Essays*, Oxford University Press: New York and Oxford.

Notaker, H. and B. Johansen (1994) *A Fairy Tale of Images. Lillehammer 1994*, Grøndahl Dreyer: Oslo.

Ringebu Historielag (Ola Rønningen) (1996) *Nedlagde heimar i Ringebu, og folket som budde der*, Ringebu Historielag: Ringebu.

Ringebu kommune (1986) Fylkesplanprosjekt reiseliv. Delprosjekt private hytter. Ringebu.

Ringebu Kommune (1990). *Byggeskikk på Ringebu. Designguide. En estetisk rettleder.* Ringebu.

Rygh, O. (1964[1897]) *Norske Gaardnavne: Oplysninger samlede til brug ved Matrikelens Revision,* Børsum: Oslo.

Seamon, D. and R. Mugerauer (1985) *Dwelling, Place and Environment. Towards a Phenomenology of Person and World,* Martinus Nijhof Publishers: Dortrecht, Boston, Lancaster.

Tilley, C. (1994) *A Phenomenology of Landscape: Places Paths and Monuments,* Berg: Oxford.

Williams, R. (1973) *The Country and the City,* Pimlico: London.

Chapter 8

EQUALITY, HIERARCHY AND PURE CATEGORIES:
Gender Images in the Winter Olympics

Ingrid Rudie

Introduction

This paper springs from a fascination with the communicative power of elite sport. I am mainly interested in how the celebration of the athlete links up to notions of human excellence and, in turn, to the possible hard programming[1] of ideas about a 'natural' social order. More particularly, I will try to sort out some strands in the discourse on the gender of elite sport, taking as my point of departure some of its most salient symbolic shifts between 'feminine' and 'unfeminine' disciplines, and the double messages about gender equality and inequality that the history of sport exhibits. The focus will be on the images of female athletes as they are communicated on the arenas and the mass media. The empirical examples are drawn from cross-country and downhill skiing and figure skating, three disciplines that carry widely different symbolic loads and have different historical backgrounds.

The questions that will be posed revolve around problems of interpretation and shared meaning: can meaning be shared, and on what level? Can the images of different individuals be merged into a conception of a Generalised Female Athlete? What are the processes through which national and international myths about sport and gender develop and possibly change? These questions are nested within a more fundamental one that I will only approach on a speculative level: what is the possible impact of sport on the gender discourses in society at large? The Olympic event with its ritual and dramatic appeal is a rich field for exploring such questions.

MacAloon (1984:258 ff.) has described the Games as consisting of different layers in Chinese-box fashion – layers that he presents as game, ritual, festival, and spectacle.[2] This has inspired Handelman (1990:59) to formulate a more general characteristic of public events in which *genres of performance* are nested within one another. Gusfield (1987) has suggested that the appeal of sport can be explained by its likeness to a drama that speaks immediately to the spectators' life experience. Drama and ritual are forms of communication that convey messages in an allusive and metaphoric way. For this reason, and because they are stylised and set apart from the disarray of everyday life, they are compelling to the mind. Sport is well suited as a medium for drama and ritual because of its communicability: it is good to think with and to speak with.

Sport: Universals and Particulars

Sport has a unique power of fascinating and setting standards for human excellence across boundaries that usually divide: boundaries of cultural traditions, class, sex and age. On another level, different disciplines carry specific meanings that are not easily communicated in any full extent outside the ranks of practitioners and fans. Both these features, only seemingly contradictory, can be traced back to the same roots – to fundamental properties of sportive activities. These are bodily activities following universally shared principles of human kinetics. These kinetic experiences are in part pre-discursive or unarticulated, at the same time as their universality makes them easily understood and communicated on a certain level. But specific disciplines have also developed in close conjunction with specific local cultural traditions, and have acquired a rich load of tacit social memory. They are still to a large extent pre-discursive and non-articulated, but now the meanings separate and become inaccessible to outsiders. We are therefore facing the challenge of trying to distinguish between universals and particulars. Two attempts to define universal cognitive structures seem particularly relevant to the problems at hand – one is based in the creation of metaphor, the other in a universal 'grammar' of relational modes.

Lakoff and Johnson's theoretical experientialism builds on the assumption that a fundamental experience of existing and functioning in a physical world of contact, direction, and movement creates fundamentally similar patterns of understanding – a pre-conceptual understanding lying *beneath* language, but giving rise to universally identifiable metaphors *within* language (Lakoff and Johnson 1980; Lakoff 1987; Johnson 1987). As a cognitive linguist, Lakoff lodges the abstract conception of a cognitive structure within the physical and kinaesthetic space of the body. Some critics in the anthropological camp have found Lakoff's intent overly universalistic and philosophic (Fernandez 1991:10), and have felt the need to offer a correction by focusing on how metaphor is specifically shaped in specific cultural contexts (Quinn 1991). The unresolved question seems to be how to strike the balance between the universal and the specific, and my attempt to distinguish between levels in the communicability of sport addresses the same problem.

Relational modes provide another intake to ponder the symbolic or dramatic messages in sport. To this effect MacAloon, quoting DaMatta, draws attention to how athletic games both produce hierarchies in egalitarian societies, and egality in hierarchical societies (MacAloon 1984:256-257). The struggle for gender equality in sport fits in here, it is another theme explored by many (e.g., Birrell and Cole 1994; Blue 1988; Willis 1994). We may place these observations into a bolder hypothesis provided in Alan Fiske's book about elemental modes of sociality (Fiske 1991). Fiske argues that all social life can be read as configurations built up from four basic and universally shared relational modes which he labels Authority Ranking, Communal Sharing, Equality Matching, and Market Pricing. These modes, Fiske suggests, constitute a universal cognitive model, an inborn 'grammar' of sociality.

It is tempting to apply this schema to describe the heroism, fairplay ideals, and communality of sport: athletic competitions create ranking orders. The competitions for rank are designed and organised according to strict rules about equal opportunity. The triumphs of winners are shared communally, both by the winners' teams and their 'natural' communities (township, nation, etc.). Both the communal sharing, the absolute demands for equal conditions during competitions, and the celebration of the ranking that results, are ritualised and elevated to sacred principles.

The issue of gender enters here. For about a century women have fought for territory in elite sport, getting access to one discipline after the other, and this fight still goes on. The roles that typically emerge in this struggle, are those of gatekeepers and gatecrashers. Gatecrashing women's main argument in their thrust for participation has been about fairness and equality; the struggle for participation in sport has been one version of the general struggle for gender equalisation in society at large. To elaborate on the idea of relational modes, women claim *equal access* to competitions for rank in order to become objects of *communal worship*. However, the principle of equality acquires a double bottom, as men's and women's ranking orders remain separate. The conception of *nature* plays this trick: the biological properties of men and women become the ultimate sorting principle. The importance of this principle lies behind the introduction of sex testing in elite sport in 1968. The biological differences are expected to deliver final justice, a principle underwritten by athletes as well as organisers, whatever their attitude to sex testing *per se*. In this understanding, 'nature' equals biology. However, the category of 'nature' is a wide and fuzzy one in popular discourse: hard-programmed ideas about proper gender images are given 'nature' status. Hence the gatekeepers' resistance to women's participation in competitive sports was also grounded in arguments about nature, be it medical beliefs about the frailty of the female physique, or conventional moral and aesthetic views on the proper 'female nature'.

Hoberman (1992:111) suggests that the great concern about doping in sport can be understood as an obsession with purity and the genuine that comes as a reaction to civilisation: there is a need to see athletes as 'the last true performers'. The same argument can be made about gender in sport. To sum up so far, we may suggest that purity takes on the status of a supreme value in sport: the purity of natural categories, and of elemental social modes. These are guarded by strict rules of control and measurement, and each faultlessly completed ritual sequence of competition and victory culminates in a series of celebrations of a communal nature. Sport creates a social space in which different social modes, be they equality, rank, or communal sharing are cultivated in a form that is purer and more unambiguous than the more opaque and complex forms of everyday life. This purity accounts for easy understanding and fascination.

Underneath this level of simple messages lies another level at which the specific symbolism of separate disciplines can only be fully fathomed by insiders. Only in a limited sense can the Nordic enthusiasm for cross-country skiing and the North American enthusiasm for figure skating speak to each other. And, for that matter, it is doubtful whether a Nordic public, even if it rids itself of national pretentiousness, can fully appreciate the image of a Russian or an Italian champion. The male Russian cross-country skier Vladimir Smirnoff became immensely popular with the Norwegian public in 1994, to the point that his victory over the Norwegian favourites in the fifty-kilo-metre race on the final day of the Games was received with joy and – almost – a sigh of relief. But we must also remember that Smirnoff has partially appropriated a Scandinavian identity: he has lived in Sweden for several years, and speaks a hybrid but fluent Scandinavian.

We have now moved to the second level of communication, at which specific disciplines have become symbolically loaded in specific cultural traditions. I shall narrow my scope down to three examples that expose different aspects of the negotiations about gender images in sport. The first example shows how the image of the female cross-country skier has developed in Norway over a period of several decades, and how a global event like the Winter Olympics adds nuances to it. The second example is a classical case of the struggle for gender equality which was fought out around two alpine courses a year before the Winter Games of 1994. The third example – from figure skating – shows a sport in which glamour is an integrated part of the female image.

The Problematic Gendering of Cross-Country Skiing

As has generally been the case in typical 'track and field' sports, cross-country skiing was slow to admit women to elite competitions. The first Olympics in which women took part in the cross-country discipline was in Oslo in 1952, and it is a point worth mentioning that the Norwegian representative voted against their admission. Cross-country skiing in the Nordic countries carries a heavy symbolic load of male heroism, associated with military trials, Arctic expeditions, and everyday toil in the countryside in the olden days. Some of the early competitors after skiing became sportified grew directly out of two of these roots: the military, and rural occupations (Sami reindeer herders and Norwegian lumberjacks were prototypes from various historical eras). Against this background, women cross-country skiers were looked upon as an anomaly; it was commonly believed that they lacked the strength and stamina for such an arduous sport, and the toil and sweating in the track were seen as unbecoming. The traditional symbolic load of Norwegian cross-country skiing – the dominant image of the sport until the 1960s – could be taken as a popular image of Male Nature. Women's plea for equality was taken as an attempt to become like men – the purity of categories was threatened.[3]

Women's conquering of cross-country skiing in Norway is described in a book by Ingrid Wigernæs, leading skier in the late fifties and early sixties, later coach, and an important source of inspiration behind the decisive breakthrough when the Norwegians won the women's relay at the 1968 Winter Olympics. She describes the standard gate keeping arguments both from the points of view of medical expertise and sports journalists. The latter were frequently preoccupied with aesthetics – partly repulsed by the unattractive sight of exhausted, perspiring women, partly expressing admiration for those (like Wigernæs herself) who crossed the finish with makeup intact. Both Wigernæs's book and a photo exhibit[4] at Lillehammer in 1994 quote a sports journalist who, back in 1947, recommended that women cross-country skiers should refrain from competing for speed, but rather concentrate on making an elegant and graceful performance that would be pleasant to watch!

Soviet or Russian women have been the surest winners in international cross-country competitions for several decades. The Norwegian women have been among the better nations since the sixties, although not at the very top as often as their male counterparts. Italian women have made their way to the top during the last decade. All the time the image of female skiers has been a topic that has attracted attention. Glamour and grace were not the most striking characteristics of the Soviet women in their cross-country skiing superiority; they were frequently described as 'amazonic', and in the days before sex testing was introduced there were rumours that some of them might not be one-hundred per cent female. Ingrid Wigernæs was often complimented for her good looks, and this was certainly not to the detriment of her success as an inspiration and role model for younger skiers. This can perhaps also be an apt characterisation of the situation of the contemporary woman skier in Norway: good looks are a positive asset, but she should not be too openly playing on glamour. Her behaviour and speech should be task-oriented and no-nonsense.

The Winter Olympics in 1994 has been described as a friendly occasion at which an enthusiastic public hailed the winners regardless of their nationality. The cross-country stadium was crowded whether the competitors were male or female. Although the track had been engineered so as to make the skiers maximally visible around the start and finish area, it mostly ran through hilly woodland. This means that it was not possible to have more than a limited overview at any point along the track, and if it is a characteristic of the major sports event that it is thoroughly permeated by the media, this was especially true here. Commentators and giant television screens kept the spectators in the stadium informed of the situation at critical points along the track, and the speaker frequently broke in and directed the cheering, so that the voice of the audience was completely merged with that of the loudspeaker. This careful monitoring kept the public focused. Extra effort was made to present the women skiers as individuals before they started. After each presentation an athlete's voice was heard saying: 'Hello, my name is ... and I come from...' in her own language, or in a newly learnt Norwegian phrase, after which she was sent into the track accompanied by a burst of lively music.

Russia's Ljubov Jegorova and Italy's Manuela di Centa were the great winners of the 1994 Olympics. A stereotype of 'charmless amazon' stuck to Jegorova before the Games. After she had appeared in the daily television show that presented the winners, the public noticed her sweetness, and points were made of the fact that she enjoyed knitting. But her image remained demure and a little solemn. Di Centa's image is one of cheerful, extrovert, sparkling femininity. She played this out pointedly at the presentations in press and television, and this seems to be part of a conscious effort. At some competitions she has been known to wear a miniskirt over her tights because she wants to remind the public of her femininity (Stefania Righetti, personal communication).

The conception of gender in cross-country skiing has come a long way since the sports journalist in 1947 deplored the lack of grace and elegance in the track. Gradually, over the decades, the gap has narrowed between men and women in social roles as well as in some aspects of performative rules and body aesthetics. Waves of unisex fashion, the fitness craze, and the preference for a slimmer and harder female body ideal have been moves in this direction. But the expectation and celebration of a specifically female attractiveness has not been removed, its criteria have only changed subtly. Manuela di Centa and many before her have convinced a public that it is possible to be both strong and swift *and* attractive at the same time. When Jegorova became more visible as a total person, it was a more quiet and homely femininity that was revealed.

The images of the champions are broadcast and magnified by the media: if it were not for the television screen, they would not have been as clear and striking as they have become. Seen from the point of view of a Norwegian public, di Centa and Jegorova expose two different aspects of femininity that are widely celebrated, and join forces with the Norwegian models to form a fuller conception of what a female cross-country skier can be like. The symbol acts in an elaborating manner (Ortner 1973), adding nuances and opening new perspectives. This is an effect of globalisation as well as of parallel developments within specific local traditions.

Friedman has said about global processes that they consist in two constitutive trends of fragmentation and modernist homogenisation.[5] As a global and globalising event, the Olympic Games work fragmentation and homogenisation on the institutional or social structural level as well as on the level of meaning. It brings together different experiential worlds, splits open the local world of the host society, and provides simultaneous local and global belonging for individuals.

This may be where the fourth mode in Fiske's scheme, the market mode, becomes relevant. The market mode is often looked upon with some moral suspicion. What it does, is to split open the three previous modes; social life is made less predictable when the principle of choice between alternatives takes priority. In an analogous way,[6] a global sports event may be seen as a market of meaning in which popularity is the standard of pricing, and images are the traded items. But this idea must be examined critically. Is it really so that meanings and person images *are* traded? Can one image be discarded for another, and who does the trading, and for what purposes?

The expansion of the image of the skier is available as evidence to all onlookers, but it may be perceived and interpreted in different ways. Some onlookers may read national character into the images of di Centa and Jegorova, interpreting them as typically Italian and Russian forms of femininity.[7] Others again may see them as two sides of a generalised and ideal femininity. And yet another reading may see them as options for role modelling by aspiring younger sportswomen. A young Norwegian recruit is confronted with a more varied gallery of models than those of her own country. The expanded and fortified image may increase her confidence, but she may still not 'shop' for a personal style among a seemingly widened array of options. Personal style will have to strike a balance that tunes in with the tacit layers of each local tradition, layers that are hard to change because they are acquired early in primary socialisation, consist of specific layouts and movement patterns in physical space, specific configurations of modes of relationships, and specific mythologies tied to history, landscape and heroic figures. Elite sport is the most international of all activities, subject to uniform rules and standards. *Homogenisation* within each discipline, although more than skin-deep, may not penetrate to the bones. *Fragmentation* seems to come from two sources: from a widened pool of impulses that allow a larger number of different interpretations, and from the persistence of embodied social memory that channels processes of cultural reproduction (as a blend of change and continuity) into specific and distinguishable local 'breeds'.

A Tale of Two Hills – or a Prelude to the 1994 Games

We shall now move to another discipline and, at the same time, redirect attention from symbolic development over time to a close-up of one specific dispute that unfolded during a hectic week in 1993. It is an example of women acquiring territory in a quest for equality, and as such it is a very classical story about gate keeping and gate crashing, with some standard arguments on both sides.

The background and the events are, in brief, these: Hafjell was originally meant to be the only alpine arena during the Olympics, but shortly after Lillehammer had been chosen for the Games, it was decided that Hafjell did not offer sufficient challenge for all competitions, and Kvitfjell was developed. By early 1993 it had been decided that the men's downhill and giant slalom as well as the women's giant slalom were to take place there, while all slalom competitions and the women's downhill would take place at Hafjell. However, repeated criticism was launched against Hafjell as a downhill course. On Friday 12 March one of the major Norwegian newspapers (*Dagbladet*) specifically referred to criticism of the placement of the women's downhill, also revealing that the international skiing organisation (FIS) and the Lillehammer Olympic Organising Committee (LOOC) mutually tried to place responsibility on each other. On the same day thirteen leading women alpinists refused to run the last training heat before Saturday's downhill World Cup competition at Hafjell. They claimed that the standard of the course was not up to their level of skill and ambition. The women's protest thus completed a long history of dissatisfaction with Hafjell as an Olympic arena, and we could say that public attention was well prepared for such an action.

During their sit-down boycott the girls gave a press conference, and on Saturday 13 March all the major Norwegian newspapers as well as the local papers brought reports paying considerable attention to the event. The newspapers focused on the content of the women's argument as well as on the style of their action. It was also made clear that only a hard core took part in the boycott. Among those who did not was Astrid Lødemel, the one Norwegian woman alpinist who was believed to have real chances to win a medal in an international competition. She had won the training heat on Friday. On Sunday 14 March the actual competition took place, and everyone took part in it. Incidentally, none of the activists managed a result among the best. After the World Cup competition had come to an end, the discussions about the alpine arenas were moved to the inner circles of LOOC and FIS, and a final decision was reached in June: the women's downhill during the Olympics would be moved to Kvitfjell.

The following analysis deals with the newspaper coverage that followed immediately after the action and which lasted for about a week. The material is thus textual in the classical sense in that it is detached from its authors, and open to interpretative readings. We do not get access to any final 'truth' in the sense of the authors' 'true' intention, but we do get the signs and metaphors that are implicitly and explicitly used in the textual and pictorial material.

Dialogues and comments

Various newspapers bring similar reports in their 13 March issues. There are slightly different versions of a large photo showing several women alpinists seated on the stands, looking serious and determined. In one version they appear to be absorbed in discussion, in another they sit with arms crossed and feet resting high on the rail in front. All the reports make it clear that the women are entering into a dialogue with LOOC and FIS. The content of their argument is also made clear, and centres on the fast development in women's downhill over the last few years, a development that had far outpaced the challenge that Hafjell could offer. Kvitfjell would be a more appropriate match. Development had also outpaced the recognition of the skiing organisations: FIS has not yet discovered how good they have become. The main message is that time is overdue for increased challenges. It was also made explicit that Kvitfjell would offer a better spectacle and better television.

The women's claims are not met with direct counterarguments either from FIS or LOOC, but LOOCs sports manager Martin Burkhalter doubts the possibility of moving the competition due to practical reasons: plans may already have gone too far for the competition to be altered. A straightforward claim is thus met with practical and technical reservations.

Some press commentators are very supportive of, almost echoing, the activists' claim. *Dagbladet's* commentator (20 March) concludes his article by listing three good reasons for moving the match: that the women's downhill in Kvitfjell will guarantee great TV, that it will be a tribute to the women's policy in which Norwegian sports leaders take pride, and that it would enhance the probabilities for after-use of the hill. In other words, he lifts the discussion onto a level of political, practical, and entertainment concerns.

But newspapers also admitted doubts in various ways: by contrasting the complacent with the activists; by suggesting that the latter over-dramatised and had better 'make the best of the situation'; by reminding of the rules of the game; and by suggesting that women should possibly stay away from the toughest hills.

Astrid Lødemel got a great deal of attention, not least because she won the training heat. She was presented as one who sympathised with the activists' wish, but chose not to boycott because she was on her home arena. *Aftenposten* makes the most of the contrast, juxtaposing the photo of the determined and serious activists on the stand with a carefully studied picture of Lødemel, smiling, holding on to one ski raised vertically with helmet poised on top. The subtext says: best and boycott. In the text *Aftenposten* comments on the activists' claim in these words:

> What they did not mention, was that two months ago they were let into Cortina's challenging downhill course, so far reserved for men, with the result that many were injured. The Germans lost Katherine Guthenson and Michaela Gerg-Leitner for the rest of the season. Two weeks later American Hilary Lindh was so badly injured that she also was left out of the WC competition.

Winners and losers

At the actual World Cup competition on Sunday 14 March the winner was American Kate Pace, another woman who had not taken part in the boycott. None of the activists obtained a top result, and on Monday 15 March one of the local newspapers (*GLT*) took this as a proof that the activists fought for themselves rather than common interests.

The same issue focuses much attention on Kate Pace, who claims that she likes the Hafjell course – it reminds her of the one she grew up with, and the one on which she won the World Championship. The same issue also reports how Pace was celebrated by a local ski club of men who have made a speciality of preserving and dramatising the cultural history of skiing 'not only because she won, but because she preferred the women's downhill to take place in Hafjell next year'. This text is accompanied with a photo of the men carrying the medalists in triumph.

The next day's issue (16 March) brings the headline 'Praise at last in Hafjell. Ingress: 'Veteran Anne Berg (no. 4) and ski president Johan Bauman were beaming in competition with the sun in Hafjell yesterday'. This text is accompanied with a picture of the two in happy tête-à-tête.

These eventful three days brought out several inversions of winning and losing. As we now know, the activists eventually won their fight when the decision was made to move the Olympic competition, and their action had also been met with a great deal of respect and positive comments in the press. But the World Cup competition brought out other winners, and the comment that the activists had fought for their own interests instead of the common benefit of women alpinists suggested that there may be qualitatively different downhill styles more than one absolute standard, and that the activists wanted an arena that favoured their particular strengths.

The political victory of the activists was in tune with the main thrust of women athletes' struggle for territory: once again the gap was narrowed between the sexes and women were let into the prestige arena that had been the men's prerogative. But the sportive victory in the actual World Cup competition in Hafjell was the victory of women who accepted the conditions that were offered to them. Part of their reward was the amiable celebration by important men: the ski president, coaches, and the local historical ski club.

Voices of alpine authority

The press also brought interviews with Bernhard Russi, the architect behind Kvitfjell, and with male alpinists training there. Russi said in unambiguous terms that the hill was built for men, it was never meant to be a hill for women, and he supported his opinion on a technical argument about the limitations of the female physical capacity: 'To illustrate the difference simply, let me say that one bend in a track for men becomes one and a half bends in a track for women. Physically the sexes are different, and even among the 15 best female alpinists many will have problems with the Kvitfjell course.' He also likens the supreme satisfaction of having created this hill with the satisfaction that he presumes a woman must feel after having given birth (*Aftenposten*, 23 March 1993). In this way he efficiently contrasts male and female types of fulfilment in a way that echoes classical arguments about man the creator and woman the procreator.

On the same page, under the headlines 'No doubt, the best down-hill course' there are interviews with some of the leading Norwegian and foreign male alpinists, who all testify to the excellence of the course, and its excitement and challenge. Atle Skårdal, who is quoted at length, does not agree with Bernhard Russi's view that Kvitfjell is too tough for women skiers: 'The girls will have no problems running here. Most of them are good enough skiers, and by changing the track just a little bit ... they could have a suitable course.'

Russi speaks with the authority of one who has been a prominent alpinist and later created a superb hill, Skårdal speaks with the authority of the alpine elite of the 1990s. Russi underlines the limits of women's physical performative capacity, Skårdal underlines the flexibility of these limits, and the importance of recent developments. The absolute limits stand for unnegotiable nature, the flexible limits stand for culture and the possibility of acquiring skills. Thus we may say that the statements of these two experts represent the two poles in modern gender discourse. Attaching importance to the difference in age and nationality between the two commentators would be stretching the case too far. What can be said, however, is that Skårdal's view is more 'politically correct' and in accordance with women's struggle for new territory.

Metaphors and pictures

Two strong verbal metaphors emerge from the press coverage: the ironic characterisation of the activists as the 'trade union', and Russi's suggestive comparison between his own satisfaction with Kvitfjell and a woman's satisfaction at giving birth. 'Trade union' and 'strike' allude to the determined and argumentative style of the activists, and also suggests a contrast between amateurism and professionalism in sport. This is completed by the voice of an athlete who did not take part in the boycott, who underlines the importance of playfulness, fun, and acceptance as a better strategy than the activists' 'yelling' and complaints. The dominant photo, the large one of the determined women on the tribune, can then be juxtaposed to a series of other photos – of Kerrin Lee-Gartner in serious discussion with Martin Burkhalter, of smiling Astrid Lødemel who skied the training heat and won it, of Kate Pace being celebrated by the ski club after her victory, and of Anne Berg and ski president Johan Bauman 'beaming in competition with the sun'. One reading of these pictures together with their sub-texts and headlines and the verbal metaphors can be summed up in a series of contrasting characterisations:

'Trade union' and 'strike'	plain athletes
professionalism	play and fun
complaining attitude	acceptance
against the rules	by the rules
serious	smiling
conditional respect	celebration

This case is a contest in which the roles of gatecrashers and gate-keepers emerge with unusual clarity, and the arguments and symbols used by the two sides are inversions of each other. The main issue and its final outcome – the decision to move the competition – was in tune with the general development in the history of women's sport: a barrier was broken, women were moved closer to the men, the gap was narrowed, formal equalisation was moved a step forward. But some of the comments during the hectic week paid a tribute to other views: men and women are fundamentally different, and if that is not paid attention to, retaliation may result. The cultural process of equalisation took its course, but the reminder of nature's revenge lurks beneath. And, in line with this, victory became a conditional affair: the rewards of the activists and the complacent were of different kinds. The rewards of the latter were sweet and immediate, but the reward reaped by the activists was more costly at the same time as it was an investment in the coming Olympic event.

A short note must be added as a postscript to this case: in 1994 Germany's Katja Seizinger won the women's downhill in Kvitfjell. She was featured by LOOC's official newspaper HUGIN as the 'speed queen', but no mention was made of the fact that she had been among the activists in 1993. The regular Norwegian newspapers were remarkably silent on the event, which had its obvious explanation. No Norwegian woman alpinists were among the best, but Norwegian male skaters and cross-country skiers won some of their most solid victories on the same day, and unavoidably made the headlines.

Mythical Prototypes in Figure Skating

Figure skating is the most glamorous of winter sports, and the one most closely associated with a female aesthetic, although both men and women perform in it. According to Abigail Feder (1995:23) the stress put on conventional femininity may be a strategy to ensure the difference between the sexes in a sport in which the actual performances of men and women are very similar. Youth is also an issue; the sport favours lightness and flexibility over the strength and perseverance of adulthood, and is in this respect almost an antithesis to cross-country skiing. While many cross-country skiers follow up their best successes well into their thirties, 29-year-old Katarina Witt was described by the newspapers as the 'grand old lady' of figure skating. Many figure skating champions are in their teens, and the staging of the competitions also signals dependence and vulnerability. The athlete is maximally exposed in a solo or dual performance, and the woman is dressed in a ballet-like costume that exposes arms, legs and neck. After the performance the athlete joins the coach and waits anxiously for the results, and the suspense is released in an emotional reaction and hugs of joy or comfort visible to all.

The ice rink at Hamar, where the 1994 competitions took place, is a steep amphitheatre constructed so that the audience gets a feeling of sitting close to the performers. The women's free skating on 25 February was an event at which several mythical themes were worked through. Four performers will suffice to convey a concentrate of the dramatic content of the sport: Katarina Witt, who had won Olympic gold twice, performed in her last Olympic competition. She ended up with a seventh place, and was dethroned by a sixteen-year-old girl, Oksana Baiul, from Ukraine. These two – the winner of the past and of the present – got a great deal of positive attention before and after the competition. Katarina Witt just wanted to experience another Olympic event, she was prepared to withdraw in dignity. She was warmly cheered by the public, not least because she had engaged herself in Olympic Aid to Sarajevo.

Oksana Baiul was an orphan from a poor background and a society at a dramatic historical crossroads, and was quite unknown before the Lillehammer Olympics. She was very young and looked childlike; she had fought against odds, and there are sad features in her life history. Two other performers, Tonya Harding and Nancy Kerrigan, had an immense amount of attention before and during the Games because of the jealousy and conflict between them, a conflict made into a true soap opera by American media . 'The beauty and the beast' was the analogy frequently used to describe the style of the American media coverage, and the Norwegian press kept an ironic distance to the story. This ability to keep distance is probably also because the Norwegian public had nothing at stake in this competition: no Norwegian athlete took part. In fact, Norway has not had a figure skater of international class since Sonja Henie, and there is little emotional involvement in the sport.[8]

In the audience at Hamar Americans were numerous, and they expressed their sympathies very clearly. There were banners with slogans like 'Go home, Tonya' and 'We Love Nancy'. Tonya Harding's performance was beset with tension and bad luck; she interrupted her first attempt because of a broken bootlace, and was allowed a second try. She had an asthmatic fit after the performance, and she ended up number eight. Nancy Kerrigan won the silver medal, not quite up to the expectations of her warmest supporters, who had hoped for her to win the gold. Another dramatic twist to the story was an incident that had happened during a training session the day before the competition: Oksana Baiul had an accident on the ice while practising, and most of the competitors rushed to help her, including – as one newspaper wrote – 'doubly gold-handed Katarina Witt', but Nancy Kerrigan continued with her programme without paying attention. This, according to some commentators, made the ideal picture of her crack a little. And Oksana was on painkillers when she skated her winning performance.

Figure skating is antithetical to cross-country skiing in more than one respect: cross-country events are extensive in space, there is a larger distance between public and performer, and many stimuli compete with the race itself for the attention of the spectators. A figure skating event is like a *cabaret intime* in comparison, and the whole aesthetics and character of the performance are such that more aspects of the person in focus are made visible. In his analysis of sport as drama, Gusfield (1987) mentions the 'David and Goliath' myth as one popular theme that is sometimes the outcome of a sports competition when the unknown athlete or team wins over the famous one. The romantic setting of figure skating brings in other stories – more directly linked to ballet, opera, and movies. The figure skating event in 1994 was partly beset with the theme of beauty and the beast. The outcome of the competition was more than anything a Cinderella story.[9] Vulnerability is also an important theme. Of course all athletes are vulnerable; elite sport takes its toll in the form of skeletal and muscular injuries, and in some disciplines even fatal accidents occur. In the figure skating of 1994 the vulnerability was woven into the myths about the individual athletes and given an additional moral twist: there was Nancy Kerrigan's leg injury for which Tonya Harding was blamed; for some time it looked doubtful if either of them would make it to the Olympics. There was Oksana Baiul's accident on the ice, when some points were subtracted from Nancy Kerrigan's moral account and an extra heroic tinge was added to Oksana's victory. Finally there was Tonya Harding's bad luck, partly blamed on the strain and stress that she had been going through, partly interpreted as deserved punishment for having purportedly injured Nancy Kerrigan's leg earlier in the season.

Concluding Points

I began this discussion by stating a fascination with the communicative power of sport. The gender discourses of sport has been the main topic explored, and analytical importance has been attached to the specific way in which athletic activities work symbolically, and to the specific nature of major sports events, particularly the Olympics, as performative genres. In an attempt to sum up the discussion and reach some conclusive points, let me retrace these topics briefly.

Gender discourses in modern society are complex and contain contradictory messages, and the dramas and rituals of sport exhibit them in distilled form. The Olympic Games stand for a complexity and ritual elaboration unmatched by any other sports events. The Olympic event conveys within one organisational frame a multitude of different sports disciplines that are in their turn loaded with meaning according to different cultural traditions, as our examples have shown. The history of cross-country skiing, at least since mid-century, is beset with a struggle for gender equality that forms part of the struggle going on in modern society at large, and out of this struggle – in sport and in society – emerges a person construction in which strength and female attractiveness are not mutually exclusive. We have also seen that this picture develops and gives room for multiple interpretations even if we limit our standpoint to that of a Norwegian public, and the Olympic event contributes to this development.

Figure skating occupies a space in which struggle for gender equality seems distant. In fact, efforts seem more set on exaggerating gender difference not only through romantic trappings, but also by the stress put on technical and artistic criteria that may camouflage the purely athletic strength of a woman skater (Feder 1995:29-32). Here is a space in which the illusion of the female athlete as junior, dependent, and vulnerable is allowed to be cultivated. Again, the depth of appreciation of this imagery will vary with the cultural background of the public – for instance between the US and Norway, and, again, specific persons and events in the Olympic Games have added to the symbolic load of the discipline.

Seen more broadly, these two examples represent two opposing trends which also compete in modern society at large: between challenging and confirming the gender gap. In the case of the alpine activists, this tension came to a bursting point, and an intensive phase in the ongoing dispute was released.

So far, we have stressed negotiations and complexity. But can we also detect a general message about gender in sport, a message that may be of an overarching or homogenising nature? Earlier in this paper I suggested that an important clue lies in how sport opens up for – indeed is modelled on – ritualisation and cultivation of pure categories, whether they be the pure social modes of equality, hierarchy and communality, or the purity of 'natural' human categories.

In her influential article from 1974 Sherry Ortner created an equation about nature and culture in order to demonstrate why men rank above women in human societies. Later critics have argued that she got it wrong on most points, but the intention and the intellectual adventure of her reasoning are none the less thought-provoking. Ortner believed that culture was valued above nature universally. I will venture to suggest that in modern society Nature is about to gain rank over Culture as final truth, perhaps as a recent phenomenon, perhaps as a result of civilisation pessimism and environmental concern (see also Hoberman 1992). Nature is awesome and final, Culture is treacherous and potentially destructive.

Nature	*Culture*
final	temporary
true	treacherous
absolute	negotiable
striking back	tampering
inborn	acquired
capacity	training

The first four pairs apply to the nature/culture distinction in general, the two last carry special reference to human qualities. As a result of the political activity that has taken place in society at large, and in sport, the number of male and female qualities that are seen as inborn has been greatly reduced. Further, male and female hierarchies have become merged at the same time as the very idea of hierarchy has tended to fall from grace. Sport efficiently sorts them out again with its concern for both pure categories and unambiguous ranking resulting from the competitions.

Will male hierarchy finally rank above the female? Unambiguous rank implies comparability. In some sports where the criteria are simple, comparison also becomes simple. In cross-country skiing the criterion is speed over a certain distance, and physical qualities like muscular mass and lung capacity give an advantage to the male body. Although women's performances have closed considerably in on those of men, there are few who believe that the biological advantage of maleness will be completely overcome in this discipline, therefore the new image of strong and swift women is not really seen as eliminating the categorical distinction between male and female. In figure skating flexibility and acrobatic ability are more important than mere strength, and there is no obvious advantage in being male.[10] If Feder is correct, hierarchies must be kept separate by holding on to a culturally hard-programmed conception of Female Nature. It is, perhaps, also not coincidental that this elaboration is created in societies where a conservative gender ideology dominates in broad groups of the population.

We must ask some questions about the power of these messages. Can the truth of sport affect our view of social order in general, and what, anyway, constitutes the truth of sport? Gusfield's suggestion that sport is drama underlines the immediate recognisability of failures and successes in sport and 'real life'. The recognisability itself rests in the simplicity of sport on one level: bodily activities is a sub-linguistic or even pre-symbolic field of experience that will always guarantee some degree of understanding across even the deepest cultural cleavages. On the next level of understanding ascription of specific meaning takes place as signs are interpreted against specific cultural luggages. The signs then act metaphorically, or as elaborating symbols, in such a way that new paths of understanding can be opened. Therefore we can also not exclude the possibility that the carefully guarded gender ranks in sport can make their way back into world views that have recently striven to rid themselves of such hierarchies.

The nesting of performative genres within one another (Handelman 1990) secures the redundancy needed in order to efficiently sediment the 'truths' communicated. MacAloon stresses game and ritual, Gusfield stresses drama. It may be discussed how thoroughly drama and ritual should be distinguished – in my opinion the following distinction seems useful: a drama is an enacted story that speaks to an audience because it contains elements that are immediately appealing or understandable in terms of people's own experience. It unfolds as a specific story with a certain illusion of realism in the sense that there are at least sequences, motifs, problems or 'truths' that could have been taken directly out of 'real life'. A ritual is an ordered sequence that adds a cosmic dimension to the drama. A ritual speaks through its strict patterns and predictability; it is at the same time more real and more unreal than the drama. It is unreal in the sense that it need not tell a story with any claim to real life credibility. It is real in the sense that it unites the participants instantly in a common experience. The layer of *game* in MacAloon's 'Chinese boxes' secures the ambiguity of truth. A game is make-believe, but at the same time also a model for 'reality' (Geertz 1966), and ritual imbues it with a kind of sacredness and finality.

Notes

1. According to Bateson (1972:502) 'hard-programmed ideas become nuclear or nodal within constellations of other ideas, because the survival of these other ideas depends on how they fit with the hard-programmed ideas'.
2. According to MacAloon, spectacle and festival are 'metagenres... distinguished by their capacity to link organically...differentiated forms of symbolic action into new wholes by means of a common spatiotemporal location, expressive theme, affective style, ideological intention, or social function. In each of these ways, Olympism attempts to marry the genres of ritual and game.' (MacAloon 1984:250).
3. See Gullestad 1986 and 1989 on the difficulty of distinguishing between *equality* and *sameness*.
4. The exhibit was produced by the OL 1994 Women's Forum at Lillehammer.
5. '[Ethnic and cultural] fragmentation and modernist homogenisation are not two arguments, two opposing views of what is happening in the world today, but two constitutive trends of global reality' (Friedman 1994:102).
6. Of course, the market principle enters sports in a direct way through sponsorship, bonuses, professionalism and the 'trade' in team game players. This, however, is a vast topic in itself, and can not be covered in this study of gender discourse.
7. Needless to say, such interpretations are bound to be stereotypical and superficial. In a portrait interview of di Centa and Belmondo in Sciare (n.d.), Stefania Righetti draws a different and more nuanced picture.
8. At the peak of her skating career Sonja Henie went to Hollywood, made a series of movies and staged a commercial ice show. Her activities probably contributed a great deal to the glamourisation of figure skating.
9. After this was written, I became acquainted with Baugham's book *Women on Ice* (1995) in which a number of parallel observations are made.
10. This also applies to a new discipline, freestyle skiing, but freestyle competitions lack the romantic trappings of figure skating. At the 1994 Olympics freestyle events drew a young public and were accompanied by rock music. Men and women competed in the same event, although in different classes. The whole arrangement gave off a message of unisex youthfulness. This is yet another interesting voice in the negotiations about gender categories.

References

Baugham, C (ed.) (1995) *Women on Ice. Feminist Essays on the Tonya Harding/Nancy Kerrigan Spectacle,* Routledge: New York.

Bateson, G. (1972) *Steps to an ecology of mind,* Ballantine Books: New York.

Birrell, S. and S. Cole (eds) (1994) *Women, Sport, and Culture,* Human Kinetics: Champaign, Ill.

Blue, A. (1988) *Faster, Higher, Further. Women's Triumphs and Disasters at the Olympics,* Virago Press Ltd: London.

Feder, A.M. (1995) 'A radiant Smile from the Lovely Lady' in C. Baughman (ed.), *Women on Ice. Feminist Essays on the Tonya Harding/Nancy Kerrigan Spectacle,* Routledge: New York.

Fernandez J.W. (1991) 'Introduction: Confluences of Inquiry' in J.W. Fernandez (ed.), *Beyond Metaphor. The Theory of Tropes in Anthropology,* Stanford University Press: Stanford.

Fiske, A.P. (1991) *Structures of Social Life. The Four Elementary forms of Human Relations,* The Free Press: New York.

Friedman, J. (1994) *Cultural Identity and Global Process,* Sage Publications: London.

Geertz, C. (1966) 'Religion as a Cultural System' in M. Banton (ed.) *Anthropological Approaches to the Study of Religion,* Tavistock Publications: London.

Gullestad, M. (1986) 'Symbolic fences in urban Norwegian neighbourhoods' in *Ethnos* 51:1-2, pp. 52-69.

Gullestad, M. (1989) *Kultur og hverdagsliv,* Universitetsforlaget: Oslo.

Gusfield J. (1987) 'Sports as Story: Content and Form in Agonistic Games' in Kang Shin-pyo, J.J. MacAloon and R. DaMatta (eds.) *The Olympics and Cultural Exchange,* The Institute for Ethnological Studies, Hanyang University, Korea.

Handelman, D. (1990) *Models and mirrors: towards an anthropology of public events,* Cambridge University Press: Cambridge.

Hoberman, J. (1992) *Mortal Engines. The Science of Performance and the Dehumanization of Sport,* The Free Press: New York.

Johnson, M. (1987) *The Body in the Mind: The Bodily Basis of Meaning, Imagination, and Reason,* Chicago University Press: Chicago.

Lakoff, G. (1987) *Women, Fire, and Dangerous Things. What Categories Reveal About the Mind,* The University of Chicago Press: Chicago and London.

Lakoff, G. and M. Johnson (1980) *Metaphors We Live By,* University of Chicago Press: Chicago.

MacAloon, J.J. (1984) 'Olympic Games and the Theory of Spectacle in Modern Societies' in J.J. MacAloon (ed.) *Rite, Drama, Festival, Spectacle. Rehearsals toward a Theory of Cultural Performance,* Institute for the Study of Human Issues: Philadelphia.

MacAloon, J.J. (1987) 'An Observer's View of Sport Sociology', *Sociology of Sport Journal*, 4:103-115.

Ortner, S. (1973) 'On Key Symbols', *American Anthropologist*, 75:1338-46.

Ortner, S. (1974) 'Is Female to Male as Nature is to Culture?' in Rosaldo, M. and L. Lamphere (eds) *Woman, Culture & Society*, Stanford University Press: Stanford.

Quinn, N. (1991)'The cultural basis of metaphor' in J.W. Fernandez (ed.), *Beyond Metaphor. The Theory of Tropes in Anthropology*, Stanford University Press: Stanford.

Righetti, S. (n.d.) 'Temaer for to' Translated from the Italian by the author. Originally published in *Sciare*.

Wigernæs, I (1968) *Mot mål med jentutn*, Aschehoug: Oslo.

Willis, P. (1994) 'Women in sport and ideology' in Birrell, S. and S. Cole (eds.) (1994) *Women, Sport, and Culture*, Human Kinetics: Champaign, Ill.

Chapter 9

THE SPECTACLE OF HEROIC MASCULINITY:
Vegard Ulvang and Alberto Tomba in the Olympic Winter Games of Albertville

Eduardo P. Archetti

The ideology of the Olympic Games is based on the cult of humanity and the celebration of a true internationalism. These values are displayed periodically in a highly ritualistic context: the Games themselves. The Games are then seen as a communion of the humanity, of equal human beings, of independent and free persons. Thus, thinkers of modernity like Coubertin imagined that in a world of increasing complexity and differentiation, the only traits which members of modern societies retained in common was their humanity. The modern Coubertinian ideal became consecrated in the context of the Games. The Games made possible the realisation of the Olympic idea: the existence of a common global humanity, in spite of not only social and cultural differences but also conflict, war, and hate. MacAloon has emphasised the fact that the Olympic ideology is based on the following statement: 'We respect one another because we are the same in our differences' (1989:30). Therefore, Olympism, as ideology, is based on a heterogeneous synthesis in which the unity of mankind, the complementarity of gender (separate competitions for men and women), the existence (the need) for, and the respect of, cultural differences crystallised in 'nations' (and team-sport competitions) and the cult of the competitive (honest) individual human being (athlete) constitute the main values to be celebrated. The Olympic Games proclaim simultaneously the idea of universal sameness and of the resiliently particular: 'We are the same, we are different'. Logically, the celebration of humanity is also paralleled by the complementarity of gender as a universal and the cult of outstanding performing individuals as a model to be admired. The respect of cultural differences is, in this context, also related to the cultural and political existence of sovereign 'nations'.

The complex intermingling of individuality, gender (masculinity), and nationhood will be viewed in this paper through the concrete analysis of the performances and the social repercussion of two male athletes who stood out in 1992 during the XVI Olympic Winter Games at Albertville: Vegard Ulvang, a Norwegian Nordic skier, and Alberto Tomba, an Italian alpine skier. It has been observed that different images and behaviours contained in the notion of masculinity are not always coherent and that they may be competing, contradictory, and mutually undermining (Cornwall and Lindisfarne 1994). The same can be said of the construction of nationhood and national imageries. Male athletes deploy their manhood in contexts conditioned by values and expectations conveyed by Olympic ideals, media, and the adoring audiences. Competing forms of masculinity are produced and negotiated in different social arenas with different actors.

A sports hero can be any person admired for given qualities or achievements and regarded as an ideal or model.[1] A sports hero is an idol and an icon who belongs to a specific time: the time of heroes. The time of heroes, opposed to other times which encapsulate daily routines or scheduled rituals, represents in the mind of the adoring public a glorious dream-like time during which the daily mediocrity of normal life is suddenly transcended. Christian, one of my informants, clearly stated this idea when saying: 'we need sport heroes because they give us relief from our monotonous daily life through their magical performances. I always follow Nordic and alpine skiing, or other sports, with a real hope of experiencing something unique, a great performance.' The world of sports heroes is a world of creative enchantments because, in some moments, like flashes of intense light, athletes become mythical icons representing mastery over mortality (Novak 1993:163). The heroes stand *alone*, alone against a world of opponents and alone against an underworld full of dangers. The solitude of heroes is of great value in their transformation into cultural icons (see Rank 1990).

The heroic sports figures must be seen in their cultural context in order to understand their social meaning and to observe their communal impact (see Holt and Mangan 1996). In this paper, my analysis of heroic masculinities will touch upon the logic of creating differences and how this impacts on discourses on agency, personhood, morality, and identity. Oriard has shown that sport is a privileged arena in the production and presentation of heroes in American society (1982). The athlete-hero in America is the hero of the 'land of opportunity' and, in this sense, is the most widely popular and most attractive self-made man. The hero sustains the American Dream, personifies the democratic ideal of open accessibility to prestige and allows all citizens to share in his glory. Moreover, the athlete-hero represents the American belief in the possibility of perfection (Oriard 1982:55). These dimensions are found in the career and perception of different popular sports heroes in America. They are very general and close to the common-sense description of American fundamental values. However, a detailed analysis of different sports is needed when different heroic qualities are tied to a discussion of masculinity. In relation to American football, Oriard has demonstrated that in the historical production of a restricted heroic masculinity certain competing qualities were at stake (1993:191). On the one side, simple, unambiguous physical force was emphasised - what he calls an antimodern value. On the other side, the required 'manly' qualities were temperance, patience, self-denial and self-control – which lie behind the modern and technocratic aspects of modernity (1993:192). Oriard asserts that football's cultural power derived in large part from this collision of the modern and the antimodern, one aspect of which was this dialectical embrace of competing notions of manliness (1993:201).

Heroes are not only national or limited to a given sport. In many cases sporting heroes are a source of collective identity and pride in both national and supra-national settings. The case of Maradona, an Argentinian football player, is a clear illustration of 'transnational' heroism. He was a God-like hero in Naples while he was playing for the Naples Football Club and in Argentina while playing on the national team. His heroism was related to mythological figures in the respective local traditions: in Naples he was identified with the mythical figure of the *scugnizzo* and in Argentina with the *pibe*. These prototypes have something in common: they are human beings endowed with grace, elegance, creativity, and freedom (Dini 1994 and Archetti 1997).

The comparative analysis of the heroic status of Ulvang and Tomba in the context of the Olympic Winter Games at Albertville will enable us to answer some of the questions related to heroism and masculinity.[2] How are ideas of heroism and power connected to maleness? How and why are particular images and behaviours given heroic labels? Is a hero always the same kind of hero? How can we interpret commonalities or divergences in definitions and meanings? How are heroic figures imbued with strength, moral qualities and bodily faculties? These questions were asked and were answered by my informants during my fieldwork at the Olympic Winter Games at Albertville.

The Fieldwork

I arrived and stayed in Mégève, Haute Savoie, ten days before the beginning of the Games, on 8 February 1992, and stayed until 28 February, five days after the competitions and closing ceremony were over. The Albertville Games were not compact and centralised. In the 'warm' valley of Tarantaise with no snow at all, where Albertville is situated, individual competitions on ice were programmed, while the snow disciplines were spread over different mountain ski stations. Thus, during the two weeks of the Games, there were several centres and several peripheries in the Savoie region, all of them conditioned by the different competitions and social and cultural arrangements that are also a part of the official programme of the Olympic Games. This spatial dispersion and the considerable distances between different places made it practically impossible to be present at all or most of the competitions. I decided to concentrate my fieldwork on the disciplines that allowed a more or less systematic gathering of information among my French and Norwegian informants: the men's cross-country skiing and the alpine skiing.

Before the Games, I had conducted several visits to Mégève and made some acquaintances among the people engaged in winter sports, both as spectators and practitioners. I attended some competitions with them and they kindly introduced me to other informants. During the Games, I stayed at a hotel in Mégève, which only hosted Norwegian supporters with whom I watched many competitions and prize ceremonies. We spent several hours in the same buses, travelling from the hotel to the different competition sites. What could be considered to be more extended individual cases, extensive dialogues, and open exchanges of opinions, were few and spring out of these two milieus. In relation to Tomba, my fieldwork was limited to one competition: the slalom in Les Menuires on Saturday 22 February. I arrived very early in the morning and worked desperately to contact as many Italian supporters as possible. I was able to spend seven hours with a group of them. On the day of Tomba's victory in the giant slalom in Val d'Isère I was, however, in Les Saisies, very far away, watching the classic 4 x 10 km cross-country skiing and hoping that Ulvang would get his third gold medal.

My data from the field are a mixture of the seen, the lived, the said, and the written. Regarding the seen, I daily supplemented my own data with the extensive summaries given by the French television. My main intention was to check my observations with pictures that I could not see while limited to a small area during the competitions. Listening to interviews and following the journalistic coverage of events and the rhetoric used was also very useful. I discovered, especially in relation to my French informants, that television and newspapers generated important information that I could use in the conversations with my informants (see Rapport 1994: 172-87). The media creates and recreates mythological and magical moments and also consecrates great heroes. The adoring audiences and the journalists share the same social and symbolic reality and the hermeneutic codes mobilised are, in many cases, very similar. Reading newspapers the day after each competition was one of my more relaxing fieldwork rituals. Reading different newspapers gave me the opportunity to control my 'vision' of events and individual performances and, at the same time, opened up the possibility of depicting differences in the way the Games and heroes were locally perceived and defined.

The competitions in the Games are 'ranked' differently according to local traditions and practices. The universal appeal of figure skating is unmatched in the context of the Winter Games. The choice of alpine and cross-country skiing made it possible to follow different audiences and compare the opinions and interpretations of French people with those of the Norwegians. It was clear that in alpine and Nordic disciplines the audience was very international: Scandinavians, French, Swiss, Austrians, Italians, Americans, Spaniards, and even Mexicans and Costa Ricans. The most local of all competitions I attended was, without doubt, all-round speed skating: a real local Derby between Norwegian and Dutch skaters. The spectators in general and the spirited fans belonged to these two nationalities. The few French nationals who followed the exhausting 5,000 or 10,000 m competitions never understood why the Norwegians or Dutch shouted so enthusiastically during some moments but remain silent in others, and, of course, they were unable to interpret the round times or to relate them to the physical strength exhibited by the skaters. My French informants in Mégève confessed a total ignorance of this sport and they had no interest in following me to Albertville where the competitions took place. The Dutch or Norwegian stars of speed skating were unknown to my French informants. On the other hand, the best alpine and cross-country skiers, including the Norwegian champions, were relatively well known.

The concrete development of competitions in the Games confronts athletes and spectators with a variety of experiences constrained by the type of sport practices, rules, and locations. I will argue that the Games are one of the best contemporary examples of a true modern ideology because a mechanical social unity is postulated as the result of complex diversity. This argument permits us to understand the diversity of the qualities and achievements associated with sports heroes and to explain the continuous expansion of new disciplines (new local cultures) in both Winter and Summer Olympic Games as well as the real difficulties of getting rid of the most archaic and less popular competitions. Ulvang and Tomba touch the individual imagination and the collective sensibility in a different way and represent different bodily performances and sport traditions. The comparison is relevant in order to discuss the complexities of sport heroism.

Ulvang: The Serenity and the Natural Force

For Norwegians, cross-country skiing is the discipline identified with their old tradition of mastering the difficulties of snowy and icy terrains in the forests and mountains. Norway is still presented as 'the land of skiing' (Johannesen 1952:9). A gentle communion with nature is a key element in the imagery of cross-country skiing. In this imagery, the human practitioners are naturalised and, at the same time, nature is humanised. The skier is supposed to find an animated environment of enjoyment and creative dependency in the particular landscape. Nature is perceived as a substance with a transformative capacity, and not as an entirely pure object. The massive popular participation in great cross-country competitions can be seen as representing an ambiguous dimension because the skier is identified with nature in order to experience the flow of freedom. Pierre, an engaged French alpinist and one of my best informants, confessed his recent enchantment with cross-country skiing. He stressed his feeling of freedom in empty spaces and the importance of mastering the monotony of the long journeys in a landscape with continuous ups and downs. Pierre pointed out that the cross-country boom in France was intimately associated with a 'snobbish urban attitude', a kind of ecological revival and a return to what was imagined more natural, less modern. He agrees with the element of premodernity when comparing cross-country skiing with other disciplines. For him, alpine skiing is pure modernity because the practice is based on the display of a sophisticated technology for the fulfilment of a race of two or three minutes. According to Pierre, cross-country skiing is a mixture of patience and sustained physical effort because the skiers and the spectators can be hours and hours in the track. He compared cross-country with the Tour de France, the epical French cycling competition.[3] As he explained to me,

> In the Tour de France, nature is there to be conquered and mastered. Some laps require supernatural qualities: a capacity for suffering that is above what we can imagine, the result of scientific training and individual technical attributes. The Tour renders the contemplation of the victory of the human will and the expression of the superiority of the human forces over the obstacles of the nature possible. You just need to think of the ascending of the Ventoux mountain! I always imagined cross-country, especially 30 and 50 km competitions, as a kind of a Scandinavian miniature of the Tour de France. An Alpine competition is different and, perhaps, the technical qualities and the equipment of the skier are more important than his determination and his capacity of physical suffering.

I believe that the majority, if not all, of my Norwegian informants during Albertville will concur with this vivid description. However, I would like to add some of the arguments given by Norwegian supporters while watching competitions or waiting for the prize ceremonies. One key argument is related to what I can call 'the moral of struggle'. '30 km or 50 km races are not just suffering;' said Audun, 'it is a combat (*kamp*), a continuous combat lasting for hours.' When I asked for a further explanation, Audun expanded his ideas in the following way:

> You see, in a cross-country competition, the runner is given information by his team, the assistants, every 2 or 5 kilometres. He will know his time, his position, who is behind him, who is in front of him, who is approaching him, and consequently he will deduce his pace, or, if you prefer, how his effort is transformed into time. You need a real morale, a strong morale, in order to maintain your accidental superiority or to overcome your inferiority. In a 30 or 50 km it is a continuous fight and you must surpass yourself every kilometre in order to win. We Norwegians speak of the Finnish *sisu*. This word expresses the Finnish skiers' capacity to struggle. In Alpine skiing, the skier just goes, he is not informed of his

time in relation to the time of the other skiers. Thus, when they finish, the first thing they will do is to look for the elapsed time. In cross-country, with the exception of the very closed races, the runners can know some kilometres before the end of the competition what their positions and their real possibilities are.

Wilhem, a devoted supporter and follower of Norwegian skiers in the last three Olympic Games, pointed out the importance of uncontrollable forces of nature. He elaborated on the fact that for the success of an Alpine competition 'the weather, the snow, everything, must be perfect, because the risks are very high.' He confidently said as far as cross-country is concerned:

> there is the weight of natural forces: a sudden change of temperature, a heavy snow fall, lack of snow, a very low temperature, all these add magic to the development of the course. The runner needs a lot of support, he must be in a team; the experts advising him in all the technical aspects. We can call it a lottery, the role of randomness, but I prefer to call all this magic, the magic of the elements, the magic of nature.

In the discussions with Audun and Wilhem, what I would like to call 'utopian aspects of cross-country skiing' were clearly presented. I felt that cross-country was a kind of bodily performance and a spectacle through which human beings try to generate a balance between themselves and the forces of nature. The fragility of this balance is expressed by the idea of uncontrollable magical forces. From the point of view of the athlete he will attempt to achieve a simultaneous double communion, with the spectators on the one hand and with nature on the other. In the case of Norway, where cross-country skiing is a key social and symbolic event, a fascinating national ceremony, a perfect race of an admired runner can express a historical moment full of meaning because this man, through his performance, becomes linked to the aspirations of a community and is able to control the forces of nature (including his own nature, his own bodily agency). It is in relation to this context that the significance of Ulvang must be seen and understood.

Since the beginning of modern competitions, at the end of nineteenth century, and after the first Winter Olympic Games held in Chamonix in 1924, Norway has produced great sports heroes, some of them globally consecrated, in cross-country skiing as well as in the other Nordic disciplines of ski jumping and combined. The winning skiers consolidated Norwegian power and prestige, and, at the same time, were central figures in propagating Winter Sports (*'vise verden vinterveien*) all over the world (Olstad and Tønnesson 1986:184). The sunny and cold morning of the Monday, 10 February 1992, in Les Saisies was not an ordinary day for the hundreds of Norwegian supporters arriving at the cross-country skiing stadium. Norway had not won a single gold medal in the men's cross-country skiing in the last three Olympic Games. This was a period of Swedish domination and changes in skiing style and rules. A revolutionary skating style had been adopted in addition to the classic style. This was done despite opposition from Norwegians who thus were seen as the defenders of tradition, conservative, and bad losers. Moreover, in the entire history of the Olympic Games, the 30 km, a middle-distance competition and a mixture of sprint and endurance, was never won by a Norwegian. Today's race was, in many ways, an appointment with destiny which could turn into a historical reversal, a return to a winning tradition. While walking among so many Norwegian supporters with their flags, their cow bells, their shouts and their uniforms with logos indicating which company they belonged to (Gjensidige, Uni-Storebrand, Noiseless, Ali-kafe, Vital), many sporting typical Telemark clothes (and among them a numerous group from Notodden in Telemark, with giant bells), their friendly provocation of Swedish fans, their irony over the Italians or the Finns, I remembered a recent conversation with Christian on the meaning of sports in general. It has been said and written that sport is joy, public display of concrete individual bodies and abstract virtues, play, time-out, alienation, poetry, excitement, primitiveness, civilisation, passion and fever, true boredom, violence, corruption, madness, risk, carnival, suffering, socialisation in the acceptance of rules, discipline, sacrifice, and we agreed. Christian added something more:

> It has been stated that the difference between us, human beings, and the animal kingdom is related to making fire and cooking, language, reason and religion. Well, all this is true, I am quite sure, but what you learn through sport is also fundamental. You learn about hope. I think that hope is more important than reason. I think that hope is a state of mind that keeps us human until the very end. Without hope, why live?

This Monday there was hope, plenty of hope, and confidence among Norwegian supporters at Les Saisies. They knew that the Norwegian team was the strongest, that the Swedish and the Finnish teams were not as good, and that Smirnoff, the great Russian skier, was out of form at that particular moment. The only threat came from the other side of the Alps, from Italy, in the name of Marco Albarello. The

Italians knew this and were noisily present in the stadium and in the track by their hundreds. Most of them came from Aosta and other small cities located in the Aosta valley.

The 30 km classic style was historic and signalled the start of the majestic epic of Winter Sports. Norway won the three medals: Vegard Ulvang, gold; Bjørn Dæhlie, silver; and Terje Langli, bronze. Vegard Ulvang was almost one minute ahead of Dæhlie. The long march in the desert ended in triumph. In the flower ceremony, carried out in the stadium just after the competition, there was a real explosion of joy among the Norwegian supporters. Hundreds sang '*seier'n er vår*' (the triumph is ours) and greeted Norway and the athletes with great energy. The atmosphere was of a genuine feast; it was as if all Norwegians had known each other for ages. Victory created liminality. Social and territorial boundaries were suspended for twenty minutes.

The celebrations continued in the afternoon when the medals were awarded to the Norwegian champions in a formal and beautiful ceremony in the centre of Les Saisies. There was an indescribable atmosphere of happiness (I could write ecstasy without exaggeration), among the Norwegian fans who had returned to Les Saisies for this occasion. It was clear to me that Ulvang's victory had a special meaning for many Norwegian supporters. Olav, a sixty-year-old entrepreneur who could remember three Olympic Games and six World Championships, told me that:

> Vegard Ulvang represents many years of frustration and defeat in the national team. For almost a decade, the Swedish cross-country skiers dominated the world scene and we were satisfied with second or third places. Vegard is the symbol of endurance, of always being prepared to fight, to lose, and to come back at the next competition. Sometimes, I thought how difficult it was for him just to compete and, I imagine, how difficult it was to be motivated. I think that he was a kind of moral example for younger skiers. Vegard is a very balanced person, he knows the limits of his capacities very well. He is intelligent and he has been very supportive of other skiers. Dæhlie, for instance: he is younger, more talented than Vegard, but always accepts his seniority. I am very happy today; his victory implies that he is no longer the eternal second. Sport must also be an arena where justice is experienced.

I am quite sure that these words could have been voiced by the majority of the Norwegian fans. After the prize ceremony, hundreds of supporters literally occupied Les Saisies and organised a spontaneous march towards the parking lot where the buses were waiting. In the middle of the main street, Tom, one of the most enthusiastic Norwegians throughout the Games, announced that a song had been composed for the occasion. He distributed copies and invited one of the Gjensidige (an insurance company) fans to accompany the song on his accordion. The song was sung several times that night, in Les Saisies, in Mégève, and in our hotel. The lyrics, literally translated went:

> Tonight we are together,
> a special occasion will be celebrated:
> An Olympic gold medal was won !!!
> Vegard, Bjørn, and Terje ran
> and all nice prizes got.
> Yes, everything went very well
> now we can grin broadly !!!
> Hei, cheers !!! Hei, cheers !!!
> An Olympic gold medal in 30 km
> we did not manage to get before
> but when we finally got it
> we took all three.
> It was joy to be here,
> we will never forget it !!!
> Yes, this was history,
> and we were present.
> Hei, cheers !!! Hei, cheers !!!

It was historical, and they were there at that historical moment. This is, after all, the privilege of the adoring and engaged supporters. In the car park, an improvised dancing party was organised and many waltzes were danced with panache and grace. The celebrations continued in our hotel until very late in the night.

The Parisian newspaper *Libération* described the Norwegian triumph the next day as 'sweet vengeance' because the Swedish skiers came sixth, seventh, and eighth (11 February 1992:35). They described the Norwegian supporters and their celebrations, concluding that such happiness would only be conceivable in France in the event of the national football team winning the World Cup. In a long interview Ulvang explained that cross-country skiing is part of a national tradition, that the best skiers have been competing since they were ten years old and that the national team is united and bonded because they live together 200 days a year (ibid.). In the same article Ulvang is described as unmarried, though associated with some mysterious love stories, skiing across Greenland in the company of a French co-skier, and climbing Mount McKinley in

Alaska. The image conveyed is, in many ways, that of a quiet, balanced, and mature sportsman, and a romantic character in his free time (ibid.).

In the special issue of the regional newspaper *Le Dauphiné Liberé* for the Olympic Games Ulvang is depicted as a person who adores nature and who is a great hunter. It is specially mentioned that in the last hunting expedition in Northern Norway, where he lives, he managed to bag fifty white partridges in ten days (11 February 1992:1). The convinced ecologist and passionate climber is presented in great detail. Ulvang loves to take risks and to drive his Mazda along the empty roads around Kirkenes at considerable speed. He is saluted as the new, very handsome star of cross-country skiing with a powerful sex-appeal. The journalist is quite sure that French girls will notice Ulvang because he has '*l'oeil coquin*' (a playful glance).

The popular sport newspaper *L'Equipe* portrayed Ulvang as a 'patient and serene person' and his personal victory as a just reward after to a 'long wait' (11 February 1992: 2). The paper recalls that he had always been second or third in great competitions and that he had never won a gold medal. He is presented as an ecologist, interested in green issues, and a great lover of adventure in exciting natural landscapes. Ulvang says, 'I have always loved nature, the mountains and physical exploits in company with my friends. I organise ski climbing or expeditions like the one to Greenland in order to be with my best friends.' In the article it is especially mentioned that one of his best friends is French, Pierre Gay-Perret, a mountain guide, and that they were together on the Greenland expedition (ibid.). Michel Clare, one of the prominent writers, placed the Norwegian triumph in a mythological context: cross-country skiing was born in Norway, in Morgedal in Telemark, and Ulvang and the other champions are descendants of the great Sondre Norheim, the first modern sport hero, a jumper and fantastic skier. What was experienced in Les Saisies, Clare assured the reader, was an historical event: a combination of 'hard exploits, in which human limitations are overcome with violence' in the 'bucolic countryside' of Les Saisies and on a 'magnificent and sunny day' (ibid.). The combination of tradition, great athletes representing this tradition, and a perfect day was also emphasised in an article with the title 'The Stars from the North' (ibid.).

On the afternoon of the 11 February TV-1 presented a five-minute portrait of Ulvang and the same virtues were emphasised: patience, energy, serenity, love of nature, ecologist and organiser of inspiring expeditions. Pierre Gay-Perret was also interviewed. He stressed

Ulvang's imperturbability, his balanced make-up, his genuine interest in green politics and he mentioned that Ulvang was a mathemat-
ics student at Oslo University and that he had moved to Northern
Norway in order to be closer to nature and to prepare for the
Olympics. This portrait was repeated until the end of the Games. On
20 February, two days before the end of the Games, the prestigious
newspaper *Le Monde* insisted on the fact that Ulvang, 'a modest hero
of a Nordic legend', lives in a kind of pre-modern romantic equilib-
rium with the environment.

The media image of Ulvang was somewhat expected: a man close
to nature who enjoys its gifts, seeks adventure, takes risks, respects
and uses the products of the wilderness. The perfect outdoor life of
a modern man lay behind this imagery. When I summarised what
the press and television said about Ulvang to some Norwegians, they
agreed. Ulvang is a man who enjoyed nature and magnificent landscapes all over the world, who uses and takes from nature whatever
is permitted. The combination of skiing, climbing, walking in the
mountains and hunting was perfect. 'Very accurate' according to
Audun, 'all these activities are what a good Norwegian man must do
and enjoy.' With irony, Audun commented that the French will, one
day, discover that Vegard loves to go canoeing on dangerous Norwegian rivers. The 'playboy' image was much more difficult to
accept. They ignored his love-affairs with Italian women or that he
was fond of fast cars or that he was almost a kind of 'womaniser' with
a 'killing look'. These aspects of Ulvang were not denied but they
were viewed as extremely exaggerated. Wilhem said:

> You see, the French construct a hero that must be in part French. Well,
> Ulvang as an ecologist fits in well with the image of Norway and of cross-
> country skiing. But a real man, an adored idol, must have sex-appeal.
> Take Platini, the football player. He is handsome, without any doubt,
> and I think that he is portrayed as having not only control over the play-
> ers he is playing against but also over all the women of the world. I never
> imagined Vegard as a great lover. For Latins a perfect man ought to be a
> great lover. They need salt and pepper. I don't care how many Italian
> women Vegard has conquered. This has not been mentioned in the Nor-
> wegian newspapers and it is not important for the Norwegian public.

I discussed Ulvang with Christian, Pierre, and Luc (and in 1994 I
returned to this issue during a dinner with them and their respective
spouses). They had read *L'Equipe* and watched television. They were
fascinated by his character. They said to me that living in the Alps is
perhaps like living in Northern Norway and that they, like Ulvang,

carry on a life of outdoor, modern men. Christian is an agronomist, Pierre an Air Inter jet pilot, and Luc a free-lance urbanist with a degree in planning. Ulvang's life style and the values he expressed were perceived as politically honest and correct. The combination of modern sports, scientific training, discipline, and bodily suffering required for cross-country was only understandable if respect for nature and joy and freedom in contact with it were also stated clearly. Ulvang, for them, was a symbol of this kind of life. They were happy with his victory. Pierre said that he felt that Ulvang was a person with whom one could feel very close. He added that the capacity to be a real sports hero was related to this dimension.

Ulvang continued to win medals. Three days later, on 13 February, he won the 10 km classic style twenty seconds in front of the Italian Marco Albarello. On 15 February he won a silver medal in the 15 km skating, behind Bjørn Dæhlie, the other great Norwegian champion. The first week of the Olympic Games was dominated by his presence. He was declared by the media to be a complete athlete, a model of a new type of idol engaged in global issues and living a life according to his ideals. Moreover, in the second week of the Games, he completed a memorable performance determining, by an astonishing acceleration in the stadium, the 4 x 10 km relay in favour of Norway. A new gold medal, the third, in the 'more noble of the cross-country competitions because in the relay the authentic standard of a nation is manifested', as Wilhem put it. The award ceremony in Les Saisies was an explosion of joy for the hundreds of devoted Norwegian supporters. The superiority of their nation was once again proclaimed. The 50 km was the last race and nobody expected Ulvang to win. Dæhlie obtained the last gold medal on behalf of Norway.

Ulvang entered in the sporting mythology of Olympic Winter Games and of his own country, Norway.[4] In France, too, he was declared a French idol. *Libération* devoted a whole page to Ulvang on 19 February, explaining to the French public how he had been transformed from being a 'Poupou', the nickname of Raymond Poulidor, the eternal number two of many Tours de France, to a real Anquetil, winner of four Tours de France (Jaurena, 19 February 1992:34). While reading this article I remembered my conversation with Pierre on the parallelism between cross-country skiing and cycling. In the article Ulvang's qualities were, in a way, stamped in the same mould as the great champions of the Tour de France: '*solitude, souffrance et masochisme*' (solitude, suffering, and masochism). The fact that he was already 29 years old and had waited a long time for this success was a privileged dimension of his heroic life marked by such moral attributes.

Ulvang, interviewed in the article, confirmed the importance of these moral and psychological attributes. He admitted that he enjoyed to be alone while training and that this could be explained by the fact that 'he was born in one of the wildest places in Europe, where you can walk for a week without meeting a soul'. The journalist asked him directly about the role of suffering in his life as a skier. Ulvang confessed that he did not enjoy suffering but that it was a necessary condition for winning in cross-country skiing, and added, 'after suffering there is a feeling of plenitude'. However, he did not accept that his life was marked by masochism. Suffering was not masochism, he insisted. To be good in cross-country skiing implies that 'you must be able to experience your own physical and psychological limitations, perhaps to surpass them, and to tell yourself this is important in order to win' (ibid.). The article ends by pointing out that Ulvang had recently been singled out, together with the Italian Marco Albarello, as a representative of the top international skiers. The journalist writes that Ulvang has become a 'trade unionist' like the other great French Tour-de-France hero, Bernard Hinault. Thus, Ulvang is today 'Hinault after having been Poulidor and transformed into Anquetil' (ibid.). Ulvang is thus presented as the synthesis of the three great contemporary French heroes of popular sports culture.

Ulvang's extremely aggressive masculinity, based on his exhibition of physical power and dominance over the other skiers during the Games, was also portrayed. The American CBS television network launched him as 'The Terminator', alluding to an extremely violent film starring the Austrian-born Arnold Schwarzenegger. The French newspapers and media rejected this image. Jaurena wrote: 'Terminator. The nickname given to Ulvang by the CBS lacks imagination and a good deal of sense' (ibid.). Ulvang was not a macho-vulgar type, he was made of other qualities. The Norwegian supporters never imagined Ulvang as being typically macho. The 'Terminator' idea was an American invention in order to sell him and the Olympic Games to a disinterested audience. However, the macho figure of the American CBS coexisted with the European and Norwegian image of the ecological and extremely balanced pre-modern sportsman. Two years later, just before the beginning of the Olympic Games in Lillehammer, Ulvang himself denied the validity of the macho image created for him by the American media. He said:

'Because I go cross-country and have been on some expeditions, I am related to a hard masculine macho image. This is completely wrong. I am not a good mountaineer. I just walk in the mountains. The truth is that I enjoy an outdoor life, building a camp fire, watching the flames, contemplating the stars in the sky. Outdoor life is enjoyable. At the same time I have a positive relation to body performances. I like to feel tired. (*Dagbladet* 5 February 1994:10).

Ulvang won three gold medals and one silver, the same as Bjørn Dæhlie. The Scandinavian Airlines System named two aircraft after them. The pair of them were great athletes during the Olympic Games in Albertville but only one hero was created, imagined and adored by the various audiences. Audun tried to explain to me the reason for this. He was very assertive.

Ulvang has his ups and downs and will continue to do so. He is not the best in the world, and not even in Norway. Dæhlie is a much better skier, he is more technical and, above all, he is complete; he is as good in classical as in skating. But Ulvang is the 'boy' (*gutt*), is our 'boy'. He is always restrained, suffers in silence, and respects all the other competitors. He will never complain when life is hard and unjust. He will never explain his bad results because he has physical pains. He will be satisfied with a fifth or a seventh place. He knows that the life is made of ups and downs. After all, he is at the same time Poulidor, Anquetil and Hinault.

Tomba: The Charisma and the Excess

Max Weber argues that individuals who are perceived to possess certain attributes that set them apart from ordinary men, are treated as if endowed with supernatural, superhuman, or at least exceptional powers or qualities. An individual with such capacities is defined as having charisma. In sports it is the crowd that provides the legitimacy for the existence of a charismatic hero and the validity of his performance (see St. Pierre 1995). Tomba has charisma, his adoring audiences know it, as do the thousands of his fans who follow him and his career, and who re-create it well in carefully directed public spectacles. Charisma needs great performances. Without doubt, Tomba is a great performer possessed by some of the ills of charismatic heroes: excess, a hyper-realistic magnificence conveyed through his exaggerated bodily gestures, verbosity, and an extreme passion for what he does and likes (in sport and in leisure). Since his first victory at the age of 20, at Sestrière in the World Cup, he slowly transformed alpine skiing into a kind of theatre of imagery dominated by his performances.

It is through performances that humans project images of themselves and the world to their audiences (see Ehrenberg 1991; Palmer and Jankowiak 1996). The constructions created by performances may be the performances themselves, as in the ephemeral constructions of a race; or they may be more durable products, like the emblematic figure of Tomba. He is one of the few skiers with a forceful nickname which condenses some of his qualities: his way of skiing as well as his body language is explosive and he is called 'La Bomba' (the Bomb) in Italy and around the world. *Libération* describes how his physical power has been consolidated by the continuous work of a team of four experts in an almost 'scientific way'. He has been helped by a physical coach, a physiotherapist, a psychologist, and an expert on skiing equipment. His body, his mind, and the material he needs have been carefully researched. As a consequence of this he has now a compact muscular volume (90 kg for 1,82 m, he lost seven kg last year); he is extremely quick in relation to his weight (100 m in 11.8 seconds); he is very flexible (1,90 m in the high-jump), and when competing he is able to generate 38 watts. (This is considered incomparable because the best Italian volleyball players, World champions, only generate on average a potential of 27 watts) (18 February 1992:35). This article tells us that Tomba is a real bomb, a product of an exceptional biology and of modern industrial techniques, that explodes when skiing. A bomb is a cultural (scientific) product. His physical power is, however, combined with other traits. He loves his audiences and it is believed that he accepts few limits in his daily life. Thus, in Italy, he is called '*Il cavallo pazzo*' (the mad horse) and, in the French version, '*Le cheval fou*'. He is like an undomesticated animal when he is not competing, wild and pure nature.

He is a kind of postmodern hero who knows very well that in order to create and recreate his image he must continually perform in the circumscribed places and times of stadiums and competitions, as in the Olympic Games, but also in his ordinary life, full of incidents captured by photographers and sprinkled with love scandals. He must be a bomb and a horse. His imagery is dependent on what is written in newspapers and magazines and on what is shown and said on television. In this sense he is just a 'young man' for whom his symbolic value (and objective capacities) allows his fans to devour him. He is the only real masculine idol in Italy who can compete in popularity with the football stars. He can mobilise twenty thousand supporters in Italian World Cup competitions in Sestrière or Alta Badia. Pietro, a barman from Genoa, expressed this perfectly when he described the Italian *Tombamania* for me: 'Alberto is a football team on his own. Who else is followed by twenty thousand supporters?

Only him and Sampdoria, my football club'. He drew young urban people into the alpine skiing arenas and in doing so he changed the character of the competitions. He is a city boy himself, born in Bologna, and his family is rich. He is not like the other skiers, peasants from small villages in the Italian Alps speaking difficult dialects. He speaks loudly, like a perfect urbanite Italian, and gesticulates constantly. The discreet Italian mountain people know that they cannot rival the glib tongue of the son of Bologna. It is said that he lost seven kilos the last year eating *pasta*. He proudly accepted to be the figurehead and media symbol of the huge *pasta* company Barilla. Some of his fans decorate their flags with a painted dish of hot spaghetti. Pietro said that in his fan club, the dish represented *spaghetti bolognese*, the classic *pasta* dish with tomato and meat sauce. His love for *pasta* is identified with his confessed adoration for his mother, Maria-Grazia. He is a bomb, a horse, and a loving son. His mother tells the press that he is not a machine without sentiments, he is a beloved son with a great heart (*Libération*, 18 February 1992:35).[5]

Above all, he is a spectacular performer. In Albertville he acted in his own play in several acts. The morning of the opening ceremony, on Saturday, 8 February, he arrived in an Italian police helicopter. He is a non-working police sergeant (with uniform and medals) in the forces controlling the northern borders. He was the flag-bearer of the Italian national team during the ceremony. In the evening he flew back to the training camp in Sestrière in the Italian Alps. This short appearance at the opening was the first act of his master play. During the first week, dominated by the exploits of Vegard Ulvang, he was supposed to train alone with his team of experts. He never joins the Italian team and he does not consider himself as a member of an alpine tradition dominated by skiers from Friuli-Veneto or Tyrol. His absence created great expectations. He had, before the Games, announced that his two 1988 Olympic gold medals from Calgary, in slalom and in giant, would be won again. The journalists prepared the public and the public expected this to happen. We were assured that it was going to be something spectacular and exceptional, a new chapter in the history of modern winter sports. A different heroic performance. His second act was the creation of real suspense, a state of anxious uncertainty lasting a whole week. Nobody, in the history of the Games, had managed to win the same alpine skiing gold medals in two successive Games. If he managed to do this he could be the first one ever and *il unico* and *il magnifico*.

The third act was initiated with verve on his return to Albertville on Sunday February 16. In a tumultuous press conference, Tomba declared that the Games needed a star, himself, and that from this very moment the city should change its name from Albertville to Albert*o*ville. He declared the Olympic Games of Albert*o*ville to be open. The press unanimously accepted the re-naming of the city. Asked about his training in Sestrière he boastfully answered:

> What I have done in Sestrière ? I went to bed every day at five o'clock in the morning with three women. But now I am seriously in the Games, and I must be more discreet. I will go to bed at 3 o'clock in the morning but with five women. I am not afraid of any of my competitors. My greatest enemy is not Accola, or Girardelli, or any Norwegian, it is simply the unexpected and the unknown. (*L'Equipe* 17 February 1992: 2)

At the end of the conference he announced for the following Tuesday that he would win a historic double gold medal in the giant slalom.

His performance was perfect. He was co-ordinated, ironic, reflexive, acting and directing his audience. He knew what to say and he measured the impact of his words and metaphors. We can say that in this spectacle it was possible to find 'enactment of imagery, symbolic expression of imagery, awareness of audience, and experience of imagery' (Palmer and Jankowiak 1996:252). His play was individual, but it entered into a kind of collective and intersubjective construction of imagery. Since this very day the Games were known in France as the Albert*o*ville Games. In a good analysis of the impact of the Games, his capacity to create powerful images was underlined and the chapter devoted to him was entitled *Les Jeux olympiques d'Albertoville* (Mercier 1992). Tomba demonstrated that public performances are a central aspect in the creation of powerful images.

On the Sunday, while watching the press conference on television, Christian commented, 'Fortunately for him he is not only a boastful person (*un grand fanfaron*). He enjoys being a show-off and perhaps he talks too much but he also wins often, very often.' He told me that in the 1992 World Cup season, Tomba took part in eleven slalom and giant slalom races and won ten. He was convinced that in magical Val d'Isère next Tuesday, Tomba would win his second giant slalom gold medal. And he did. Girardelli, the Austrian champion representing Luxembourg, was second with the Norwegian Aamodt taking the third place and the bronze medal. He become history and myth. I was not in Val d'Isère that morning. I did not see Tomba's mythical fourth act witnessed by four thousand Italian supporters. I was in Les Saisies with Ulvang and the Norwegians. In the Olympic Games it is difficult to be in several mythical and magical arenas at the same time.

The *International Herald Tribune* wrote:

It was more than a dramatic showdown of champion skiers. It was a classic confrontation of Olympic ideals. Tomba, whom all of Italy adores, versus Marc Girardelli, the man without a country. How do you like your Olympics, with flag-waving nationalists or purely for the sake of athletic competition? For Tomba, the giant slalom course was laced Tuesday with thousands of horn-blowing, banner-toting, Tomba-worshipping zealots. For Girardelli, the only known fervent supporter was his autocratic father and coach, Helmut Girardelli, pulling for his progeny somewhere on the mountain. True to his mystique, Tomba did not let victory pass without playing it for every photograph it was worth. He hugged the beaten but unvowed Girardelli behind the finish line. He lifted his skis in the palm of his right hand. He mixed with his fans by the side of the course, telling them he loved them as much they love him. 'I did not know what happened until I saw all the flags waving' Tomba said. 'Then I know that I won.' It seemed as if all of Italy had poured through a narrow mountain pass into this icy Savoie outpost in support of Tomba. He is a rare ski champion from a city, Bologna, and he is as revered in the more rabid south of Italy as any soccer or tennis player, world-wide. Tomba fans had come the night before, hundreds standing in the cold to scream his name as he picked the sixth position for the morning run in a public draw. By the time the course was set, and the skiers were at the top, the finish line area was draped in the Italian colours, red, green and white. (19 February 1992:1 and 23)

I arrived at 6.50 a.m. on Saturday 22 February, at Les Menuires. The first leg of the slalom would start at 10.00 a.m. I read that thousands of Italians had arrived at Val d'Isère for the giant slalom early in the morning, travelling in their buses all the night (see *Le Monde* 19 February 1992). This was unbelievable. The way to the main road to Les Menuires was a surrealist vision: hundreds of Italian buses parked all over, French policemen trying to organise what was indescribable traffic chaos, and, above all, the scene of Tomba supporters walking up the seven kilometres to the stadium with their flags and horns, singing and jumping to keep themselves warm. The outside temperature was minus 10 C. It was 6.30 a.m. and my first thought was of the enduring supporters coming from Bologna: 'Yesterday, Friday. At what time did they leave the city?' The first supporters I saw at the stadium were the ones coming from Castel de Britti, the village close to Bologna where Tomba was born. Paolo, co-owner of a small construction enterprise, told me that Castel de Britti is a village with 1,000 inhabitants and that the supporters' club has 400 members. He has been following Tomba for three seasons and he confessed, 'I can get mad if I start to count the hours spent in buses and the money used up for each season. Every year I am obliged to make up for my travels by reducing my summer vacations.' With a gesture of resignation he added, 'The cult of idols is very demanding.' In order to demonstrate that he was not 'insane', with great humour he introduced me to a young couple of real 'fanatics', Alberto and Carla. Alberto explained that he and three others had created the Castel de Britti fan club in 1988 before the Olympic Games in Calgary, and that they never expected any success. In the last season he had covered 14,000 km following Tomba and insisted that I should write that each journey was always a kind of feast. Carla interrupted him and told me that they had planned to get married in 1991, but had postponed the wedding until 1992, 'we were married on 9 February in Bologna and we decided to have our honeymoon in Albertville. We were quite sure that we could tell our grandchildren that we were married the year Alberto got his third gold medal.' They told me that the journey from Bologna to Albertville takes eleven hours. I estimated that the supporters coming for the second time would have spent almost two days travelling and half a day watching the races out of a total of five. Paolo assured me that they had not wasted their time on Tuesday because Alberto won, and the same would happen today.

At 7.30 a.m. the best cheap standing places at the stadium were totally occupied by the Italian supporters. Until the end of the second leg at 2.00 p.m. it was what we might imagine a Mediterranean kermis to be: music, food, Italian flags, horns, cries, and football emblems (flags and scarves of Inter, Juventus, Verona, Sampdoria, and Genoa dominated). One of the most enthusiastic groups came from Verona and they marked the confluence of Tomba and football on a huge pennant on which was written: '*Tomba e veloce comme Caniggia. Verona Fans Club*' ('Tomba is as quick as Caniggia' - a football idol of Verona). Mixed with the Italian supporters I identified Spanish and Portuguese - a Portuguese - Galician-speaking fan club with members from Lisbon and Orense, Spain, England and America (from New York) with their flags. The British supporters came from Brighton and the 'boss' of the fan club was a barman, the son of an Italian immigrant. They had a banner saying '*Tomba number one*' and it was decorated with the emblematic steaming plate of spaghetti. On some of the banners we could read: the admiring '*Alberto cuore di leone. Forza*', '*De l'Italia: un grito forza Tomba*', the implorings '*Alberto vince per noi*' or '*Alberto regalacci e medaglione*', the poetical '*Alberto benvenuto sulla terra*', the ethnocentric '*Forza Tomba. Tomba e unico. Castel de Gritti*', the obvious '*Tomba La Bomba. Forza*', the objective '*Alberto la leggenda d'Italia*' or '*Alberto Rei*' or '*Magico Alberto*', the chauvinist '*Italia e maravigliosa. Un figlio comme Alberto*', and the ironic in French '*Albertoville c'est plus facile*'. Hundreds and hundreds of small Italian flags with '*Alberto, ti amo*' were all over the place.

It was a feast. It was an Italian carnival. It was an adoring audience performing in honour of a hero.[6] It was dramatic. After the first leg, Tomba was one-and-a-half seconds behind the leader, the Norwegian Jagge, and very far from any medal. It was a great deception, but the supporters knew that Tomba would be transformed into a real bomb during the second leg. Tomba's second leg was mythical, a real explosion and an exhibition of force and confidence. But it was not enough. In the end Jagge won the gold medal and Tomba the silver, just twenty-eight hundredth's of a second behind. It was a tragedy. Tomba had not won. However, after some minutes of disenchantment, the fans started their fans again. They will always remember Tomba's second leg. He was a man of great courage, a deep sense of honour and a great fighter. Paolo expressed this perfectly when he said, 'We waited for a miracle but it did not happen and still Alberto is our saint.' Tomba summarised his participation in Albertville as the best Games for him in spite of only one gold medal compared with the two in Calgary. He said that in Calgary he had competed with an anti-hero, the English ski jumper Eddie '*The Eagle*' Edwards, and with the grace of Katarina Witt, the German figure skater, while in Albertville he was the number one (Mercier 1992: 62). He forgot to mention Vegard Ulvang.

By Way of Conclusion

I hope that my analysis of heroic exploits in the context of the Olympic Games of Albertville has shown that the different images and behaviour contained in the notion of masculinity are not always consistent and that they may be competing, contradictory, and mutually undermining. The idealised masculinity is not just about men, it is a part of a cultural system for producing differences. In the case of Albertville, the opposition between Ulvang, a man close to nature, and Tomba, a pure product of Italian urban values, seems to me crucial for understanding the complex imagery of masculinity. The endurance and the serenity of Ulvang does not include the excess and the charismatic force of Tomba. We can say that Ulvang as a man is very Norwegian as well as that Tomba is very Italian. However, their qualities as expressed in Albertville transcend the limits of nationality and direct attention to a variety of proposals concerning how one should, or could, be a sporting hero.[7]

If we accept that there is a relation (tenuous or strong, depending on the situation) between social imageries and individual heroes, it is difficult to accept that in sporting events normal patterns of understanding performances and motives are suspended. The examination of concrete performances makes it possible to see how every performance (and every man) has some significance for the audience. I believe that it has been made clear that in the dramatic spectacles I have described, we find ideas, opinions, and symbols that reflect upon themselves, the participants, and us, the observers. An anthropological approach that takes the role of performances and sport in the production of meaning in modern life may seriously expand the field of cultural analysis. The display of the imagery associated with Ulvang and Tomba is central in such a perspective.

Notes

1. See the special issue of *The International Journal of the History of Sport* 'European Heroes. Myth, Identity, Sport', 1996, vol. 13, 1.
2. On the complex meaning of masculinity and gender in sport see the analysis of wrestling in Turkey by Stokes (1996) and of female bullfighting in Spain by MacClancey (1996).
3. On the 'deep meaning' of the French Tour de France see the classical analysis of Barthes (1957: 110-20). See also Vigarello (1992).
4. Many of the discussed qualities related to Ulvang are presented in a condensed and epic way in his biography (Aasheim 1993).
5. For a better understanding of his life see Tomba and Turrini (1992).
6. For a perceptive analysis on the meaning of the carnivalesque in sport, see Giulianotti (1991) and Armstrong (1996).
7. Metoudi (1992) has shown that in the case of male sporting heroes the attributed values are usually force and courage. The women stars in winter sports are always described as feminine and fragile. She concludes by arguing that the transformation of women stars into heroes is extremely difficult. The pantheon of heroism in winter sports is occupied by men.

References

Aasheim, S. P. (1993) *Vegard Ulvang,* J.W. Cappelens Forlag: Oslo.

Archetti, E. P. (1997) '"And Give Joy to My Heart". Ideology and Emotions in the Argentinian Cult of Maradona' in Gary Armstrong and Richard Giulianotti (eds) *Entering the Field. New Perspectives on World Football,* Berg Publishers: Oxford.

Armstrong, G. (1996) *Football Hooligans. A Case Study. The 'Blades ' of Sheffield United F.C.*, Ph.D. thesis, University College: University of London.

Barthes, R. (1957) *Mythologies*, Editions du Seuil: Paris.

Cornwall, A. and N. Lindisfarne (1994) 'Dislocating masculinity: gender, power and anthropology' in A. Cornwall and N. Lindisfarne (eds) *Dislocating Masculinity. Comparative Ethnographies*, Routledge: London.

Dini, V. (1994) 'Maradona, héros napolitain', *Actes de la recherche en sciences sociales* 103:75-8.

Ehrenberg, A. (1991) *Le culte de la performance*, Editions du Seuil: Paris.

Giulianotti, R. (1991) 'Scotland's Tartan Army in Italy: The case for the Carnivalesque', *Sociological Review* 39:503-27.

Holt, R. and Mangan, J. A. (1996) 'Prologue: Heroes of a European Past', *The International Journal of the History of Sport* 13, 1:1-13.

Jaurena, C. (1992) 'Ulvang, l'homme atteint tous les sommets', *Libération*, 19 February.

Johannesen, H. (1952) *Olympic Winter Sports in Norway. The Land of Summer and Winter Glory*, The Norwegian Ski Association: Oslo.

MacAloon, J. (1989) 'Festival, Ritual, and Television' in *International Conference Proceedings of the Olympic Movement and the Mass Media. Past, Present and Future Issues*, Hurford Enterprises Ltd: Calgary.

MacClancey, J. (1996) 'Female Bullfighting, Gender Stereotyping and the State' in J. MacClancey (ed.) *Sport, Identity and Ethnicity*, Berg Publishers: Oxford.

Mercier, A. (1992) *Albertville 92. XVIes Jeux Olympiques d'hiver*, Calmann-Lévy: Paris.

Metoudi, M. (1992) 'Pourquoi Carole Merle ne sera pas Jeanne d'Arc, ou la place des femmes dans l'héroisme sportif', *Centre de Recherche sur la Culture Européenne, Institute Universitaire Européen*, Firenze (MS).

Novak, M. (1993) 'The Joy of Sports' in C. S. Prebish (ed.) *Religion and Sport: The Meeting of the Sacred and the Profane*, Greenwood Press: Westport.

Olstad, F. and S. Tønnesson (1986) *Norsk idretts historie. Folkehelse, trim, stjerner 1939-1986*, Aschehoug: Oslo.

Oriard, M. (1982) *Dreaming of Heroes. American Sports Fiction, 1868-1980*, Nelson Hall: Chicago.

Oriard, M. (1993) *Reading Football. How the Popular Press Created an American Spectacle*, The University of North Carolina Press: Chapel Hill.

Palmer, G. B. and W. R. Jankowiak (1996) 'Performance and Imagination: Toward an Anthropology of the Spectacular and the Mundane', *Cultural Anthropology*, 11, 2:225-58.

Rank, O. (1990) *In Quest of the Hero*, Princeton University Press: Princeton, N.J.

Rapport, N. (1994) *The Prose and the Passion. Anthropology, Literature and the Writing of E.M. Forster*, Manchester University Press: Manchester.

St. Pierre, M. (1995) 'West Indian Cricket as Cultural Resistance' in M. A. Malec (ed.) *The Social Roles of Sport in Caribbean Societies*, Gordon and Breach Publishers: Reading.

Stokes, M. (1996) 'Strong as a Turk': Power, Performance and Representation in Turkish Wrestling' in J. MacClancey (ed.) *Sport, Identity and Ethnicity*, Berg Publishers: Oxford.

Tomba, A. and L.Turrini (1992) *Alberto Tomba. Il romanzo di un fuoriclasse*, Vallardi: Milan.

Vigarello, G. (1992) 'Le héros du Tour de France, les transformations d'un mythe', *Centre de Recherche sur la Culture Européenne, Institut Universitaire Européen*, Firenze (MS).

NOTES ON CONTRIBUTORS

Arne Martin Klausen (b. 1927, Norway), Dr. Philos. Professor (emeritus) of Social Anthropology, University of Oslo since 1973. Author of several anthropological textbooks in Norwegian, used at Scandinavian Universities. Fieldwork in South India 1960, 1961-1962 for the monograph *Kerala Fishermen and the Indo-Norwegian Pilot Project*, Oslo University Press/Allan and Unwin: Oslo 1968. Editor of *Den norske væremåten*, Cappelen: Oslo 1984. French translation 1991: *Le savoir-être norvégien. Regards anthropologique sur la culture norvégienne*, L´Harmattan: Paris.

John J. MacAloon (b. 1947, USA), Ph.D. University of Chicago, Professor of Social Anthropology, Master of Arts Program in the Social Sciences, University of Chicago. Has written and lectured extensively on sport, culture and politics based on fieldwork during several Olympic Games. He has edited *Rite, Drama, Festival, Spectacle. Rehearsals Towards a Theory of Cultural Performance,* Institute for the Study of Human Issues Press: Philadelphia 1984 and written the excellent biography *This Great Symbol. Pierre de Coubertin and the Origins of the Modern Olympic Games,* University of Chicago Press: Chicago 1981.

Odd Are Berkaak (b.1950, Norway), Dr. Philos, Professor of Social Anthropology, University of Oslo. Fieldwork in Jamaica, St.Vincent, Zambia and Norway. Published books in Norwegian on modern popular music, rock and roll and reggae. 'Experiencing the person: Autonomy and hierarchy in rock and roll' *Ethnos,*1990.

Roel Puijk (b. 1952, The Netherlands), Dr. Philos. Senior Lecturer, Lillehammer College. Fieldwork in France and Norway. Special interests are tourism, media and the Olympics. He has published books in Norwegian on journalism and television production. Editor of *Global Spotlights on Lillehammer. How the World Viewed Norway During the 1994 Winter Olympics,* John Libbye/University of Luton Press: Luton 1997.

Ingrid Rudie (b 1933, Norway) Mag. art. Oslo 1963. Professor of Social Anthropology, University of Oslo. Fieldwork in Norway from 1961 and Malaysia 1964-1965, 1986,1987, 1988. Author and editor of books on gender issues. Publications include 'Translating gender and autonomy over time in Malaysia' in Diane Bell et al. (eds), *Gendered Fields* Routledge: London 1993. *Visible Women in East Coast Malay Society,* Scandinavian University Press/Oxford University Press: Oslo 1994.

Eduardo Archetti (b. 1943, Argentina). Professor of Social Anthropology, University of Oslo. He has written extensively on society and culture in Ecuador and Argentina. His most recent book is *Guinea Pigs. Food, Symbol and Conflict of Knowledge in Ecuador,* Berg Publishers: Oxford 1997. Editor of *Exploring the Written. Anthropology and the Multiplicity of Writing,* Scandinavian University Press: Oslo 1994. Archetti is currently conducting research on the construction of national identity in Argentina through the study of tango, soccer and polo.

INDEX